CROP PRODUCTIVITY AND PLANT DISEASE MANAGEMENT

ENV BOOKS SERIES

CROP PRODUCTIVITY AND PLANT DISEASE MANAGEMENT

Editors

Dr. Alka Chauhan
Department of Environment Conservation
Society for Environment, Health, Awareness of Nutrition & Toxicology (SEHAT)
20, Jamaalpur Maan, Raja Ka Tajpur
Bijnore - 246 735 (U.P.) (India)

Dr. Pawan Kumar 'Bharti'
Vice President
Society for Environment, Health, Awareness of Nutrition & Toxicology (SEHAT)
1775, Sohan Ganj, Near Clock Tower
Delhi - 110 007 (India)
E-mail: *gurupawanbharti@rediffmail.com*

Ms. Deepti Sadana
Department of Plant Biotechnology
Manav Rachna International University
Faridabad - 121 004, (Haryana) (India)

Associate Editor

Mr. Jaswant Ray
F/119, Pandav Nagar
Meerut - 250 003 (U.P.) (India)

DPH

DISCOVERY PUBLISHING HOUSE PVT. LTD.
NEW DELHI-110 002

Published by:
Namit Wasan
DISCOVERY PUBLISHING HOUSE PVT. LTD.
4383/4B, Ansari Road, Darya Ganj
New Delhi-110 002 (India)
Phone : +91-11-23279245, 43596064-65
Fax : +91-11-23253475
E-mail : discoverypublishinghouse@gmail.com
namitwasan9@gmail.com
sales@discoverypublishinggroup.com
web : www.discoverypublishinggroup.com

First Edition: **2016**

ISBN: 978-93-5056-791-3

Crop Productivity and Plant Disease Management

Printed at:
Infinity Imaging Systems
Delhi

ENV Books Series, India

Calls lengthy and error free chapters for further volumes of books on various environmental issues. (Send your manuscripts to envbooks@gmail.com)

Founding Editor ***(Editor-in-Chief)***

Dr. Pawan Kumar 'Bharti'
Society for Environment, Health, Awareness of Nutrition & Toxicology (SEHAT-India)
1775, Sohanganj, Near Clock Tower, Delhi-7, (India)
E-mail:*gurupawanbharti@rediffmail.com*

Other Titles by Editor-in-Chief:

1. **Advances in Biotechnology and Ecological Sciences (2013)**
   Bharti, P.K., Chauhan, A. and Ray, J. (eds.)
   (ISBN: 978-93-5056-358-8).
2. **Advances in Agriculture and Ecology (2013)**
   Bharti, P.K.; Chauhan, A. and Ezeaku Peter Ikemefuna (eds.)
   (ISBN: 978-93-5056-362-5).
3. **Agriculture and Environmental Biotechnology (2014)**
   Bharti, P.K. and Chauhan, A. (eds.)
   (ISBN: 978-93-5056-479-0).
4. **Agriculture Development and Sustainable Environment (2015)**
   Ray, J. and Bharti, P. K. (eds.)
   (ISBN: 978-93-5056-759-3)
5. **Agriculture Ecology and Environment (2014)**
   Bharti, P.K. and Olubukola O. Babalola (eds.)
   (ISBN: 978-93-5056-480-6).
6. **Agriculture, Environment and Nano-science (2015)**
   Bharti, Pawan K. (ed.)
   (ISBN: 978-93-5056-760-5)
7. **Agro-biodiversity:** ***Conservation & Sustainable Development*** **(2016)**
   Sharma, Pankaj; Singh, Narayan; and Bharti, P.K. (eds.)
   (ISBN: 978-93-505-782-1)
8. **Agro-forestry and Climate Change (2014)**
   Bharti, Pawan K. and Singh, Narayan (eds.)
   (ISBN: 978-93-5056-514-8).

9. **Agro-forestry and Sustainable Agriculture (2016)**
Sharma, Pankaj; Bharti, P.K. (eds.)
(ISBN: 978-93-5056-786-9).
10. **Aquaculture and Fisheries Environment (2014)**
Gupta, S.K. and Pawan K. Bharti (eds.)
(ISBN: 978-93-5056-408-0).
11. **Aquatic Biodiversity and Pollution (2013)**
Bharti, P.K.; Chauhan, A. and Kaoud, H.A.H. (eds.)
(ISBN: 978-93-5056-359-5).
12. **Aquatic Ecology and Biotechnology (2014)**
Bharti, P.K. and Zaki, M.S.A. (eds.)
(ISBN: 978-93-5056-451-6).
13. **Aquatic Environment and Toxicology (2013)**
Bharti, Pawan K. (ed.)
(ISBN: 978-93-5056-236-9).
14. **Biodiversity, Biotechnology and Environmental Conservation (2015)**
Bharti, P.K. and Bhandari, G. (eds.)
(ISBN: 978-93-5056-750-0).
15. **Biodiversity of Aquatic Ecosystem: *Significance, Threat and Conservation* (2013)**
Bharti, P.K. and Kaoud, H.A.H. (eds.)
(ISBN: 978-93-5056-297-0).
16. **Biological Diversity and Ecology (2016)**
Arya, M.K.; Bharti, P.K. and Ritesh Joshi (eds.)
(ISBN: 978-93-5056-785-2).
17. **Bioremediation and Microbial Biotechnology (2016)**
Gupta, Sandeep; and Bharti, P.K. (eds.)
(ISBN: 978-93-5056-783-8)
18. **Biotechnological Approaches & Water Ecosystem (2016)**
Zaki, M.S.A.; and Bharti, P.K. (eds.)
(ISBN: 978-93-5056-779-1)
19. **Biotechnology, Agro-ecology and Environment (2015)**
Chauhan, Avnish and Bharti, P.K. (eds.)
(ISBN: 978-93-5056-757-9).
20. **Clean Technologies and Environmental Protection (2015)**
Chauhan, A.; Sharma, S. and Bharti, P.K. (eds.)
(ISBN: 978-93-5056-731-9).
21. **Climate Change and Agriculture (2012)**
Bharti, P.K. and Chauhan, Avnish (eds.)
(ISBN: 978-93-5056-148-5).

22. **Climate Change and Biodiversity (2013)**
Bharti, P.K. and Chauhan, Avnish (eds.)
(ISBN: 978-93-5056-360-1).
23. **Climate Change, Disaster Management and Environment (2016)**
Chauhan, Alka; Bharti, P.K. (eds.)
(ISBN: 978-93-5056-784-5).
24. **Conservation and Cultivation of Medicinal Plants (2015)**
Bharti, P.K. and Singh Narayan (eds.)
(ISBN: 978-93-5056-740-1).
25. **Eco-toxicology and Eco-technology (2013)**
Bharti, P.K. and Zaki, M. (eds.)
(ISBN: 978-93-5056-313-7).
26. **Environmental Biotechnology and Application (2013)**
Bharti, P.K. and Chauhan, Avnish (eds.)
(ISBN: 978-93-5056-262-8).
27. **Environmental Conservation and Biotechnology (2014)**
Chauhan, A. and P.K. Bharti (eds.)
(ISBN: 978-93-5056-512-4).
28. **Environmental Health and Problems (2013)**
Bharti, P.K. and Gajananda, Kh. (eds.)
(ISBN: 978-93-5056-263-5).
29. **Environmental Pollution and Biodiversity (2012)**
Bharti, P.K.; Chauhan, Avnish and Kumar, P. (eds.)
(ISBN: 978-93-5056-149-2).
30. **Fisheries and Toxicology (2014)**
Zaki, M.S.A.; Bharti, P.K. and Chauhan, A. (eds.)
(ISBN: 978-93-5056-452-3).
31. **Fish Habitat and Aquaculture (2015)**
Bharti, P.K.; Gupta Kr. Sanjay (eds.)
(ISBN: 978-93-5056-744-9).
32. **Fisheries and Sustainable Aquaculture (2016)**
Gupta, S.K.; Bharti, P.K (eds.)
(ISBN: 978-93-5056-797-5).
33. **Food Processing, Management and Nanotechnology (2016)**
Chauhan, Avnish; Bharti, P.K. (eds.)
(ISBN: 978-93-5056-796-8).
34. **Freshwater Ecosystem and Xenobiotics (2013)**
Bharti, P.K.; Zaki, M. and Chauhan, A. (eds.)
(ISBN: 978-93-5056-299-4).
35. **Limnology and Aquatic Science (2015)**
Sharma, S. and Bharti, P.K. (eds.)
(ISBN: 978-93-5056-735-7).

36. **Medicinal Plants: *Distribution, Utilization and Significance* (2015)**
Sharma, P.; Bharti, P.K. and Narayan Singh (eds.)
(ISBN: 978-93-5056-734-0).

37. **Microbial Applications and Environment (2014)**
Bharti, Pawan K. (ed.)
(ISBN: 978-93-5056-515-5).

38. **Microbial Ecology and Habitat (2014)**
Bharti, Pawan K. (ed.)
(ISBN: 978-93-5056-514-8).

39. **Natural Ecosystem and Climate Change (2015)**
Bharti, P.K., and Kh. Gajananda (ed.)
(ISBN: 978-93-5056-745-6).

40. **Pest Management and Agro-Techniques (2016)**
Biswas Asim; Bharti, P.K., and Chauhan Avnish (eds.)
(ISBN: 978-93-5056-794-4).

41. **Prakriti me Aushadhi (*in Hindi*) (2012)**
Singh, J.R.; Bharti, P.K. and Bharti, B.
(ISBN: 978-93-5056-200-0).

42. **Seed Technology, Plant Growth and Cropping System (2015)**
Tyagi, P.K. and Bharti, P.K. (eds.)
(ISBN: 978-93-5056-738-8).

43. **Soil Characteristics and Agro-ecology (2015)**
Avnish Chauhan and Bharti, P.K. (eds.)
(ISBN: 978-93-5056-758-6)

44. **Soil Contamination and Conservation (2015)**
Ezeaku, P.I. and Bharti, P.K. (eds.)
(ISBN: 978-93-5056-737-1).

45. **Soil Quality and Contamination (2013)**
Bharti, P.K. and Chauhan, Avnish (eds.)
(ISBN: 978-93-5056-361-8).

46. **Waste Disposal and Management (2015)**
Bharti, P.K.; Tabassum, B. and Bajaj, P. (eds.)
(ISBN: 978-93-5056-729-6).

47. **Waste Generation and Utilization (2016)**
Bajaj Priya; Tabassum, B., and Bharti, P.K. (eds.)
(ISBN: 978-93-5056-792-0).

48. **Waste Management and Environmental Health (2016)**
Tabassum, B., Bajaj Priya, and Bharti, P.K. (eds.)
(ISBN: 978-93-5056-777-7).

49. **Water Resources and Agriculture (2014)**
Bharti, P.K. and Ezeaku Peter Ikemefuna (eds.)
(ISBN: 978-93-5056-481-3).

50. **Water Resources Management: *Monitoring and Assessment* (2016)**
Gupta Sandeep and Bharti, P.K. (eds.)
(ISBN: 978-93-5056-799-9).

Preface

The global demand for plant based products, such as feed and food, is increasing dramatically, as illustrated by the recent doubling of the price of most commodity crops. Unfortunately, the poorest people on earth will be the first victims of expected food shortage. The first obvious factor is the still exponentially growing world population. It is hard to fathom, but in the coming decades three billion additional people will have to be fed while less arable land is utilized. Furthermore, the standard of living is anticipated to continue to go up in many developing countries where consumption of animal products is burgeoning, in turn necessitating a larger input of plant-derived feed because, on average, the production of one kilogram of meat requires 4 to 8 kilograms of cereals.

There is an urgent need of further improvement and to increase crop productivity. Whereas in the sixties 'green revolution', based on the use of new crop varieties and the efficient application of agrochemicals, immensely contributed to increased plant productivity, biotechnological innovations are expected to enhance the ability of plants to capture sun energy and to convert it into useful products for mankind. One major area for biotechnological improvement is boosting up intrinsic crop yield in a sustainable manner with a minimum input of water, fertilizers and agrochemicals.

As yield is the most important trait for breeding, a considerable amount of eco-physiological research has been conducted on yield performance of crops. In contrast, surprisingly little is known about the molecular networks underpinning crop yield, partly because of its multi-factorial nature in which many physiological processes, such as photosynthesis, water and mineral uptake, and stress tolerance determine the resources available to new cells, tissues, and organs. A better understanding of yield will enable scientists to select or engineer crops with a higher productivity.

Plant diseases have caused severe losses to humans in several ways. Many plant diseases cause less dramatic losses annually throughout the world but collectively constitute sizable losses to farmers and can reduce the aesthetic values of landscape plants and home gardens. The goal of plant disease management is to reduce the economic and aesthetic damage caused by plant diseases. Disease management might be viewed as proactive whereas disease control is reactive, although it is often difficult to distinguish between the two concepts, especially in the application of specific measures.

Plant disease management practices depend on anticipating occurrence of disease and attacking vulnerable points in the disease cycle. Therefore, correct diagnosis of a disease is necessary to identify the pathogen, which is the real target of any disease management program. A thorough understanding of the disease cycle, including climatic and other environmental factors that influence the cycle, and cultural requirements of the host plant, are essential to effective management of any disease.

The present book updates the subject matter and issues related to crop productivity, plant disease, plant treatment technology, plant health issues, agro-technology, sustainable agriculture and plant disease management. Thanks are due to contributors from various institutions and publisher for their interest in this book. The book will definitely provide a multidisciplinary forum to explore emerging areas in the field of crop plant productivity, plant health, agro-biodiversity, agriculture biotechnology, environmental conservation, plant disease management and agro-technology.

–Editors
(envbooks@gmail.com)

Contents

Pages: 1-18

CROP PRODUCTIVITY AND PLANT DISEASE MANAGEMENT

Edited by: Dr. Alka Chauhan; Dr. Pawan Kumar 'Bharti'; Ms. Deepti Sadana

ISBN: 978-93-5056-791-3

Edition: 2016

Published by: Discovery Publishing House Pvt. Ltd., New Delhi (India)

CHAPTER - 1

Crop Residues Management
Improving Soil Quality and *Crop Productivity*

Tripti Nayak[*1]; **Chandrakant Thakur**[2]; **Payal Devi**[3] and **Mala Kumari**[4]

ABSTRACT

Crop residues of common cultivated crops are an important resource not only as a source of significant quantities of nutrients for crop production but water and soil quality and Also affecting soil physical, chemical, and biological functions and properties and water and air quality. This can only be achieved with the better understanding of residue, soil, and management factors and their interactions, which affect the decomposition and nutrient release processes. In addition, crop residues and their proper management affect the soil quality either directly or indirectly. Crop residue management practices should be selected to enhance crop yields with a minimum adverse effect on the environment. It is suggested that in each cropping system, the constraints

[1] Department of Soil Science and Agriculture Chemistry, Indira Gandhi Krishi Vishwa Vidyalaya, Raipur - 492 012, Chhattisgarh, (India)

[2] Department of Chemical Engineering, National Institute of Technology Raipur, Chhattisgarh, (India)

[3] Department of Entomology, Indira Gandhi Krishi Vishwa Vidyalaya, Raipur - 492 012, Chhattisgarh, (India)

[4] Department of Genetics & Plant Breeding, Indira Gandhi Krishi Vishwa Vidyalaya, Raipur - 492 012, Chhattisgarh, (India)

to production and sustainability should be identified and conceptualized to guide toward the best option. Multidisciplinary and integrated efforts by soil scientists, agronomists, ecologists, environmentalists, and economists are needed to design a system approach for the best choice of crop residue management system to enhance both agricultural productivity and sustainability.

Keywords: Crop Residues Management, Soil Quality, Crop Productivity

INTRODUCTION

It is well recognized that the organic matter content of a soil is a key attribute of fertility. The beneficial effects of organic matter on the physical, chemical, and biological properties of soil are well documented. Decline in organic matter content in intensive cropping systems is considered to be the major problem in maintaining agricultural productivity in the tropics. Additions of organic materials such as crop residues play an important role in the recycling of nutrients. More than one half of all dry matter in the global harvest is in the form of residues, and in most developing countries the amount of nutrients in residues are often several orders of magnitude higher than the quantities applied as fertilizers. Thus, proper management of crop residues for the maintenance of soil fertility cannot be overstressed. This coordinated research project (CRP) focused on countries where crop production and soil fertility can be sustained by the better management of crop residues.

Organic matter contributes to plant growth through beneficial effects on the physical, chemical, and biological properties of the soil, including (*i*) provision of a carbon and energy source for soil microbes; (*ii*) improvement of soil aggregation, thus reducing the hazard of erosion; (*iii*) retaining of nutrients and water; (*iv*) provision of nutrients through decomposition; and (*v*) reduction of soil compaction. The amount of soil organic matter is controlled by the balance between additions of plant and animal materials and losses by decomposition. Both additions and losses are directly affected by management practices. For example, replacing perennial vegetation with short season vegetation and the burning of crop residues result in a reduction in organic inputs to the soil, while application of animal and crop residues, use of cover crops, and reduced tillage increase inputs or reduce losses and hence help to maintain or increase soil organic matter content. Under tropical conditions, organic matter is rapidly lost through accelerated oxidation due to hot and moist conditions. Rapid losses can be arrested through appropriate agronomic practices that include retention of crop residues (CR).

This CRP supported national efforts in eleven Member States to identify options managing crop residues for sustainable agricultural production and environmental preservation in a wide range of soils and cropping systems.

WHAT IS CROP RESIDUES?

Crop residues are a tremendous natural resource-not a waste. Residue management is receiving a great deal of attention because of its diverse effects on soil physical, chemical, and biological properties. The quantities of nutrients that can be returned annually to soils as residues of common cultivated crops are considerable, requiring worthwhile consideration. Biological nitrogen fixation (BNF) by leguminous crops and the recycling of fixed nitrogen (N) when leguminous crop residues are returned to the soil can be a significant source of N to the soil organic N pool as well as for subsequent plant uptake. The amount of N that recycles into agricultural fields through residues may add 25 to 100 Tg of N year- into agricultural soils (Mosier and Kroeze, 1998). Thus, there is a need to determine sink sizes and turnover rates of different quality residues and to increase the efficiency of nutrient cycling from residues through different soil sinks, and eventually to growing plants, with minimum loss from the system.

This may involve development of practices to enhance the immobilization of nutrients when plants are not growing, as well as practices to increase nutrient availability when plants are actively growing. Information on the kinetics of decomposition of the crop residues and mineralization-immobilization turnover of different quality residues (leguminous and non-leguminous) is required to ascertain the actual amount of crop residues needed to maintain the soil productivity and to ensure environmental protection by minimizing nutrient losses and soil erosion. Addition of organic matter (OM) to the soil through the return of crop residues also improves soil structure, influences soil water, air, and temperature relations, helps control runoff and erosion, and makes tillage easier.

DEFINITION OF CROP RESIDUES

Crop residues, in general, are parts of the plants left in the field after crops have been harvested and thrashed or left after pastures are grazed. These materials have at times been regarded as waste materials that require disposal but it has become increasingly realized that they are important natural resources and not wastes.

ENERGY FROM CROP RESIDUES

If surplus crop residues, instead of being burnt in the fuel, are used for production of commercial energy, they will become a marketable produce which will bring additional income to the farmers. Combustion of CR (crop residues)under controlled conditions in a power plant will greatly reduce air pollution caused during uncontrolled burning from emission of smoke and particulate matter. Studies at Punjab Agricultural University and in Thailand have shown that the cost of CR increases with increase in the quantity to be collected, because of the longer distances over which these have to be transported (Pathak and Bining, 1982; Anonymous, 1991). For this reasons, CR are not a suitable fuel for large power plants. They are, however, an appropriate fuel for decentralized power generation in the rural sector where these are available. CR based power generation will add to the income of the farmers in production catchments, as they will be able to sell the surplus CR. It will create self-reliance in the rural sector for power supply, encourage development of agro-processing industries in villages, create new employment opportunities and reduce migration to urban centers. The farmer, being the supplier of energy source and also the main energy consumer, will have an opportunity to influence and even participate in the management of decentralized power generation. It is important to successfully address technical and management related issues for recovery and supply of CR at a reasonable cost for power generation.

Many crop residues have high ash content which lower their calorific value and aggravate clinker formation. Presence of alkali metals like potassium in large amounts, makes some CR unsuitable for combustion and other high temperature conversion processes, because the alkali metals volatilize at relatively low temperature and foul up the user system. But the major problems in use of CR as energy source relate to their thin spread over large area after crop harvest and low bulk density. The rice husk or bagase burn each year which are collected from harvested area. Compared to the 250 to 300 kg/m^3 bulk density of sized wood, the bulk density of CR varies from 30 to 150 kg/m^3. The bulk density of residues of agro-processing like rice husk and groundnut shell does not exceed 100 kg/m^3. This creates problems in handling, transport and storage. Large volume to mass ratio of CR requires large reactor volumes. The flow ability of CR is very poor due their light weight and irregular size and shape. Without densification, most CR are not suitable for energy generation on commercial scale. Successfully tested technology packages are needed to promote CR based energy generation and these should include equipment and practices for all operations from harvest/collection of CR to their supply in the desired form to the energy generation system.

DECOMPOSITION OF CROP RESIDUES

The decomposition of crop residues is a microbial-mediated progressive breakdown of organic materials with ultimate end products C (Carbon) and nutrients released into the biological circulation in the ecosystem at both a local and a global scale. Crop residues represent only a fraction of total C in soil but these decompose very rapidly. It has been estimated that about half of the global CO, output from soil originates from the decomposition of annual litter fall (CoQ teaux *et al.*, 1995). However, there is a vast pool of stable OM in the soil, but this decomposes very slowly-over centuries or millennia (Campbell *et al.*, 1967; Jenkinson and Rayner, 1977; Goh *et al.*, 1984; Parton *et al.*, 1987).

CoQteaux et *al.* (1995) stated that plant residue decomposition involves two simultaneous and fundamental processes: the concomitant mineralization and humidification of C compounds by microorganisms and the leaching downward in the soil of soluble compounds, whose C and N are progressively mineralized and immobilized.

According to Gregorich and Janzen (1998), in natural ecosystems the decomposition synchronizes with plant growth and C and other nutrients are utilized in the system with maximum efficiency. However, disturbance of these ecosystems may retard or accelerate the decomposition process relative to the other ecosystem processes and may lead to the deterioration of some of the components of the ecosystems. An understanding of this process will help to ensure the proper management of this important resource.

FACTORAS AFFECTING CROP RESIDUE DECOMPOSITION

Residue decomposition processes are controlled by three main factors:

1. Kind of plant residues
2. Edaphic factors
3. Residue management factors

Many of these factors are not independent as a change in one factor may affect other factors. For example, high soil moisture may result in lower soil temperature and aeration and surface residue application may affect soil moisture and temperature simultaneously. Because of these strong interactions, it is often difficult to isolate the effects of specific environmental factors on residue decomposition.

1. Crop Residue Factors

(a) Residue Particle Size

Ground plant material has often been used for convenience in the study of plant residue decomposition because of their uniform substrate. There is controversy regarding the effect of plant residue particle size on the rate of residue decomposition, and mineralization-immobilization turnover (MIT) of N in the soil (Angers and Recous, 1997; Jensen, 1994; Sorensen *et al.*, 1996). Small particles may decompose faster than larger particles because of the increased surface area and greater dispersion in soil increasing the susceptibility to microbial attack due to lack of lignified barrier tissue (Summerell and Burgess, 1989), especially if residues are not penetrated readily by fungi and bacteria (Amato *et al.*, 1984; Jensen, 1994; Nelson *et al.*, 1996; Angers and Recous, 1997). Although soil fauna are responsible for only a small proportion (< 10%) of soil respiration (Juma and McGill, 1986; Anderson, 1991), they play an important role in increasing the rate of decomposition by comminuting and redistributing OM, making it more accessible to microbial attack. For example, Curry and Byrne (1992) reported a 26-47% faster decomposition of straw in mesh bags allowing earthworms than in bags that excluded earthworms during 8 to10 month period of decomposition. However, the microbial biomass and products formed during the initial decomposition of small particles may be better protected against further decomposition due to a more intimate mixing of the mineral soil (Van Schrevan, 1964; Saggar *et al.*, 1996; Skene *et al.*, 1996).

(b) Age of Residue

In general, water-soluble fractions (sugars, organic acids, proteins, and part of structural carbohydrates) are degraded first (Reber and Scharer, 1971; Knapp *et al.*, 1983) followed by structural polysaccharides (cellulose and hemicellulose) (Harper and Lynch, 1981) and then lignin (Harman *et al.*, 1977; Stout *et al.*, 1981; Collins *et al.*, 1990). Consequently, the residue of immature plants generally decomposes more readily than those of older plants (Wise and Schaefar, 1994; Cortez *et al.*, 1996) and, as a result, releases more nutrients (Luna-Orea *et al.*, 1996).

(c) Leaf Toughness

Physical leaf toughness affecting residue decomposition has received little attention. Gallardo and Merino (1993) developed a toughness index of residue and proposed leaf toughness as an index of substrate quality. Silica content is responsible for leaf toughness and has been reported to affect the digestibility of plant material and their decomposition (Goering and Van Soest, 1970; Ma and Takahashi, 1989). In general, the greater the silica content, the slower the decomposition.

(d) Desiccation

The drying of crop residues before incorporation is a common procedure in N mineralization studies. Heat drying plant materials even at low temperatures between 50 and 60°C can produce analytically significant increases in lignin concentration because of the production of artifact lignin via a nonenzymatic browning reaction that involves plant N (Goering and Van Soest, 1970; Moore *et al.*,1988)

2. Crop Residue Quality

Plants contain 15-60% cellulose, 10-30% hemicellulose, 5-30% lignin, 2-15% protein, and soluble substances, such as sugars, amino acids, amino sugars, and organic acids, which may contribute 10% of dry weight (Paul and Clark, 1989). Plants also contain cutin, polyphenols, and silica . The rate of organic matter breakdown depends on the relative proportions of each of these fractions, such as soluble sugars, cellulose, hemicellulose, and lignin (Stout *et al.*, 1981).

(a) C/N Ratio and Nitrogen Content

Crop residues contain about 40-50% C on dry weight basis, but their N content varies considerably, causing the variation in C/N ratios. It is generally accepted that residues with a wide C/N ratio decompose more slowly than those with a narrow C/N ratio (Parr and Papendick, 1978), and plant residues with high N content show high decomposition rates and nutrient release (Janzen and Kucey, 1988; Douglas and Rickman, 1992).

(b) Lignin

The role of lignin as an inhibitor in the decomposition process has been elucidated in several studies (Meentemeyer, 1978; Berendse *et al.*, 1987., Lignin is known to be a recalcitrant substance, highly resistant to microbial decomposition (Mellilo *et al.*, 1982), and only relatively few microorganisms can degrade lignin and these are exclusively aerobic (Jenkinson, 1988). Many workers have found that increasing the lignin concentration reduces the decomposition rate and nutrient release from plant residues and also enhances nutrient immobilization, especially N (Aber and Mellilo, 1982; Aber *et al.*, 1990; Tian *et al.*, 1992).

(c) Polyphenols

Vallis and Jones (1973) suggested that polyphenols bind to protein and form complexes resistant to decomposition. Polyphenols can also bind to organic N compounds (amino acids and proteins) in leaves, making N unavailable, or bind to soluble organic N released from leaves, forming resistant complexes in the soil (Northup *et al.*, 1995). The importance of polyphenols in residue decomposition and the mineralization process has been debated frequently (Swift *et al.*, 1979).

(d) Combined Chemical Composition

Herman *et al.*, (1977) and Tian *et al.*, (1995b) found that the decomposition rate of plant residues could not be predicted from individual property of the organic material such as C/N ratio, lignin content, or carbohydrate content, but when combined these properties could accurately predict relative rates of decomposition for a broad range of plant residues.

3. Methodological Problems Associated with Residue Quality Characterization

To quantify residue quality and its relationships with residue decomposition, mostly in terms of N mineralization (Bending *et al.*, 1998). Although general trends have been observed, no unique relationship has been developed (Vanlauwe *et al.*, 1997).

(a) Extraction Methods for Lignin and Polyphenols

Different methods are used for extracting polyphenols from plant tissues. Amounts of total ploypheno1s extracted from plant tissues varied from 30 to 90% according to a method used (Vanlauwe *et al.*, 1997).

(b) Age of Plant Residues and Molecular Size of Polyphenols

The concentration of polyphenol is generally greater in mature residues than in green leaves (Thomas and Asakawa, 1993), and polyphenols have different properties with respect to binding N-containing compounds, depending on their molecular weights (Scalbert, 1991).

(c) Methods of Determining Decomposition Rates

Different particle sizes of crop residues and methods of determining residue decomposition (viz. direct application to soil or application in mesh bags) are known to affect residue decomposition rates (Magid *et al.*, 1997a).

(d) Variation in Composition of Same Plant Species at Different Sites and Different Plant Parts

Several workers have reported differences in residue decomposition due to differences in N, C/N, lignin/N, and polyphenol/N ratios even for the same species. Variation of site, plant part, and environment conditions also affected the litter chemistry of residues from the same plant species (Berg and Tammy, 1991).

4. Edaphic Factors

(a) Soil pH

Soil pH is one of the most important factors influencing residue decomposition as it affects both the nature and size of population of microorganisms and the multiplicity of enzymes at the microbial level, which subsequently affect decomposition (Paul and Clark, 1989).

(b) Soil Temperature

The influence of temperature on crop residue decomposition has been described quantitatively as the temperature quotient Q_{10}, Values of Q_{10}, for the N mineralization rate of native SOM in th temperature range between 5 and 35°C have been reported to be approximately 2 (Scholes *et al.*, 1994). Microorganisms function at maximum growth and activity in the temperature range of 20-40°C and showed maximum decomposition in this range (Stott and Martin, 1989).

(c) Soil Moisture

The growth and activity of soil microorganisms rely on soil moisture, which, in turn, produces significant effects on plant residue decomposition and nutrient cycling (Schomberg *et al.*, 1994). Sommers *et al.* (1981) observed that soil dried to a water potential of - 10 Mpa evolved CO, at about half the rate of soils incubated at optimal water content (-20 to -50 kPa).

(d) Aerobic and Anaerobic Conditions

Decomposition and mineralization are slower and less complete under anaerobic than aerobic conditions (Kretzschmar and Ladd, 1993).

(e) *Available Nutrients*

The primary limiting factor in most soils for microbial growth is C. An abundance of C is added to the soil through crop residues. New cells of microorganisms require not only C, H, 0, and N, but also P, K, S, Mg, Ca, and micronutrients. When an organic material is added to the soil, microorganisms decomposing it can obtain the necessary inorganic nutrients (N, P, K, S, Ca, etc.) for growth from two sources: (*i*) those already present in the soil in plant available forms; and (*ii*) those in the added organic material itself.

(f) *Soil Texture, Clay Content, and Soil Structure*

Jenkinson (1977) and Ladd and Foster (1988) showed that the decomposition of plant materials was more rapid in soil with less clay content because the clay protected the OM from decomposition. As clay content increases, soil surface area also increases, which results in an increased SOM stabilization potential (Saggar *et al.*, 1996). This stabilized OM has turnover time ranging from 10 to 1000 years (Parton *et al.*, 1987). The role of clay in stabilizing OM appears to be more important in warmer soils where higher decomposition rates can be expected. In cold soils, cool temperature may be the main factor slowing decomposition, and clay content may be less important (Anderson, 1995).

Texture also influences the soil physical environment (Hassink *et al.*, 1993), which further affects the microbial activity (Killham *et al.*, 1993). Other effects of soil texture may be through N and P availability by influencing total OM accumulation or microbial activity (Hassink *et al.*, 1993).

(g) *Indigenous Macro and Micro-organisms*

Decomposition and mineralization are largely biological processes, mainly accounted for by the activity of the soil microflora. However, abiotic processes cannot be discounted entirely, especially in harsh environments, where appreciable plant litter mass may be lost by abiotic mechanisms, such as fragmentation, physical abrasion, photochemical breakdown, and leaching. Fungi and bacteria are ultimately responsible for the biochemical processes in the decomposition of organic residues (Juma and McGill, 1986).

EFFECTS OF RESIDUES AND MANAGEMENT ON SOIL QUALITY

1. Soil Quality Indicators

The increasing awareness of the progressive degradation of soils has led to the search for a reliable measure of soil quality. Traditionally, soil productivity has been used as a measure for soil quality (Hornick, 1992).

Soil quality has been defined as "the capacity of a soil to take up, store, and recycle water, minerals, and energy so that crop production is maximized and environmental degradation is minimized" (Trasar-Cepeda *et al.*, 1998).

Brookes (1989) stated that a high-quality soil should (*i*) assist in the reduction of contaminant levels in surface and subsurface waters; (*ii*) allow the production of healthy and nutritious crops; and (*iii*) display key characteristics of ecosystem maturity.

Soil quality depends on a large number of physical, chemical, biological, and biochemical soil properties, and its characterization requires the selection of the properties most sensitive to the management practices as soil quality indicators (Cameron *et al.*, 1996).

Crop residue management is known to either directly or indirectly affect most of these indicators. It is perceived that soil quality is improved by the adoption of crop residue management practices. Karlen *et al.* (1994) evaluated several proposed soil quality indicators and developed a "soil quality index" based on several parameters.

2. Soil Physical Properties

Crop residues play an important role in maintaining good soil physical conditions. In most climates, the removal of all crop residues from the field leads to a deterioration of soil physical properties (Kladivko, 1994).

(a) Soil Erosion

Many studies reported that incorporating residues to various degrees can reduce runoff and hence water erosion losses of soil by 27-90% (Fawcett. 1995).

(b) Soil Aggregation and Soil Structure

Information on the effect of crop residue management on soil aggregation is limited, although it is well established that OM helps maintain aggregate stability (Haynes *et al.*, 1991; Haynes and Francis, 1993). The addition of crop residues is expected to have a positive effect on soil structure and aggregation.

(c) Compaction, Bulk Density, and Penetration Resistance

Under the weight of soil mass, the impact of raindrops, or the compactive pressure of traffic, soil particles reorient themselves and pack together more tightly, while excluding air and water contained within, resulting in higher bulk density and penetration resistance. However, surface and subsurface soil density and penetration resistance may increase naturally when using a no-tillage system resulting from the raindrops effect and the structural failure (collapse) of soils having low-stability aggregates (Bautista *et al.*, 1996).

(d) Soil Hydraulic Conductivity and Infiltration

Crop residues increase soil hydraulic conductivity and infiltration by modifying mainly soil structure, proportion of macropores, and aggregate stability. These increases have been reported in treatments where crop residues were retained on the soil surface or incorporated by conservation tillage (Murphy *et al.*, 1993). Thus, although increases in soil hydraulic conductivity and infiltration can result through proper residue management practices, care should be taken because increased infiltration may lead to leaching, causing nutrient losses and groundwater pollution.

(e) Soil Temperature

Crop residue management influences soil temperature significantly. Major mechanisms involved are (*i*) a change in radiant energy balance; and (*ii*) insulation (Unger and McCalla, 1980). Residue characteristics involved in the reflectance of incoming radiations include residue age, color, orientation, distribution, and amount (Unger and McCalla, 1980).

3. Soil Chemical Properties

(a) Soil pH

One of the most important factors determining soil fertility is pH, which may, however, be influenced strongly by cultivation and crop residue management. It has been noted in Australia, New Zealand, and many other parts of the world that soil pH decreases as a result of continuous cultivation of clovers and other leguminous crops attributed mainly to BNF and to proton release by legume roots resulting in the accumulation of organic anions such as malate, citrate, and oxalate in plants.

(b) Soil Organic Matter and Nitrogen

The addition of crop residues on Organic Matter (OM) and N increases may depend on the amount of residue added, quality of the residue environment, and the duration of addition. Short-term addition in hot climates, promoting rapid decomposition, may lead to only a slight or no increase in soil OM (Aggarwal *et al.*, 1997), but long-term addition has been shown to increase both C and N contents .The effect of crop residues on SOM content is related strongly to the amount of residues added and only weakly related to the type of residue applied (Rasmussen and Collins, 1991).

(c) Phosphorus

Most workers reported increased phosphorus (P) accumulation near the soil surface no-tillage or minimum tillage systems. Stratification of P resulting from minimum tillage is believed to result in improved P availability because there is less soil contact of organic P in crop residues and hence less P fixation. Burning cereal residues also resulted in a higher extractable P content in the surface 0- to 2.5-cm soil layer and increased plant uptake. Compared to residue removal, the incorporation of residues of cluster bean, mung bean, and pearl millet has been found to increase available P, probably due to an increase in phosphatase (both acid and alkaline) enzyme activity (Aggarwal *et al.*, 1997).

(d) Other Nutrients

Nutrients are released over time by chemical, physical, and biological processes. Considerable quantities are released within a short period of time depending on the residue quality (Luna-Orea *et al.*, 1996) and the kind of nutrients. Increases in exchangeable cations (K, Ca, Mg) and base saturation have been reported (Geiger *et al.*, 1992). The greater availability of both macro- and micronutrients has been reported more under conservation tillage than other conventional tillage.

(e) Loss of Nutrients Due to Burning of Crop Residues

The burning of crop residues can result in nutrient loss as a result of the direct convective transfer of ash (Harwood and Jackson, 1975), and subsequent losses may be increased by the action of wind and water. Simultaneous losses of C, S, and N have been reported on residue burning.

4. Soil Biological Properties

Leaving crop residues on the soil surface or incorporation provides a favorable environment for soil and surface residue dwelling organisms because of reduced water loss, amelioration of temperature extremes, fluctuations, and the presence of a relatively continuous substrate for decomposers (Wardle and Lavelle, 1997). Several aspects of crop residue management practices on soil biological properties have been studied.

(a) Soil Biota

Microbial biomass/microorganisms: Soil microbial biomass (SMB) is the living component of the soil that comprises mainly fungi and bacteria, including soil microfauna and algae. Although it accounts for only 1-3% of organic C and 2-6% of organic N in soil it plays a key role in SOM and nutrient dynamics by acting as both a sink (during immobilization) and a source (mineralization) of plant nutrients. Because SMB and microbial activity are closely related to SOM content, they are influenced positively by organic amendments such as crop residues and animal manures.

Higher populations of bacteria, *Actinomycetes,* fungi, earthworms, and nematodes have been reported in residue mulch than in incorporated residues. Residue incorporation produced more microbial activity than residue removal or burning . Direct counts of viable bacteria and total fungal hyphae were consistently higher on residue from incorporated treatments compared with removed or burned treatments.

Soil fauna: Many studies have shown that earthworms and microarthropods may assume a more dominant role in OM decomposition and nutrient flux patterns in residue management systems. Although crop residue management and their effect on microclimate play a role in determining the population of macroorganisms, the nutritional quality of plant material appears to be more important in influencing earthworm population.

Mycorrhiza: Mycorrhiza play an important role in plant growth and crop production. However, effects of soil management prac tices on the abundance and activity of mycorrhiza are complex. It is reported that tillage disrupts soil networks of mycorrhizal hyphae and may impair nutrient uptake and reduce crop yields. Cropping with hosts that become colonized extensively with mycorrhiza may affect the quality of crops produced (in terms of relatively greater nutrient uptake) and improve the quality of the crop residues produced. This may improve the soil quality indirectly by improving the aggregate stabiltiy, microbial biomass, and other parameters. However, there is little published evidence on the effects of tillage and residue management on mycorrhizal associations with plants and their effects on soil and plant quality need to be explored.

(b) Microbial Processes

Crop residues and tillage have been reported to significantlyand rapidly (within few weeks) alter the composition, distribution, and activity of the soil microbial community and enzymes. Soil pH also controls either the rate of enzyme activity or the stability of some enzymes. Beare *et al.* (1993) found that microbial growth is favored in the minimum tillage soil environment, resulting in greater enzyme activities.

Carbohydrates influence soil quality mainly through their role in the formation and stabilization of aggregates.

RESPONSES OF CROP GROWTH AND YIELD

1. Germination, Seedling Establishment, and Growth

In general, the early removal of straw by burning has been used by farmers to get rid of the straw from the field for better seedbed preparation for the seeding of small seed crops and especially for crops grown for seed production and some cereals. Since the enforcement or ban on burning in some countries, crop residues are utilized on farm, either incorporated or left on the surface. As direct drilling or minimum tillage leaves the straw from a previous crop on the soil surface without or minimum incorporation, these residues are either mulched or left on the surface as such, depending on the availability of machinery and time with the farmers.

2. Crop Yields

Several workers have examined the effect of residue management practices on the harvested yield of the following crop. Results from these experiments are conflicting because of a number of factors involved, including residue quality, management, and edaphic factors and also the health of the previous crop and their complex interactions with various management factors in determining the ultimate crop yield. This indicates that no one residue management system is superior under all conditions. The constraints identified in the crop production system would guide toward the best option. Thus, effort has been made to relate the effects on yield resulting from various crop residue management practices to the constraints in crop production.

However, under different environmental and edaphic constraints, different residue management practices have been found to show different grain yield trends. In cropping systems, where the previous crop was infested with pests and disease, treatments with burning of residues generally yielded more grains (Jenkyn *et al.*, 1995; Sumner *et al.*, 1995; Prew *et al.*, 1995).

3. Biological Nitrogen Fixation

No-tillage and conservation tillage soils have often decreased amounts of soil nitrate compared to cultivated soils. which may affect N, fixation, as nodulation and N, fixation in leguminous crops are increased in soils with a low concentration of nitrates. Increased N, fixation under direct drilling as compared to cultivated soils has been reported in many leguminous crops. Crop residues with a wide C/N ratio or C-rich sources have also been added with the aim of immobilizing the soil inorganic N and to increase N, fixation

4. Phytotoxicity of Crop Residues

The decomposition of some crop residues has been found to have adverse allopathic effects on seed germination, seedling, and crop growth due to substances produced during residue decomposition. Microorganisms can produce **a** large range of substances, potentially toxic to plant roots but these toxins seldom accumulate in aerobic soils because they are metabolized rapidly by microorganisms.

EFFECT OF RESIDUE MANAGEMENT ON THE ENVIRONMENT

Crop residues and tillage management also affect the erosion of soil and the associated nutrients and chemicals and also leaching, which may pollute the groundwater or surface waters. Another important factor to consider is the fuel energy consumed and pollution created by machinery in incorporating the residues.

Management of crop residues other than by burning may also produce greenhouse gases. The presence of crop residues on soil surface may influence ammonia volatilization by acting as a source of urea. Ammonia volatilization losses may also occur when crop residues decompose on soil surface and denitrification can be stimulated on their incorporation. If, however, residues are burned on the soil surface, the ash, which is alkaline, can enhance ammonia emissions (Bacon and Freney, 1989).

CONCLUSION

This review reveals that crop residues of common cultivated crops are an important resource, not only as a source of significant amounts of nutrients for crops and hence agricultural productivity, but also affecting soil physical, chemical, and biological functions and properties and water and air quality. Crop residue management is known to affect most of these soil quality indicators either directly or indirectly. It is perceived that soil quality is improved by the adoption of proper crop residue management practices crop residue management practices should be selected to enhance crop yields with minimum adverse effects on the environment several workers have examined the effect of residue management practices on the harvested yield of the following crop. a system approach for the best choice of crop residue management practices for enhancing agricultural productivity and sustainability.

REFERANCES

Aber, J.D., and Mellilo, J.M. (1982). Nitrogen Mineralisation in Decaying Hardwood Leaf Litter as a Function of Initial Nitrogen and Lignin Content. *Can. J. Bor.* 60, 2263-2269.

Aber, J.D., Mellilo, J.M., and McClaugherty, C.A. (1990). Predicting long-term Patterns of Mass-loss, Nitrogen Dynamics and Soil Organic Matter from Initial Litter Chemistry. *Can. J. Bo!.* 68, 2201-2208.

Aggarwal, R.K., Kumar, P., and Power, J.F. (1997). Use of Crop Residue and Manure to Conserve Water and Enhance Nutrient Availability and Pearl Millet Yields in an Arid Tropical Region. *Soil Tilluge Rex* 41, 43-51.

Amato, M., Jackson, R.B., Butler, J.H.A,, and Ladd, I.N. (1984). Decomposition of Plant Materials in Australian Soils. 11. Residual Organic I4C and "N from Legume Plant Parts Decomposing Under Field and Laboratory Conditions. *Ausr. J. Soil Res.* 22, 331-341.

Anderson, D.W. (1995). Decomposition of Organic Matter and Carbon Emissions from Soils. *In* "Advances in Soil Science, Soils and Global Change" (R. Lal, J. Kimble, E. Levine, and B.A. Stewart, eds.), pp. 165-1 75. CRC Press, Boca Raton, FL.

Anderson, J.M. (199 I). The Effects of Climate Change on Decomposition Process in Grassland and Coniferous Forests. *Ecol. Appl.* 1, 326-347.

Angers, A., and Recous, S. (1997). Decomposition of Wheat and *rye* Residue as Affected by Particle Size. *Plan! Soil* 189, 197-203.

Anonymous. 1991. Baling Sugarcane Tops and Leaves. Biomass Systems and Technology Project, DHR-5737- A-00-9058-00, USAID/Thailand.

Bautista, S., Bellot, J., and Ramon-Vallejo, V. (1996). Mulching Treatment for Postfire Soil Conservation in a Semiarid Ecosystem. *Arid Snil Res. Rehab.* 10, 235-242.

Beare, M.H., Pohlad, B.R., Wright, D.H., and Coleman, D.C. (1993). Residue Placement and Fungicide Effects on Fungal Communities in Conventional and no-tillage Soils. *Soil Sci. Soc. Am. J.* 57, 392-399.

Bending, G.D., Turner, M.K., and Burns, 1.G. (I 998). Fate of Nitrogen from Crop Residues as Affected by Biochemical Quality and the Microbial Biomass. *Soil Biol. Biochem.* 30, 2055-2065.

Berendse, F., Berg, B., and Bosatta, E. (1987). The Effect of Lignin and Nitrogen on the Decomposition of Litter in Nutrient-poor Ecosystems: A Theoretical Approach. *Can. J . Bor.* 65, 11 16-1 120.

Berg, B., and Tammy, C. 0. (1991). Decomposition and Nutrient Dynamics of Litter in Long-term Optimum Nutrition Experiments. 1. Organic Matter Decomposition in *Picea abies* Needle Litter. Scand. *J.* For: *Res.* 6, 305-321.

Cameron, K.C., Cornforth, I.S. McLaren. R.G., and Beare. M.H. (1996). "Soil Quality Indicators for Sustainable Agriculture in New Zealand." Proc. of a Workshop held for MAF Policy by Lincoln Soil Quality Research Centre, Lincoln University, Canterbury, NZ.

Campbell, C.A., Paul, E.A., Rennie, D.A., and McCallum, K.J. (1967). Applicability of the Carbondating Method of Analysis to Soil Humus Studies. *Soil Sci.* 104, 217-224.

Collins, H.P., Rasmussen, P.E., and Douglas, C.L., Jr. (1992). Crop Rotation and Residue Management Effects on Soil Carbon and Microbial Dynamics. *Soil Sci. Soc. Am. J.* 56,783-788.

CoQteaux, M.M., Bottner, P., and Berg, B. (1995). Litter Decomposition, Climate and Litter Quality. Trends *Ecol. Evol.* 10, 63-66.

CoQteaux, M.M., Bottner, P., and Berg, B. (1995). Litter Decomposition, Climate and Litter Quality. Trends *Ecol. Evol.* 10, 63-66.

Curry, J.P., and Byrne, D. (1992). The Role of Earthworms in Straw Decomposition and Nitrogen Turnover in Arable Land in Ireland. *Soil Biol. Biochem.* 24, 1409-1412.

Douglas, C.L., and Rickman, R.W. (1992). Estimating Crop Residue Decomposition from Air Temperature, Initial Nitrogen Content and Residue Placement. *Soil Sci.* SOC. *Am. J. 56,* 272-278.

Fawcett, R.S. (1995). "Impact of Conservation Tillage on the Environment." North Cent. Weed Sci. SOC., Omaha, NE.

Gallardo, A,, and Merino, I. (1993). Leaf Decomposition in Two Mediterranean Ecosystems of Southwest Spain: Influence of Substrate Quality. *Ecology* 74, 152-161.

Geiger, S.C., Manu, A., and Bationo, A. (1992). Changes in Sandy Sahelian Soil Following Crop Residue and Fertiliser Additions. Soil *Sci.* Soc. *Am. J.* 56, 172-177.

Goering, H.K., and Van Soest, P.J. (1970). "Forage Fibre Analyses: Apparatus Reagents, Procedures and Some Applications." USDA Handb. No. 379. U.S. Govt. Printing Offices, Washington, DC.

Goh, K.M., Stout, J.D., and O'Brien, B.J. (1984). The Significance of Fractionation in Dating the Age and Turnover of Soil Organic Matter. *N.Z. J*. Sci. 27, 413-416.

Gregorich, E.G., and Janzen, H.H. (1998). Microbially Mediated Processes: Decomposition. In "Handbook of Soil Science" (M. Sumner, ed.). pp. 106-119. CRC Press, Boca Raton, FL.

Harman, W.A,, McGill, W.B.. and Dormaar, J.E (1977). Effects of Initial Chemical Composition on Decomposition of Roots of Three Grass Species. *Can. J. Soil Sci.* 57, 205-215.

Harwood. C.E., and Jackson, W.D. (1975). Atmospheric Losses of Four Plant Nutrient during a Forest Tire. *Aust. For.* 38, 92-99.

Hassink, J., Bouwman, L.A., Zwart, K.B., and Brussard, L. (1993). Relationships Between Habitable Pore Space. Soil Biota and Mineralizable Rates in Grassland Soils. *Soil Biol. Biochem.* 25, 47-55.

Haynes, R.J., Swift, R.S., and Stephen, R.C. (1991). Influence of Mixed Cropping Rotations (Pasturearable) on Organic Matter Content, Water Stable Aggregation and Clod Porosity in a Group of Soils. *Soil Tillage Res.* 19, 77-87.

Hornick, S.B. (1992). Factors Affecting the Nutritional Quality of Crops. *Am. J. Alrern. Agric.* 7, 63-68.

Janzen. H.H., and Kucey, R.M.N. (1988). C,N, and S Mineralization of Crop Residues as Influenced by Crop Species and Nutrient Regime. *Plant Soil* 106, 35-41.

Jenkinson, D.S. (1988). Soil Organic Matter and its Dynamics. *In* "Russel's Soil Condition and Plant Growth" (A. Wild, ed.), 11th ed., pp. 564-507. Longman, London.

Jenkinson, D.S., and Rayner, J.H. (1977). The Turnover of Soil Organic Matter in Some of the Rothemsted Classical Experiments. *Soil Sci.* 123, 298-305.

Jensen, E.S. (1994). Mineralisation-immobilisation of Nitrogen in Soil Amended with Low C:N Ratio Plant Residues with Different Panicle Sizes. *Soil Biol. Biochem.* 26, 519-521.

Juma, N.G., and McGill, W.B. (1986). Decomposition and Nutrient Cycling in Agroecosystems. *In* "Microfloral and Faunal Interactions in Natural and Agro-Ecosystems" (M.J. Mitchell and J.0. Nakas, eds.), pp. 74-136. Martinus Nijhoff, Dordrecht, The Netherlands.

Karlen, D.L., Wollenhaupt, N.C., Erbach, D.C., Berry, E.C., Swan, J.B., Eash, N. S., and Jordahl, J.L. (1994). Crop Residue Effects on Soil Quality Following 10-years of No-till Corn. *Soil Till. Res.* 31, 149-167.

Killham, K., Amato, M., and Ladd, J.N. (1993). Effect of Substrate Location in Soil and Soil Pore Water Regime on Carbon Turnover. *Soil Biol. Eiochem.* 25, 57-62.

Knapp, E.B., Elliott, L.F., and Campbell, G.S. (1983). Microbial Respiration and Growth during the Decomposition of Wheat Straw. Soil *Bid. Biochem.* 15, 319-323.

Kretzschmar. A., and Ladd, J.N. (1993). Decomposition of 14C-labelledp Lant Material in Soil: The Influence of Substrate Location, Soil Compaction and Earthworm Numbers. Soil *Bid. Biochem.* 25, 803-809.

Kumar. K. and Goh, K.M., Crop Residues and Management Practicees Effects on Soil Quality, Soil Nitrogen Dynamics, Crop Yield, and Nitrogerne Covery. *Soil, Plant, and Ecological Sciences* Division Lincoln University Canterbury, New Zealand.

Luna-Orea, P., Wagger. M.G., and Gumpertz, M.L. (1996). Decomposition and Nutrient Release Dynamics of Two Tropical Legume Cover. *Agmn.* J. 88, 758-764.

Ma, J.F., and Takahashi, E. (1989). Release of Silicon from Rice Straw Under Flooded Conditions. *Soil Sci. Plant Nurr* 35, 663-667.

Magid, J., Jensen, L.S., Mueller, T., and Nielsen, N.E. (1997a). Size-density Fractionantion for *01 situ* Measurements of Rape Straw Decomposition-an Alternative to the Litter Bag Approach' *Soil Bid.Biochem.* 29, 1125-1 133.

Meentemeyer, V. (1978). Macroclimate and Lignin Control of Litter Decomposition Rates. Ecology 59, 465-472.

Mellilo, J.M., Aber, J.D., and Muratore, J.F. (1982). Nitrogen and Lignin Control of Hardwood Leaf Litter Decomposition Dynamics. *Ecology* 63, 621-626.

Moore, J.C., Walter, D.E., and Hunt, H.W. (1988). Arthopod Regulation of Micro-and Mesobiota in Below-ground Detrital Food Webs. *Annu. Rev. Enromol.* 33, 419-439.

Mosier, A., and Kroeze, C. (1998). A New Approach to Estimate Emissions of Nitrous Oxide from Agriculture and its Implications for the Global N, O Budget. Global *Change N e d* 34, 8-13.

Murphy, B.W., Koen, T.B., Jones, B.A,. and Huxedrup. L.M. (1993). Temporal Variation of Hydraulic Properties for Some Soils with Fragile Structure. *Aust. J . Soil Reu.* 31,179-197.

Nelson, C.J. (1996). Allelopathy in Cropping Systems. *Agmn. J.* 88, 991-996.

Nelson, P.N., Ladd, J.N., and Oades, J.M. (1996). Decomposition of I4C- labelled Plant Material in a Salt-affected Soil. *Soil Bid. Biochem.* 28, 433-441.

Northup, R.R., Yu, Z.S., Dahlgren, R.A., and Vogt, K.A. (1995). Polyphenol Control of Nitrogen Release from Pine Litter. *Nature (London)* 377, 227-229.

Pam, J.F., and Papendick, R.I. (1978). Factors Affecting the Decomposition of Crop Residues by Microorganisms. *In* "Crop Residue Management Systems" (W.R. Oschwald, ed.), pp. 101-129. Am. Soc. Agron., Madison, W1.

Parton, W.J., Schimel, D.S., Cole, C.V., and Ojima, D.S. (1987). Analysis of Factors Controlling Soil Organic Matter Levels in Great Plains Grasslands. *Soil Sci. SOC. Am. J.* 51, 1173-1179.

Pathak, B.S. and Bining, A.S. 1982. Economics of Rice Straw Collection for Power Generation, Tech. Report, Punjab Agricultural University, Ludhiana.

Paul, E.A., and Clark, F.E. (1989). "Soil Microbiology and Biochemistry." Academic Press, Orlando, FL.

Rasmussen, P.E., and Collins. H.P. (1991). Long-term Impacts of Tillage, Fertiher, and Crop Residue on Soil Organic Matter in Temperate Semi-arid Regions. *Adv. Agron.* 45, 93-134.

Reber, H., and Scharer, A. (1971). Degradation Sequences in Wheat Straw Extracts Inoculated with Soil Suspensions. *Soil Biol. Biochem.* 3, 381-383.

Saggar, S., Parshotom, A., Sparling, G.P., Feltham, C.W., and Hart, P.B.S. (1996). 14C Labelled Ryegrass Times in Soils Varying in Clay Content and Mineralogy. *Soil Eiol.* Biochem. 28, 1677-1686.

Scalbert, A. (1991). Antimicrobial Properties of Tannins. *Phytochemistry* 30, 3875-3883.

Scholes, R.J., Dalal, R.. and Singer, S. (1994). Soil Physics and Fertility: The Effects of Water, Temperature and Texture. *In* "The Biological Management of Tropical Soil Fertility" (P.L. Woomer and M.J. Swift, eds.), pp. 117-136. Wiley, New York.

Schomberg, H.H., Steiner, J.L., and Unger, P.W. (1994). Decomposition and Nitrogen Dynamics of Crop Residues: Residue Quality and Water Effects. *Soil Sci. Sue. Am. J.* 58, 372-38 1.

Skene, T.M., Skjemstad, J. O.O ades, J.M., and Clarke, P.J. (1996). The Influence of Inorganic Matrices on the Decomposition of Straw. *Ausr. J. Soil Res.* 34, 413-426.

Sommers, L.E., Gilmour, C.M., Wildung. R.E., and Beck, S.M. (1981). The Effect of Water Potential on Decomposition Processes in Soils. *In* "Water Potential Relations in Soil Microbiology" (J.F. Parr. W.R. Gardner and L.F. Elliott, eds.), Spec. Publ. No. 9, pp. 97-117. Soil Sci. *Soc.* Am., Madison, W1.

Sorensen. P., Ladd, J.N., and Amato. M. (1996). Microbial Assimilation od I4C of Ground and Unground Plant Materials Decomposing in a Loamy Sand and a Clay Soil. *Soil Biol. Biochem.* 28, 1425-1434.

Stott, D.E., and Martin, J.P. (1989). Organic Matter Decomposition and Retention in Arid Soils. *Arid Soil Res. Rehab. 3,* 115-148.

Stout, J.D., Goh, K.M., and Rafter, T.A. (1981). Chemistry and Turnover of Naturally Occurring Resistant Organic Compounds in Soil. *In* "Soil Biochemistry" (E.A. Paul and J.N. Ladd, eds.), Vol. 5, pp. 1-73. Dekker, New York.

Summerell, B.A., and Burgess, L.W. (1989). Decomposition and Chemical Composition of Cereal Straw. *Soil Biol. Biochem.* 21, 551-559.

Swift, M.J., Heal, O.W., and Anderson, J.M. (1979). "Decomposition in Terrestrial Ecosystems," Stud. Ecol., Vol. 1. California University Press, Berkeley.

Thomas, R.J., and Asakawa, N.M. (1993). Decomposition of Leaf Litter from Tropical Forage Grasses and Legumes. *Soil Bid. Biochem.* 25, 1351-1361.

Tian, G., Brussaard, L., and Kang, B. T. (1995a). Breakdown of Plant Residues with Contrasting Chemical Compositions Under Humid Tropical Conditions: Effects of Earthworms and Millipedes. *Soil Eiol. Biochem.* 27, 277-280.

Tian, G., Brussaard, L., and Kang. B.T. (1995b). An Index for Assessing the Quality of Plant Residues and Evaluating Their Effects on Soil and Crop in the (sub-) Humid Tropics. *Appl. Soil Ecol.* 2, 25-32.

Tian, G. Kang. B.T., and Brussaard. L. (1992a). Biological Effects of Plant Residues with Contrasting Chemical Compositions Under Humid Tropical Conditions-decomposition and Nutrient Release. *Soil Eiol. Biochem.* 24, 1051-1060.

Trasar-Cepeda, C., Leiros, C., Gil-Stores. F., and Seoane. S. (1998). Towards a Biochemical Index for Soils: An Expression Relating Several Biological and Biochemical Properties. *Eiol. Fertil. Soils* 26, 100-106.

Unger, P.W., and McCalla, T.M. (1980). Conservation Tillage Systems. *A ~ IAJg.r on.* 33, 2-53.

Vallis, I., and Jones, R.J. (1973). Net Mineralization of Nitrogen in Leaves and Leaf Litter of *Desmodium Inrortum* and *Phaseolus Arropupureus* Mixed with Soil. *Soil Eiol. Eiochem.* 5, 391-398.

Van Schrevan, D.A. (1964). Acomparison Between the Effect of Fresh and Dried Organic Materials Added to Soil on Carbon and Nitrogen Mineralization. *Planr* Soil 20, 149-165.

Vanlauwe, B., Diels, J., Sanginga, N., and Merckx, R. (1997). Residue Quality and Decomposition: An Unsteady Relationship? *In* "Driven by Nature: Plant Litter Quality and Decomposition" (G. Cadisch and K.E. Giller, eds.), pp. 157-166. CAB International, Wallingford, UK.

Wardle, D.A., and Lavelle, P. (1997). Linkages Between Soil Biota, Plant Litter Quality and Decomposition. *In* "Driven by Nature: Plant Litter Quality and Decomposition" (G. Cadisch and K.E. Giller, eds.), pp. 107-124. CAB International, Wallingford, UK.

Pages: 19-37

CROP PRODUCTIVITY AND PLANT DISEASE MANAGEMENT

Edited by: Dr. Alka Chauhan; Dr. Pawan Kumar 'Bharti'; Ms. Deepti Sadana

ISBN: 978-93-5056-791-3

Edition: 2016

Published by: Discovery Publishing House Pvt. Ltd., New Delhi (India)

CHAPTER – 2

Pulse Based Cropping System

Paramount for Nutritional and Soil Health Security in Bihar, India

Rakesh Deo Ranjan[1]; Shivnath Das[2]
Sanjeev Kumar[3]; Archana Rani[4] and Sanjay Kumar[5]

ABSTRACT

Pulses and other legumes have significant roles in Indian agriculture because they maintain productivity in different cropping system as a result of their nitrogen fixing ability with soil- inhabiting root-nodule bacteria. They play an additional role in sustainability because their use in rotation systems can help restore soil fertility, increase yield of succeeding crops, conserve soil ,control weeds and so on. At the same time, the increased demand and prices of

1 Jr. Scientist cum Assistant Professor (Plant Physiology) Bihar Agricultural University, Sabour, Bhagalpur - 813 210 (Bihar), (India).

2 Jr. Scientist cum Assistant Professor (Agronomy) Bihar Agricultural University, Sabour, Bhagalpur - 813 210 (Bihar), (India).

3 Assistant Professor/Scientist, Plant Pathology, J.N. Krishi Vishwa Vidyalaya, Jabalpur - 482 004 (MP), (India).

4 Research Associate, Department of Plant breeding & Genetics J.N. Krishi Vishwa Vidyalaya, Jabalpur - 482 004 (MP), (India).

5 Jr. Scientist cum Assistant Professor (Plant Breeding) Bihar Agricultural University, Sabour, Bhagalpur - 813 210 (Bihar), (India).

oilseed and pulse legumes is a cause of concern, especially for low income group in India. However, there is possibility of area expansion of pulse crops into less fertile soils and fitting them in the cropping systems. Pulses are valued for their importance in nutritional security, soil amelioration and sustainable crop production. They also play an important role in protecting the environment from the risk associated with high input agriculture.

INTRODUCTION

Concept of cropping system is as old agriculture in India. Multiplicity of cropping system has been one of the main feature of Indian agriculture and it is mainly attributed to prevailing socio-economic situations of farming community. The term cropping system essentially represents a philosophy of maximum crop production per unit area of land within the calendar year or relevant time unit with minimum natural resources degradation. Gangwar *et al.* (2012) reported India's targeted food production of 450 to 500 mt in 2050. In order to achieve this target, cropping system research has to play vital role of enhancing the land use efficiency as per capita availability of agriculture land is decreasing at a the fast rate (0.48 ha in 1951 to 0.14 ha in 2001). Cropping system will continue to form as a major module in farming systems management which are pursued to provide sustainable livelihood for about 90% of land holding consisting of small, marginal and semi-medium categories of farm house hold.

PRODUCTION TRENDS AND GEOGRAPHICAL DISTRIBUTION IN INDIA

Pulses are grown in an area of 22-23 million hectares with an annual production of 13-18 million tons (MT). India accounts for 33% of the world area and 22% of the world production of pulses. About 90% of the global pigeonpea, 65% of chickpea and 37% of lentil area falls in India, corresponding to 93%, 68% and 32% of the global production, respectively (FAOSTAT 2011). There is a steep increase in the prices of pulses due to supply constraints to meet the growing demand due to population increase. The net availability of pulses has come down from 70.1g/day/person (1951) to 31.6 g/day/person (2010). However, ICMR recommends 70 g/day/capita requirement of pulse (Economic Survey 2011-12). More recently, under the National Food Security Mission (NFSM), high priority has been given to increasing the production of pulses across the country to curtail growing imports, reduce protein malnutrition and make pulses affordable to the common man.

Pulses are grown across the country with the highest share coming from Madhya Pradesh (24%), Uttar Pradesh (16%),Maharashtra (14%), Andhra Pradesh (10%), Karnataka (7%) and Rajasthan (6%), which together share about 77% of the total pulse production, while the remaining 23% is contributed by Gujarat, Chhattisgarh, Bihar, Orissa and Jharkhand. Among pulses, chickpea (45.1%) occupies the major share, followed by pigeonpea

(15.7%), mungbean (9.9%), urdbean (9.6%) and lentil (7.3%), which together account for 87% of the total pulses production. Much of the pulses production has been slowly shifted from *kharif* to *rabi* and now the *rabi* share is increased to about 61.0% of the total pulses production. The research and development investments on each crop should be in proportion to the share of the crop in the respective category. More emphasis should be given to *rabi* pulse crops as their production share is much higher and increasing in recent years.

PRODUCTION AND PRODUCTIVITY OF PULSES IN BIHAR

Bihar has unique feature of agro-climatic conditions suited for growing a wide variety of pulses indifferent season and regions (Table 2.1) and capacity to surpass the productivity in compression to national levels.

Table 2.1: Diversity and Seasonal Distribution of Pulses in Bihar

Sl. No.	Crop Season	Pulses Crops
1.	Rabi (Winter)	Chickpea, lentil Pea, lathyrus, faba bean, rajmash
2.	Summer	Moong bean, urd bean cow pea
3.	Kharif	Pigeonpea, urdbean horse gram cow pea
4.	Pre-Rabi	Pigeonpea
5.	Autumn	Moong bean, urd bean
6.	Spring	Moong bean

Table 2.2: Comparative Pulses Productivity Level in Bihar Vs. India (2009-10)

Crop	Productivity (kg/ha)		
	Bihar (A)	India (B)	Difference (A-B)
Pigeon pea	1513	728	785
Chickpea	1014	793	221
Lentil	793	591	202
Green gram	685	513	172
Black gram	837	543	294
Field pea	1001	910	91

EXISTING CROPPING SYSTEMS IN BIHAR

Cropping system is a kind of sequence and arrangement of crops grown on a given area of land over a period of time. Cropping systems are the outcome of the technological innovations, household needs, reflection of government policies, and availability of production inputs, market forces and socio-economic compulsion. An ideal cropping system should use natural resources efficiently, provide stable and high returns and do not damage the ecological balance. Cropping system is broadly grouped into sequential cropping and intercropping. It may be a regular rotation of different crops in which the crops follow a definite order of appearance on the land or it may consist of only one crop grown year after year on the same area so there is great potential for enhancing legumes production both under irrigated and rainfed conditions in Bihar.

Table 2.3: Cropping Systems in Bihar

Zone	Rainfed			Irrigated		
	Kharif	Rabi	Summer	Kharif	Rabi	Summer
• North West Gangetic plains	Paddy	Chickpea	–	E. Paddy	Maize	–
	Paddy	Wheat	–	Maize	Potato	Green gram
	Paddy	Paira lentil	–	Maize/E. Paddy	Rai	Green gram
	Paddy	S/cane	S/Cane	Paddy	Wheat	–
	Fallow	Tobacco		Paddy Maize E. Paddy	S/cane Potato Pulses	S/cane Onion Green gram
• North East Gangetic plains	Jute	Pulses	–	Paddy	Wheat	–
	Jute	Wheat	–	Paddy	Wheat	Green gram
	Paddy	Chickpea	–	Paddy	Paddy	–
	Paddy	Oilseed	–	Jute	Mustard	Maize
	Maize	Pigeonpea		E. Paddy, Jute Paddy, Jute, Jute Maize	Potato Maize Potato Potato IS Wheat Vegetables	G/nut Onion Green gram
• South Gangetic plains	Maize	G/nut	–	Paddy	Wheat	–
	Maize	Pigeonpea	–	Paddy	Wheat	Green gram
	Paddy	Paira Lentil	–	Paddy	Maize	–

INCLUSION OF PULSE WITH DIFFERENT CROPPING SYSTEM IN BIHAR

(A) Pigeonpea in Short-duration Sequence with Wheat

On uplands of Bihar, short-duration pigeonpea can be successfully grown. As this region receives more precipitation, pigeonpea planting should be done in ridges in the first fortnight of June with pre-planting irrigation so that by the time monsoon rains start, the seedlings are strong enough to tolerate adverse effects of excess moisture. Short-duration pigeonpea can be popularized with the availability of disease resistant genotypes having tolerance to excess soil moisture

(B) Spring and Summer Cultivation of Black Gram and Mungbean

Bihar also offers good scope for cultivation of spring black gram and mungbean as well as summer mungbean. Both mungbean and black gram are cultivated after harvest of mustard, potato, pea, wheat, and sugarcane. They can also be intercropped with spring-planted sugarcane and sunflower.

(C) Rice-Chickpea/Lentil Sequential Cropping

Chickpea verities (e.g., KPG 59 and Pusa 372) amenable for late planting in mid-December are cultivated after rice. Under resource constraints, rice-chickpea is more remunerative than rice-wheat. In lowland areas with excessive moisture, lentil is a more assured crop than chickpea. Hence, the rice-lentil system is popular in the lowlands. The adoption of the high-yielding, bold seeded, wilt- resistant varieties such as DPL 62 and Noori, and small-seeded, rust-resistant varieties such as DPL 15, PL 406, and PL 639 may encourage expansion of lentil.

(D) Post-Rainy Season Pigeonpea

Bihar receives heavy rains and experiences frequent floods during July-August, which cause considerable or complete loss of July-planted pigeonpea. Under such situations, post rainy season pigeon pea can be grown successfully. Varieties (e.g., Sharad and Pusa 9) that are resistant to Alternaria blight with yield of 2 tons per ha and suitable for September planting have proved a boon for extension of post-rainy season pigeonpea. As these varieties are highly thermo-sensitive, their planting period is restricted up to mid-September. Delayed planting causes considerable yield loss. Hence, varieties which can be successfully planted until early October will provide greater opportunities to expand pigeonpea cultivation under sequential cropping with short duration upland crops such as maize.

(E) Post-Rainy Season Common Bean

High yielding genotypes (e.g., Udai, Amber, HUR 15, and HUR 137) that yield 2.5 to 3.0 tons per ha and suitable for planting in October-November have been adopted. Common bean is a high-value and short-duration (115 to 125 days) crop with few problems of insect pests and diseases. This legume has the potential to cover large areas under irrigated conditions. It can be intercropped with potato.

PARAMOUNT ROLE OF PULSE CULTIVATION IN CROPPING SYSTEM

Pulses are known for their soil fertility restoration value. Deep rooting, nitrogen fixation, leaf shedding ability and mobilization of insoluble soil nutrients are some of the unique characteristics of pulses. By improving chemical, biological and Physical environment in the soil, pulses can arrest the declining trend in productivity of cereal-cereal system. Inclusion of pulses in intensive cereal based system itself is a component of integrated plant nutrient supply system. Therefore, pulses have become viable alternative to improve the soil health and conserve the natural Resources and agricultural sustainability.

(a) Contribution to sustainability and profitability of cropping systems
(b) Daily item in food basket – poor man's meat
(c) Nutrient recycling
(d) Enhancement of nutrient availability
(e) Improvement in Bio-physiochemical properties of soil

Aggregate stability : Enhanced

Bulk density and hydraulic conductivity	: Decreased
Soil penetration and soil porosity	: Increased
Soil pH	: Decreased
Organic matter and nutrients (N &P)	: Enhanced
Microbial population and enzymatic activity	: Increased
Weed population	: Reduced

1. Contribution to sustainability and profitability of cropping systems

Pulses are usually cultivated as mixed crops along with crops such as cotton, mustard, or as catch crops between two cereal crops. A comparison of the economics of pulse-based cropping systems with non-pulse-based cropping systems was done by Materne and Reddy (2007). The input utilization (fertilizers, pesticides, labor and water) was less for the pulse-based cropping systems. The benefit-cost ratio was almost the same (1.8) for both the cropping systems. Overall, pulse-based cropping systems are more suitable for resource-poor farmers and waterscarce regions. The pulse-based cropping systems are environmentally sustainable also, as they require lower use of fertilizers, pesticides and irrigation in addition to enhancing the productivity of cropping systems by increasing yield of subsequent crops (Reddy 2004, Reddy 2009a). With this background, this policy brief tries to examine the reasons for the success of pulses production in recent years at the all-India level with special reference to chickpea and pigeonpea and suggest policy options to increase production and competitiveness. The study used secondary data collected from FAO and Directorate of Economics and Statistics, Ministry of Agriculture to depict trends in area, production and yield, and prices of pulse crops over a period. The cost of cultivation scheme data was used to examine the relative cost advantage of pulses in different states

2. Daily item in food basket – poor man's meat

Pulses are good sources of proteins and commonly called the poor man's meat (Reddy 2010). The frequency of pulses consumption is much higher than any other source of protein; about 89 percent consume pulses at least once a week, while only 35.4 percent of persons consume fish or chicken/ meat at least once a week in India (IIPS, ORC Macro, 2007). Further, any reduction in prices of pulses will increase consumption by the poor more than the rich consumers (Mittal 2006). Further, pulses provide healthy proteins compared to other protein rich sources like meat and meat products. Lastly, pulses meet tastes of different sections of society across India. The major chickpea consuming states are Punjab, Haryana, Rajasthan and Madhya Pradesh. The major pigeonpea consuming states are Karnataka, Maharashtra, Andhra Pradesh and Madhya Pradesh. Some pulses, like chickpea, are used in multiple ways viz dal, wholegrain, flour and preparation of snacks while pigeonpea is used in preparation of dal and sambhar (Reddy 2004; Reddy and Bantilan 2012; Reddy 2013).

3. Nutrient Recycling

Nutrient recycling by legumes in different cropping system is an important way to improve soil fertility through partial or complete recycling. It has been estimated that 668,000 tonnes of nitrogen can be incorporated in the soil through the inclusion of legumes in cropping systems(Singh *et al*, 2009). For recycling, short-duration legumes such as mungbean, black gram (urd bean), or cowpea can be either grown as a catch crop during spring or summer, or intercropped with cereals (e.g., maize,), and commercial crops (e.g., sugarcane). This system not only provides a bonus yield of legumes but also benefits the succeeding or companion crop. Cultivation of cowpea during summer enhanced yield of succeeding rice by 0.33 tons per ha. Legumes not only provide an excellent cover to soil surface due to their dance canopy but also leave substantial amount of easily decomposable crop residue. In rice-wheat cropping system, growing a summer mungbean and intercropping its residue after harvesting the matured pods resulted in recycling of 77-113 kg N/ha and increased the productivity of rice-wheat cropping system by 0.5-1.3 t/ha/year and N –uptake by 12-35 kg/ha/year over summer fallow (Sharma and Prasad,1999). The low harvest index in legumes eventually provides large amount of residues. A good crop of chickpea may provide 8-10 tonnes straw (crop residues). Winter grain legumes and pigeonpea shed a large number of their leaves at maturity which provide a thin soil cover.

4. Enhancement of Nutrient availability

Leguminous plants have a special relationship with nitrogen-fixing bacteria called *Rhizobium*. By biologically fixing nitrogen in the soil, legumes provide a relatively low-cost method of replacing nitrogen in the soil, enhancing soil fertility and boosting subsequent crop yields.

Different legumes have different capacity to leave behind varying amounts of N for use by the succeeding crops. In sequential cropping involving pulses, the preceding pulse may contribute 18-70 kg N/ha to the soil and thereby considerable amount of nitrogen to succeeding crop (Ali and Mishra 2000). Growing of short duration legumes such as green gram and cowpea in widely spaced crops and ploughing back the same in the soil after picking the grains resulted in an advantage of 30 kg N/ha on fertilizer basis in Alfisol.

Rekhi and Meelu (1983) found that incorporation of crop residue of mungbean in rice-wheat system not only added 100 kg N/ha to the soil but also maintained high availability of N during various growth stages of rice.

Table 2.4: Enhancement of Nitrogen Economy due to Inclusion of Pulses

Preceding Legume	Following Cereal	Fertilizer Nequivalent (kg N/ha)	Reference
Chickpea	Maize Pearlmillet	60-70 40	Subbarao (1988)
Pigeonpea	Wheat Maize Pearlmillet Pearlmillet	40 20-49 30 40	
Lentil	Maize	18-30	Lee and Wani (1989)
Peas	Pearlmillet Maize	40 20-32	
Greengram	Pearlmillet	30	
Lathyrus	Maize	36-48	
Cowpea	pearlmillet	60	
Pigeonpea	Sorghum	51	
Chickpea	Rice	40	
Rajmash	Rice	40	Ali (1984-87)
Fodder cowpea	Rice	40	
Mungbean	Rice	40	

Combined application of NPK to major cereal based cropping system (rice-rice, rice-wheat, rice-green gram and maize-wheat), increases the efficiency of applied N, P and K nutrient. The efficiency increases ranges from 110 to 230% in various systems. Influence of *rabi* pulses on productivity and N economy in succeeding rice revealed that chickpea and lentil exhibited most favourable effect in economizing nitrogen to the extent of 40 kg/ha.

Inclusion of legume in cropping system not only economizes nitrogen requirement of cropping system but also helps in efficient utilization of native phosphorus due to secretion of certain acids that helps in solubilisation of various forms of phosphorus. This capacity of legumes makes them efficient in native utilization of phosphorus present in different forms. Increased available P is a result of P acquisition from insoluble phosphates through root exudates. Chickpea has the ability to access P normally not available to other crops by mobilizing sparingly soluble Ca-P by acidification of rhizospere through its citric acid root exudates in Vertisols and pigeon pea have been characterized for dissolution of Fe-P in Alfisol.

5. Improvement in Bio-physiochemical properties of soil

The legume play an important role in conserving natural conserving natural resources (soil, water and micro flora) by proving excellent soil cover (cowpea, urdbean, mungbean, grass pea, ricebean, etc.); adding huge amount of organic matter through profuge root system. Leaf fall and biomass and improving soil physical conditions (soil aggregates, infiltration rae and water holding capacity),Vyas *et al.* (2014)

Aggregate stability: is an important soil quality parameter, which can be used as an index to compare the long-term shift in soil quality The fungi present in the pulse crop rhizosphere produces a glycoprotein called "Glomalin". The sticky part of glomalin entraps soil mineral, organic matter and debris to form stable soil aggregates. Hence, microbial activity of rhizosphere is directly responsible for the improved soil structure in crop rotations Involving pulses. In a long-term rotational experiment, higher percentage of soil aggregates exceeding 0.25 mm were recorded where preceding crop was a legume (Sharma *et al.* 2000).

Bulk density and hydraulic conductivity: are another soil quality parameter, which responds to change in management over a long period of time. Incorporation of mungbean stover in rice-wheatmungbean sequence resulted in lower bulk density and hydraulic conductivity (Ganeshamurthy *et al.* 2006).

Soil penetration and soil porosity: Legume roots being rich in nitrogen content and having ability of deep penetration in the soil also encourage earthworm activity. The root channels and earthworm burrows increase soil porosity promoting air movements and water percolation deep into the soil.

Soil pH: Pulse crops have the ability to reduce the pH of soil in the rhizosphere and make micro-environment favourable for nutrient availability. Among grain legumes, chickpea reduces the pH most followed by pea and pigeonpea. Some of the legumes like alfalfa and soybean can reduce the pH of soil by one complete unit.

Organic matter and nutrients (N &P): Pulses with their unique ability in atmospheric N fixation, leaf shedding and higher below ground biomass add significant amount of organic carbon to the soil (Ganeshamurthy 2009). Therefore, pulses are often considered as an important component of system diversification and maintainer of soil health.

Pulses add significant amount of organic residues to the soil in the form of root biomass and leaf litter. Roots and leaf litter being rich in N facilitate decomposition of crop residues in soil and increases microbial activity. *Rabi* pulses contributed 7-14 kg N, 3-5 kg P and 8-20 kg K/ha. Pigeonpea added 8-16 kg N, 2.5-5.0 kg P and 13.5-24.0 kg K/ha through leaf drop in the entire crop growth cycle. In a study conducted over three years, mungbean green manuring or incorporation of mungbean stover after picking of pods in ricewheat system considerably improved the available P status of soil, due to root exudates capable of mobilizing sparingly soluble P in soil (Saxena ,1995). Also Singh et al, 2009, reported that green manuring with *Sesbania* sp. in rice wheat system increased organic carbon (OC) of soil from 0.29% to 0.45% over a period of six years. Similarly, on sandy loam OC, total N, and available P increased by 0.01%, 15 kg per ha, and 13.8 kg per ha respectively. The OC content and available P also increased under rice lentil and pigeon pea-wheat sequential cropping. The effect of increased fertility status was also reflected on grain yields of rice and wheat. Change in fertility status of soil under different cropping system are reflected in table ... too Singh *et al.* (1996).

Table 2.5: Effect of Different Rice-based Cropping Sequences on Final Soil Fertility Status in Bihar, (Roy *et al*, 2011)

Cropping Sequences	Organic Carbon (%)	Nitrogen (kg ha-1)	Phosphorus (kg ha-1)	Potassium (kg ha-1)
Initial soil fertility status	0.413	250	18.0	140.0
Rice-Lentil-Green gram	0.448	287	20.5	148.7
Rice-Linseed-Green gram	0.421	252.5	19.9	143.5
Rice-Wheat-Green gram	0.425	258.8	18.8	146.5
Rice-Indian mustard-Green gram	0.416	251.5	18.3	141.5
Rice-Coriander-Green gram	0.428	256.4	18.8	144.7
Rice-Pea-Green gram	0.433	19.8	264.7	147.6
CD(P=0.05)	0.03	0.09	0.03	0.07

Microbial Population and Enzymatic Activity

Inclusion of pulses in crop rotation improves soil microbial biomass and their activity that could be vital for long-term soil health and productivity. Singh, 2014 reported while Soil analysis after six year of cropping sequence involving cereal-cereal and legume-cereal, revealed the increase in population of soil bacteria and fungi along with considerable improvement in the soil enzymatic activity due to legumes in the cropping sequence (Table 2.6)

Table 2.6: Effect of Legume in Cropping Systems on Soil Microbial Population and Enzymatic Activity after Six Year of Rotation

Crop Rotation	Microbial Population		Enzymatic Activity	
	Bacteria (10^6)	Fungi (10^3)	Dehydrogenase (μ gTPFg^{-1}soil h^{-1})	Phosphatase (μ gTPFg^{-1}soil h^{-1})
Fallow-Wheat	16.8	58	47.3	30.2
Wheat-Wheat	27.5	66	63.7	42.3
Lentil-Wheat	73.0	130	109.1	97.0
Fieldpea-Wheat	63.0	142	89.0	90.0

Recent studies have observed changes in composition and diversity of microbial species in soils under legumes - cereals as compared to the cereal-cereal or follow-cereal rotation (Chao Yang *et al.*, 2013). These changes in microbial community composition due to legumes are probably responsible for the observed enhanced use efficiency of inputs as well as increase in grain yields of crops so called the "rotation effects". A diverse community of microorganism derived through addition of high quality organic matter also suppresses growth and activity of diseases producing microorganisms in soil and helps in improvements in the quality & health (Jan *et al.*, 2012)

6. Reduce/suppress weed population

Many legumes, on account of their fast growth habit and dense canopy, suppress weed flora due to their sheding and smothering effect. Cowpea, urdbean, mungbean, rice bean, horse gram which are often grown as intercrop with maize, sorghum, pearl millet, cotton etc. considerably reduce weed flora. The suppression of weed growth/population is mainly due to increased crop leaf area index and light interception (Ali, 1988). Among different close growing pulses, the weed-suppressing efficiency was found to be highest in cowpea followed by urdbean and mungbean (Table 2.7). The magnitude of crop-weed competition is generally dependent on component crops. Reduction in nutrient drain by weeds in pigeon pea-based intercropping system. Cowpea with a good canopy cover was more efficient than sesame in weed control. In another study, it was found that inclusion of green gram or cowpea as smother crops in sorghum/pigeon pea intercropping system suppressed the weed growth and proved as effective as two hand weeding. Green gram was more efficient in initial stage, while cowpea was more efficient at later stages.

Table 2.7: Weed Suppressing Ability of Legumes Under Intercropping Systems

Intercropping systems	(%)
Pigeonpea + urdbean	32.8
Pigeonpea + mungbean	31.0
Pigeonpea + cowpea	39.1
Pigeonpea + soybean	22.0
Pigeonpea + sorghum	22.3

Table 2.8: Economics of Pulse-Based Cropping Systems vs. Rice-Wheat Systems Constraints of pulse production

Crop Rotation	Cost (Rs/ha)	Gross Return (Rs/ha)	Net Return (Rs/ha)	B/C Ratio
Moong-lentil	13,685	42,540	28,855	3.2
Maize-lentil	9,985	37,000	27,015	3.7
Urad-wheat	25,310	45,000	19,690	1.8
Pigeonpea + sorghum	6,548	25,820	19,272	3.9
Pigeonpea-wheat-moong	32,730	51,500	18,770	1.6
Moong-wheat	25,310	43,500	18,190	1.7
Paddy-veg pea	35,022	52,000	16,978	1.5
Paddy-lentil	26,871	41,400	14,529	1.5
Paddy-wheat-moong	46,129	60,190	14,061	1.3
Paddy-wheat	38,497	45,190	6,693	1.2

7. Enhance B: C ratio

There are several constraints that limit the area expansion and productivity of legume crop. The low priority accorded to pulse crops may be related to their relatively low status in the cropping system. The important ones are:

(i) Production constraints
(ii) Lack of Awareness and access to new technology
(iii) Lack of Semi-formal seed system
(iv) Physiological constraints
(v) Lack of Cash and Credits facility
(vi) Problem in Farm mechanization
(vii) Lack of Supplemental irrigation
(viii) Lack of Marketing facility

HOW OVERCOMING THE CONSTRAINTS OF PULSE PRODUCTION

(A) Production constraints

Production of major pulses is constrained by both biotic and abiotic stresses. For example, pod borers (*Helicoverpa armigera*), fusarium wilt, root rots, ascochyta blight and botrytis gray mold are some of the major biotic constraints to increasing the productivity of chickpea. The major constraints to productivity in pigeonpea are biotic stresses such as pod borer, pod fly, Fusarium wilt, andsterility mosaic disease. Similarly, pod borer, aphids, cutworm, powdery mildew, rust and wilt are the major pests and diseases affecting lentil production in India. The richness of legumes in N and P, makes them attractive for insect pests and diseases (Sinclair and Vadez, 2012). Most of the pulses in India are grown in low fertility, problematic soils and unpredictable environmental conditions. More than 87% of the area under pulses is rainfed. Drought and heat stress may reduce seed yields by 50%, especially in arid and semi-arid regions. Another major problem is salinity and alkalinity of soils which is high both in semi-arid tropics and in the Indo-Gangetic plains. With recent changes in the global temperatures the grain yield is likely to be drastically affected by temperature extremities. Poor drainage/water logging during the rainy season causes heavy losses to pigeonpea on account of low plant stand and increased incidence of phytophthora blight disease, particularly in the states of UP, Bihar, West Bengal, Chhattisgarh, MP and Jharkhand (Table 2.9.)

Table 2.9: Biotic and Abiotic Constraint (Reddy, 2006)

Crop	Seasons	Stress Biotic	Abiotic
Chickpea	Timely sown	FW, root rot, chickpea stunt, BGM, pod-borer	Low temperature
	Early sown	FW, root rot, AB, or chickpea stunt, pod borer	Terminal drought, salt stress
Pigeonpea	Late sown	FW, pod borer	Terminal drought, cold
	Kharif-early	FW, PB, pod-borer complex	Water logging
	Medium late	FW, SM, pod-borer complex	Cold, terminal, drought, water logging
Moong	Pre-rabi	FW, ALB, Pod fly	Cold, terminal drought
	Kharif	MYMV, CLS, WB, sucking insect pests, Pre-harvest sprouting	Terminal drought
Urad	Zaid sucking insect pests stress, drought	MYMV, root and stem rot, stem agromyza, Pre-harvest sprouting	Temperature
	Rabi	PM, Rust, CLS	Terminal drought
	Kharif	MYMV, anthracnose, WB, LCV	Terminal drought
	Zaid	MYMV, root and stem rot, stem agromyza Pre-harvest sprouting	Temperature stress, drought
	Rabi/rice fallow	Spot	Terminal drought
Lentil		FW, root rot, rust	Moisture temperature

FW= Fusarium wilt, PB= Phytophthora blight, SM= Sterility mosaic, ALB= Alternaria leaf blight, MYMV= Moongbean yellow mosaic virus, BGM= Botrytis gray mould, AB= Ascochyta blight.

(B) Awareness and access to new technology

Farmers' awareness on improved varieties and seed availability of improved varieties are the key factors in the spread of improved varieties. The television will be the most popular media for increasing awareness; FPVS trials and farmers' fairs/field days will also be helpful. The identified technology needs to be subsidized for wider adoption.

(C) Semi-formal seed systems

Even though there is a good number of High Yielding Varieties (HYVs) released for all major pulses in India, and there is enough Breeder seed and Foundation seed produced, there is a shortage of Certified/Truthful seed at farmers' level. Both public and private agencies have not been able to meet the requirement of quality seed and the seed replacement ratio is very low. There has There has been some success in establishing semi-formal seed systems to produce Truthfully Labelled seed, in which linkages were established between the formal and informal seed sectors through supply of basic quality seed by the NARS, and quality of seed production is monitored by universities/non-governmental organisations/farmers' associations. If this system is continued, there will be enough quantity of seed production at the local level. It should also be coupled with FPVS, which gives farmers an opportunity to select from a range of improved varieties (Abate 2012).

(D) Physiological constaints

There is a general feeling that pulses (C-3 plants) suffer from inherently low yield potential and are a physiologically inefficient group of plants compared to cereals (C-4 plants) such asmsorghum and maize. However Aggarwal *et al* (1997), reviewed the comparative advantages of C-3 and C-4 group of plants and argued that C-3 and C-4 plants seem to compete on fairly even terms in hot dry environments. The fact that C-3 plants usually do better in cool climates suggests that C-3 plants are better for rabi season. However, the disturbing future is that the harvest index (HI) in pulses is low compared to cereals. HI is defined as seed yield per unit of recoverable biomass. In pulses it is only 15-20% compared to 45-50% in case of cereals such as wheat and rice. Low HI results from excessive vegetative growth, but can be overcome by early partitioning of dry matter into seeds (Saxena and Johansen 1990) and evolving biotechnology and genomic tools to incorporate good features of C-4 plants into C-3 plants. Pulses in general have a high rate of flower drop. In pigeonpea, over 80% of the flowers produced in a plant are shed; by decreasing flower drop, yield can be increased considerably. This can be done either by breeding lines which retain a large proportion of flowers producing pods or through physiological manipulations, such as spray of hormones which reduce flower drop. Physiological studies at ICRISAT, involving removal of flowers and young pods of pigeonpea, have shown that plants compensate for the loss of flowers and young pods by setting pods from later formed owners, which otherwise would have dropped. This compensatory mechanism provides substantial plasticity of adaptation to intermittent adverse conditions such as moisture stress or insect attack, which are common in warm rainfed areas of south India. Recent increase in yield levels in pigeonpea is due to release of long duration (annual) varieties, which maximise utilisation of assimilates in filling the available sink of a large number of flowers (Rego and Wani 2002).

(E) Cash and Credit

Cash is a key element for enabling smallholder farmers to shift from low input-lowoutput to high-input-high-output agriculture. But access to credit by these farmers is low because oftheir low asset base, low risk bearing ability and high risk environments. This can be effectively tackled by the insurance-linked credit to pulse crops without any collateral security. The scale of finance should be sufficient enough to cover all the costs of the recommended practices (Reddy 2009).

(F) Farm mechanization

One of the reasons for success of expansion of area under chickpea in Andhra Pradesh is the increased mechanization of farm operations. Farm mechanization can further be enhanced by developing varieties suitable for harvesting by combine harvesters.

Hence, farm mechanization in peak season activities such as harvesting and threshing needs to be encouragedthrough the distribution of subsidized farm machinery to cope with labor shortage and higher wage rates.

(G) Supplemental irrigation

With the expansion of irrigation facilities through groundwater and also through canal irrigation systems, there is a scope for expansion of irrigated area under pulse crops, especially summer, rabi and spring season crops, as yield response is higher. Harvesting and management of rainwater through watersheds rather than exploitation of costly groundwater needs to be emphasized.

(H) Marketing

Markets for legumes are thin and fragmented due to scattered production and consumption across states. Farmers sell their marketed surplus immediately after harvest, while some large traders/wholesalers trade between major markets and hoard pulses to take advantageof speculative gains in the off-season. Due to this, farmers do not benefit from the higher market prices of pulses. Investments in market infrastructure, warehouses, market information systems both in public and private sectors through Public-Private Partnership (PPP) models and economic viability gap funding models need to be encouraged in SAT India.

Even though India is the largest pulses producer in the world, it imports large amount of pulses from rest of the world. Farmers in India treat pulses as secondary crops. Until recently the government also gave less importance to pulses compared to the staple cereals. In general farmers' access to inputs is limited, both because of low purchasing power and accessibility to markets to sell the excess produce of pulses. Because of this situation, the farmers give first priority to staple cereals and cash crops for allocating inputs and the second priority to pulses. As a result, pulses continue to be grown on poor soils with low inputs. In addition, there is lack of policy support and post-harvest innovations related to pulse crops. Availability of quality seed of improved varieties and other inputs is one of the major constraints in increasing the production of grain legumes (David *et al*, 2002).

CONCLUSION

In short, to increase area and production of pulse crops, we need crop specific and region specific approaches. Already ICAR and ICRISAT, with the support of state and central governments, are involved in the development of short duration photo-thermo insensitive varieties for different agro-ecology and cropping system. Production of Breeder seed of pulses of the latest released varieties and organizing frontline demonstrations on pulses based cropping system in farmers' fields which leads to sustainable crop production and enhanced flow of nutrients to crops. This in turn will involve larger nutrient reserves in soils, and higher nutrient uptake and utilization by crops. Thus inclusion of pulses in cropping system is necessary not only for small and marginal farmer but also larger farmers in order to meet his various requirements in terms of quantity & quality of food as well as soil health.

Major Thrust Area

The efforts under NFSM-Pulses and R & D under NARS needs to be further strengthened with the major thrust on:

- Replacement of cereal crops in the prevailing rice-wheat cropping systems with high yield varieties of pulses, viz. Urd, moong etc. Tal area promoted as efficient pulses cultivation of gram and lentil as sole crop as well as inters crop with wheat.
- Including shortduration varieties of pulses as catch crop through introducing urdbean/mungbean (spring), which will utilize unutilized land and water in the spring/summer season with high returns.
- Encouraging R & D on extra early maturity pigeonpea suited to multiple cropping and improved crop management.
- Developing pigeonpea genotype suitable for *rabi*/spring and summer seasons.
- Developing varieties amenable to mechanical harvesting and tolerant to herbicides.

- Developing varieties tolerant to drought and heat stresses.
- Developing varieties responsive to high input conditions.
- Developing varieties with market-preferred seed traits, for example, large seed size in *kabuli* chickpea.
- Using biotechnology tools for developing multiple diseaseand pest-resistant varieties to reduce yield loss of standing crop and to increase yields.
- Coordinating research, extension and farmers through institutional innovations as technology dissemination and input delivery mechanisms are too weak for pulses.
- Reducing storage losses and improving market information and infrastructure; and
- Linking MSP to market prices, with in-build mechanism to protect farmers from wide price fluctuations that will incentivize farmers to adopt new technology.

REFERENCES

Abate T, ed. 2012. Four Seasons of Learning and Engaging Small Framers: Progress of Phase 1. PO Box 39063, Nairobi, Kenya: International Crops Research Institute for the Semi-Arid-Tropics. 258 pp.

Ali M, 1988. Weed Suppressing Ability and Productivity of Short Duration Legumes Intercropped with Pigeonpea Under Rainfed Conditions.Ttopical Pest Management 34(4): 384-87.

Ali, M (2004): "Pulses Research and Development in India: An Overview", Agri Watch, Vol. 3, (10), pp. 79-83.

Ali, M. (1984-1987) Annual Report, IIPR, Kanpur.

Ali, M. and Mishra, J.P. 2000. Nutrient Management in Pulses and Pulse Based Cropping Systems. Fertilizer News, 45(4): 57-69.

Ali, M. and Singh, B.N. (1991-92), Annual Report, IIPR, Kanpur.

Aggarwal, P K, M J Kropff, K G Cassman and H F M ten Berge (1997): "Simulating Genotypic Strategies for Increasing Rice Yield Potential" in Irrigated Tropical Environments", Field Crops Research, 51: 5-17

Chao Yang & Chantal Hamel & Yantai Gan & Vladimir Vujanovic (2013) Pyrosequencing Reveals how Pulses Influence Rhizobacterial Communities with Feedback on Wheat Growth in Semiarid Prairie Plant Soil 367: 493-505.

Roy, D.K., Rakesh Kumar and Anjani Kumar, 2011. Production Potentiality and Sustainability of Rice-based Cropping Sequences in Flood Prone Lowlands of North Bihar, Oryza Vol. 48. No.1, 2011 (47-51)

David S, Mukandala L and Mafuru J. 2002. Seed Availability, an Ignored Factor in Crop Varietal Adoption Studies: A Case Study of Beans in Tanzania. Journal of Sustainable Agriculture 21, 5-20.

FAO STAT. 2012. FAOSTAT - Statistical Database, 2012.

Ganeshamurthy, A.N., Masood Ali and Srinivasarao, Ch. 2006. Role of Pulses in Sustaining Soil Health and Crop Production. Indian Journal of Fertilizers, 1(12): 29-40.

Ganeshamurthy AN (2009) Soil Changes Following Long-term Cultivation of Pulses. J Agric Sci 147: 699-706.

Gangwar B , Ravisankar N and Prasad K, 2012. Agronomic Research on Cropping System in India, Indian Journal of Agronomy 57 (3rd IAC Special Issue): 105 -115.

Gaur PM, Jukanti AK, Srinivasan S and Gowda CLL. 2012. Chickpea (Cicer Arietinum L.). Pages 165-194 In: Breeding of Field Crops (Bharadwaj DN, ed). Agrobios (India), Jodhpur, India.

IIPS and ORC Macro. 2007. National Family Health Survey (NFHS-3), 2005-06: India. Mumbai, India: International Institute for Population Sciences.

Jan Drick van Elsas, Mario Chiurazzi, Cyrus A. Mallon ,Dana Elhottova, Vaclav Kris^tu" fek and Joana Falcao Salles (2012). Microbial Diversity Determines the Invasion of Soil by a Bacterial Pathogen, PNAS, 109: 1159-1164.

Materne M and Reddy AA. 2007. Commercial Cultivation and Profitability. Pages 173-186 in The Lentil-An Ancient Crop for Modern Times (Yadav SS, Mc Neil DL and Stevenson PC, eds.). Netherlands: Springer.

Meena, N.L. and Ali, M. (1984-87). Annual Report, IIPR, Kanpur.

Mittal S. 2006. Structural Shift in Demand for Food: Projections to 2020. Working Paper No. 184. New Delhi: Indian Council for Research on International Economic Relations.

Reddy AA, Mature VC, Yadav M and Yadav SS. 2007. Profitability in Chickpea cultivation. Pages 292-321 in The Chickpea Breeding and Management (Yadav SS).

Redden B, Chen W and Sharma B, eds.). Wallingford, Oxon, UK: CAB International.

Reddy, A A (2005): "Utilisation Pattern of Pulses", Paper Presented at International Food Legumes Research Conference-IV, Indian Agricultural Research Institute, New Delhi, 18-22 October 2005.

Reddy, A A (2008): "Supply Side Constraints in Production of Pulses in India: A Case Study of Lentils", Agricultural Economics Research Review, Vol. 21, Conference issue, pp. 281-83.

Reddy, A A. (2004): "Consumption Pattern, Trade and Production Potential of Pulses", Economic & Political Weekly, 30 October, pp. 4854-60.

Reddy, A A (2006): "Impact Assessment of Pulses Production Technology", Research Report No 3, Indian Institute of Pulses Research, Kanpur.

Reddy, AA. 2009. Pulses Production Technology: Status and Way Forward. Economic and Political Weekly, Vol. 44, (52): 73-80, December 2009.

Reddy, AA. 2009 a. Policy Options for India's Edible Oil Complex. Economic and Political Weekly, 44(4): 22-24.

Reddy A A. 2010. Regional Disparities in Food Habits and Nutritional Intake in Andhra Pradesh, India, Regional and Sectoral Economic Studies Vol. 10-2.

Reddy AA and Bantilan MCS. 2012. Competitiveness and Technical Efficiency: Determinants in the Groundnut Oil Sector of India. Food Policy, Vol. 37(3): 255-263.

Reddy AA. 2013. Strategies for Reducing Mismatch Between Demand and Supply of Grain Legumes. Indian Journal of Agricultural Sciences, 83(3) 243-59.

Reddy, Narayana, M. and Surekha, K. 1999. Role of Chickpea in Enhancing AvailableP in Chickpea-upland Rice System in Vertisol. Journal of the Indian Society of SoilScience, 47(4): 805-808.

Rego, T J and S P Wani (2002): "Environment-Friendly Management Options for Sustaining Productivity in the Asian Semi-Arid Tropics", SANREM CRSP South Asia 2001 Annual Conference, Manila, Philippines, 28-30 May, http://www.aae.wisc.edu/sanrem-sea/Conference/Papers/Paper-Rego.doc

Rekhi, R.S and Meelu, O.P. 1983. Effect of Complementary Use of Mung Straw and Inorganic Fertilizer-N on N Availability and Yield of Rice. Oryza, 20: 125-129.

Saxena, A. 1995. Agronomic Management of Mungbean in Rice-wheat-mungbean System. Ph.D. Thesis, NDUA & T, Faizabad, pp. 243.

Saxena, N P and C Johansen (1990): "Realised Yield Potential in Chickpea and Physiological Considerations for Further Genetic Improvement" in S K Sinha, P V Sane.

S C Bhargava and P K Aggarwal (ed.), Proceedings of the International Congress of Plant Physiology, Vol. 1, Indian Society for Plant Physiology and Biochemistry, Indian Agricultural Research Institute, New Delhi, pp. 279-88.

Sharma, S N and Prasad, R 1999. Effect of Sesbania Green Manuring and Mungbean Residue Incorporation on Productivity and Nitrogen Uptake in Rice-wheat Cropping System. Bioresource Technology 67: 171-75.

Sharma, Shivesh, Upadhyay, R.G., and Sharma, C.R. 2000. Effect of Rhizobium Inoculation and Nitrogen on Growth, Dry Matter Accumulation and Yield.

Sinclair TR and Vadez V. 2002. Physiological Traits for Crop Yield Improvement in Low N and P Environments. Plant and Soil 245, 1-15.

Singh A K, 2012, Nutrient Management : Need for a Paradigm Shift. Souvenir, Third International Agronomy Congress on Agriculture Diversification, Climate Change Management and Livelihoods Nov. 26-30, pp. 54-62.

Singh K K , Ali M and Venkatesh M S, 2009. Effect of Pulses on System Productivity and N Economy: In Technical Bulletin Pulses in Cropping Systems, pp. 1-34.

Singh, Y., Choudhary, D.C., Singh, S.P., Bhardwaj, A.K. and Singh, D. 1996. Sustainability of Rice (Oryza sativa) - wheat (Triticum aestivum) Sequential Cropping Through Introduction of Legume Crops and Green Manure Crop in the System. Indian Journal of Agronomy, 41: 510-514.

Singh M,2014. Soil Microbial Potential in Augmenting Nutrients Supply and Improving Pulse Productivity in a World of Declining Renewable Resources. In: Souvenir, National Conference on Soil Health: A Key to Unlock and Sustain Production Potential, JNKVV(MP), Sep 3-4, pp. 23-29.

Vyas A.K, Kumar D, Ali M, Prasad R and Rana K S, 2014. Legumes in Crop Production System: In Text Book of Plant Nutrient Management (1st edition), Indian Society of Agronomy, New Delhi, pp. 295-310.

Pages: 38-59

CROP PRODUCTIVITY AND PLANT DISEASE MANAGEMENT

Edited by: Dr. Alka Chauhan; Dr. Pawan Kumar 'Bharti'; Ms. Deepti Sadana

ISBN: 978-93-5056-791-3

Edition: 2016

Published by: Discovery Publishing House Pvt. Ltd., New Delhi (India)

CHAPTER – 3

Indices Based Study of Major Crops and Their Cropping Systems Scenario of NARP Zones in Uttar Pradesh, India

Avadhesh Kumar Koshal

ABSTRACT

Uttar Pradesh is located on the North of India between 23° 50' N to 31° 28' N latitudes and 77° 4' E to 84° 38 E longitudes. The central Plain region has highest geographical coverage 23.8% and Bhabar and Tarai zone has lowest 1.9%. It has been divided in to nine agro-climatic zones; the largest zone covered area is Central Plain Region. The Indian cropping season is classified into three seasons; Kharif (autumn) crops, Rabi (spring) crops and Zaid crops (Vegetables, fruits. The dominant five cropping systems categories are observed namely CS1, CS2, CS3, CS4 & CS5 and crops *viz.* rice, maize, arhar, pearlmillet and sorghum based systems are observed.

The crops and cropping system indices RSI, RYI, CII and REY are used for sustainable development and CLUI and MCI used for land use management. The cropping systems analysis observed Bhabar Tarai zone has maximum CLUI 26.3 in CS1 and lowest value 6.0 observed in Vindhyan zone in CS5. The average MCI of the state derived was 121.3. At NARP zones level it varied

Research Associate (GIS), NICRA Project P.D.F.S.R., Modipuram, Meerut - 250 110 (U.P.), India.

from 88.4 to 145.8. The south western semi arid region has most efficient region for maize, pearl millet, barley, potato and mustard. The Bundelkhand and Vindhyan zones are less and not efficient zones for pearlmillet and barley crops. The Rice Equivalent Yield observed potato crops has maximum value in all zones. But the Bundelkhand and Vindhyan zone has lowest value 746 and 811 for Barley and pearlmillet. The NARP zones based are useful for overall sustainability of agricultural system study. It develops many important parameters and indices are useful for dynamic efficient zone management.

Keywords: Agro-Climatic Zone, Cropping system, Efficient zone, GIS & Indices.

INTRODUCTION

The Uttar Pradesh is the main part of Indo- Gangetic Plain with river Ganges makes large fertile land of Gangetic land, having alluvial soil with rich quantity of an organic carbon. It is also called food basket of Indo-Gangetic Plain states. Uttar Pradesh is the fifth largest state having the population of 19.96 crores (Census 2011). The population density is 828 people per square kilometre, making it one of the densest states in the country (Provisional population totals, 2011). It spreads over a large area, and the plains of the state are quite distinctly different from the high mountains in the north. Planning commission has divided Uttar Pradesh into two parts 47 districts belong to Upper Gangetic Plain Region and rest 23 districts belong to Middle Gangetic Plain Region (most of the eastern parts) (Planning Commission Report, 2005). The diverse and suitable agro-climatic situations have enormous potential for agricultural crops production in the state. The agriculture crops provide food as cereal, pulses, oil and vegetables and other forms. Other forms are used as dried form after processing. Mixed Type of crops are grown in rabi, kharif and zaid season in agricultural land. Every crop have key role in agriculture food market based on the requirement of healthy environment for human beings. The important crops are grown in the Gangetic plain are rice, wheat, maize, sugarcane, mustard etc. The state receives rainfall from mid June to mid September from south-west monsoon clouds of the Bay of Bengal.

Most of the kharif crops are dependent on south-west rainfall because water is much require than Rabi crops. A cropping system is defined as the management of a cropping pattern to optimize benefits from a given resource base under specific environmental conditions (Zandastra, 1977). Cropping system is an important component of farming system. That system is based on the principles and practices of farm resources (technology and adaphic environment). When annual crops are considered, a cropping system usually means the combination of crops within a given year (Willey, 1989). The cropping systems are develop most of district develop to availability of soil water seed agriculture input and output storage. The rice-wheat cropping system is pre-dominant system (Ali *et al.*).

The agriculture provides basic source economic growth and development of society and country. The 77.73% populations are living in villages including tribal population and are dependent on agriculture and related works. The Gross cropped area is 25,414 thousand ha with the cropping intensity of 153%. In Uttar Pradesh size of holding is around 0.83 ha and per capita land area is 0.14 ha, which is less than a half of the national average of 0.32 ha. The cropping intensity is 153%. In view of the crop production pattern, the Indian IGP can also be divided into two major zones: (1) the western part, parts of Uttar Pradesh (northern, central, and western), which is largely dominated by rice-wheat cropping systems (RWCS); and (2) the eastern part, comprising eastern Uttar Pradesh, which is largely dominated by rice-based cropping systems (NRAA, 2012).

National Agricultural Research project (NARP) was launched in 1979 by ICAR for initiating agriculture research in the agro climatic zones of the country. The programme based on natural resources, major crops farming systems, production constraints and socio-economic conditions prevalent in that zone. Generally each NARP zone covers 2-4 districts and is spread over an area as high as 40-50 thousand sq.km. Under NARP, the country was divided into 127 agro-climatic NARP zones falling under 17 major states and 6 states/Union Territories of North Eastern Hills Region. Agro climatic zones corresponding to each of the 15 agro climatic regions as defined by NARP were identified (Devasenapathy *et al.* 2008). According to NARP zonation; 9 zones are covered Uttar Pradesh state. The Central Plain zone covered maximum 23.8% geographical and 24.4% cultivated area than other regions. Land use management essential for changing agriculture land control environmental loss natural disaster. The suitable management for mitigation of climate change and preserving biodiversity are essential for natural resources.

Land cover is one of the most important elements for the describing and studying the environment. Some indices are used to seek the degree of competition between the component crops in an inter cropping system based on the competiveness the advantages of intercropping are judged over pure crop and we can able to derive a possible ratio of crops in the cropping systems (Subbian *et al.* 2000). Indices are use for the dynamic analysis of distribution of crop coverage in land uses coverage. Various indices are used to assess system performance (Virmani & Singh 1997). The different types of available lands are used for agriculture, forest, fallow land and population habitation (rural or urban) etc. The lands are alternate continuous use in agriculture purpose in three seasons. The crops and cropping system indices RSI, RYI, CII and REY are used for sustainable development and CLUI and MCI used for land use management.

Objective

NARP zones based indices study of Uttar Pradesh cropping systems levels are useful to understand for overall sustainability of agricultural system. It develops many important parameters and indices are useful for dynamic efficient zone management.

Study Area

Uttar Pradesh is India's one of the largest state having area 2, 40,928 Km^2 in terms of land area which constitutes 7.3% of the total area of the country (India Forest Report 2011). It is located on the North of India between 23° 50′ N to 31° 28′ N latitudes and 77° 4′ E to 84° 38 E longitudes. It shares boundary with 10 Indian states. The Madhya Pradesh state boundary is touch maximum districts of Uttar Pradesh (Fig. 3.1a & 3.1b). The state has an international boundary with starches 1,690 km of Nepal. Uttar Pradesh has 71 Districts, 18 Divisions, 820 Blocks and 1,07,452 villages. Based on rainfall patterns, temperature, soil types and existing cropping patterns, the state has been divided in to 9 agro climatic zones; the Tarai Region, Western Plain Region, Central Western Region, South-Western Region, Central Plain Region, Bundelkhand Region, North Eastern Plain Region, Eastern Plain Region and Vindhyachal Region.

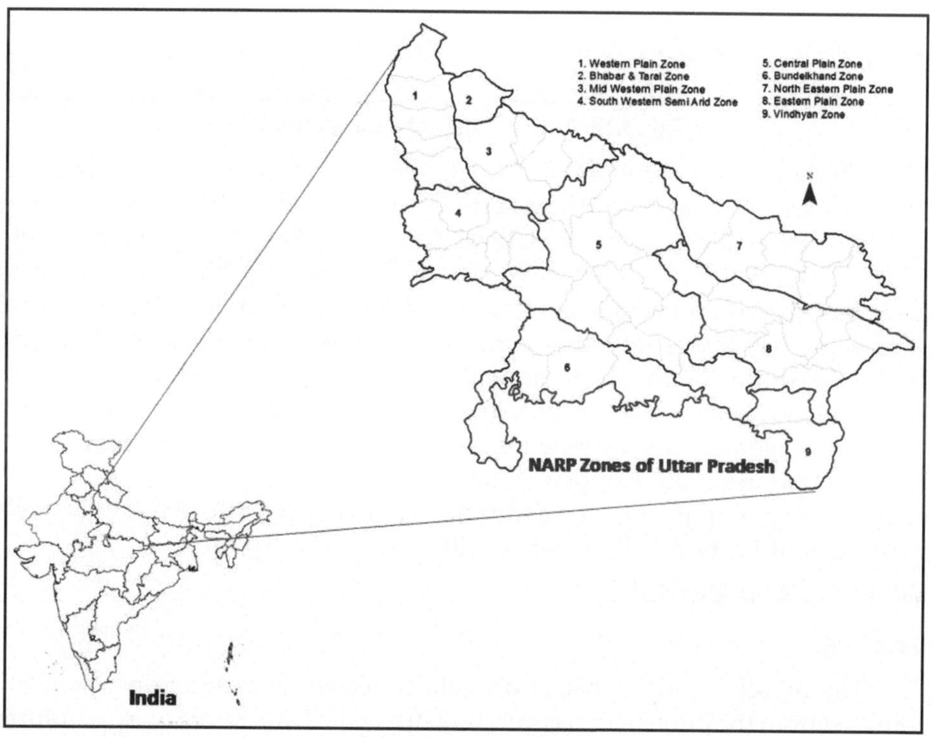

Fig. 3.1a: Study Area

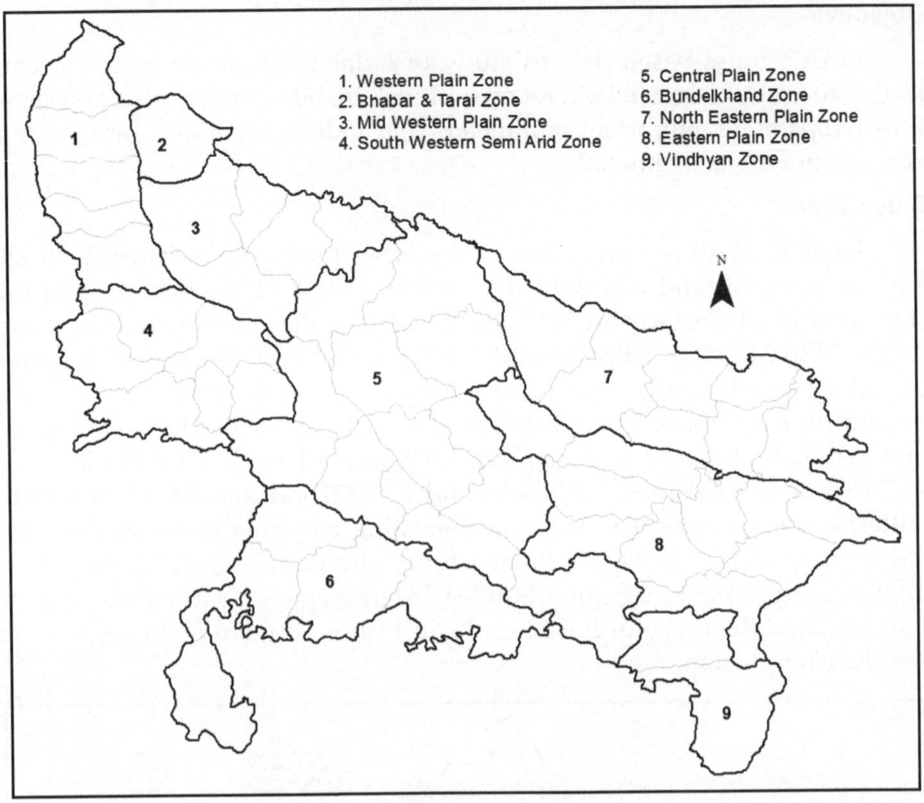

Fig. 3.1b: NARP Zones of Uttar Pradesh

The maximum numbers of districts are coverage of Central Plain zone, Eastern Plain zone and North eastern Plain zone have fifteen, thirteen and eleven districts and Bhabhar and Tarai Zone, and Vindhayan zone have one and two districts, rest zones have seven districts. The Bhabhar and Tarai Zone has maximum average annual rainfall 1400 mm but Mid Western Semi Arid Zone has lowest average annual rainfall 662 mm (Ghosh,1991). The NARP Zones are dominant alluvial soil with normal pH rich of organic matter. The dominant crops are rice, wheat and sugarcane. Uttar Pradesh has a humid subtropical climate and experiences four seasons (Upkar Prakashan, 2008). However based on the Koppen climatic classification (based on the concept of native vegetation), mostly as humid subtropical with dry winter type with parts of Eastern U.P. as Semi-Arid type.

MATERIAL AND METHODS

Data Use

The present study is based on data collected from secondary sources, collected from the published records, bulletin of the Directorate of Agricultural Statistics and the Institute of State Planning, U.P., ICAR, CENSUS India,

Vegetable Institute & other national level institutes. Besides different journals, papers, reports (NARP & Agro climatic zones report) and government websites are also used for study. The digital map of India with Uttar Pradesh state and districts, NARP zones were used for study, district and states information were taken from Census & planning commission report. National Agricultural Research Project (NARP) and Agro-Climatic Zone (ACZ) maps are used for sustainable agricultural land use planning analysis. The cropping systems maps were prepared in ARC GIS 10.2.2 software. The time series data of triennium years 2007-10 were arranged for analysis.

Methodology

In generation of cropping systems database, the steps taken was identification of crop mapping characteristics followed by computer storage of cropping systems data and finalized. Cropping pattern refers to proportions of total cropped area under different crops in a specified area under different crops in a specified area as a whole in a year. Cropped area refers to the area net cropped area plus area sown more than once during a year. The dominant cropping systems were identified based on crops coverage of kharif and Rabi season.

The detail methodology is divided in three parts for database analysis (Fig. 3.2):

1. Crop and cropping system analysis;
2. Land Use Efficiency & Cropping system Indices; and
3. Indices for delineating efficient cropping zone.

Crop and Cropping System Analysis

The important crops grown in the NARP zone of Uttar Pradesh are rice (*Oryza sativa*), maize (*Zea mays*), pearl millet (*Pennisetum glaucum*), wheat (Triticum aestivum), barley (*Hordeum vulgare*), and sorghum (*Sorghum bicolor*) among cereals; chickpea (*Cicer arietinum*), lentil (Lens culinaris), Pigeonpea (*Cajanus cajan*), and pea (*Pisum sativum*) among pulses; rapeseed/mustard (*Brassica napus* & *Brassica sp*), sunflower (*Helianthus annuus*), among oilseeds; and sugarcane (*Saccharum officinarum*), and potato (*Solarium tuberosum* L.) among cash crops. The state ranks 3rd in the country in production of rice. Rice is the single most dominant crop of the state, occupying about 32.94% of the total geographical area during the kharif season. Maize/jowar was the second major cereal crop, accounting for 13.77% of the total geographical area of the state. The major crops grown during the Rabi season were wheat and pulses/oilseed (Singh *et al.* 2011).

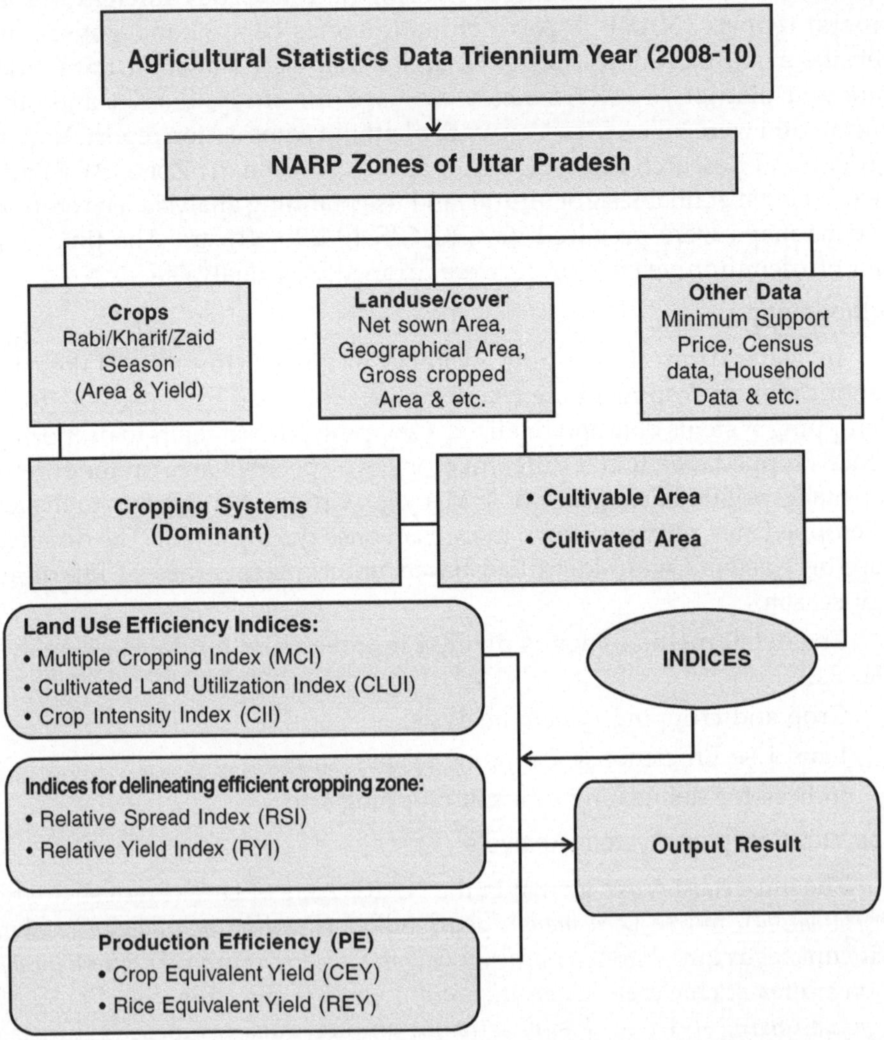

Fig. 3.2: Flow Chart of Detailed Methodology Used in the Study

Crop Calendar

The agricultural crop year in India is from July to June. The Indian cropping season is classified into three seasons; Kharif (autumn) crops, Rabi (spring) crops and Zaid crops (Vegetables, fruits) are grown in throughout year in the agriculture land of state. The kharif cropping season is from July to October during the South-west monsoon and the Rabi cropping season is from October to March (winter). The crops grown between March and June are summer crops. The South-west monsoon is having potential rainfall to cover almost all districts. It provides irrigation to agriculture land in kharif season. The Kharif crops are including Rice, Sorghum, Pearlmillet, Maize and Arhar. The rabi (spring) crops are Wheat, Barley, Gram, Lentil, Rapeseed/ mustard, Sugarcane, Potato, Pea and Sunflower and Zaid crops Vegetables and fruits (Fig. 3.3).

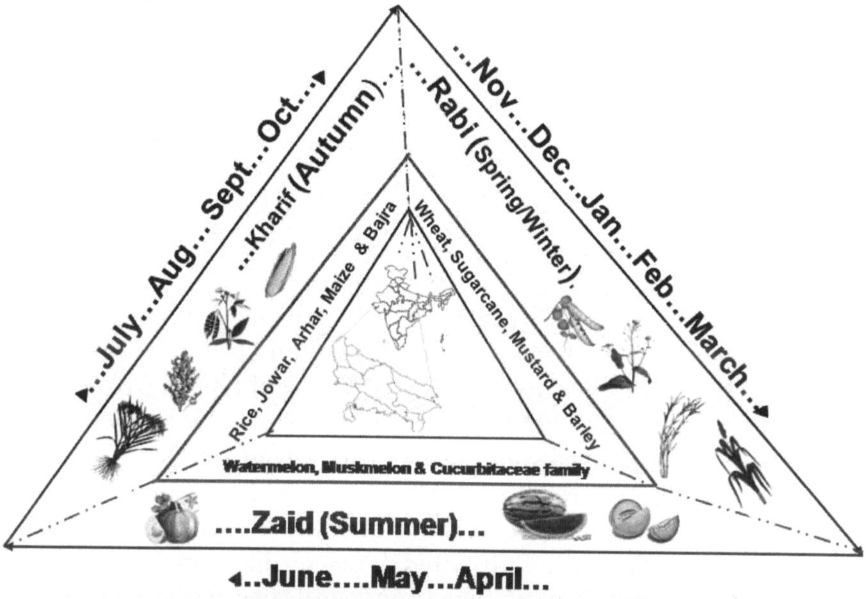

Fig.3.3: Crop calendar of NARP zones of Uttar Pradesh during Rabi, Kharif & Zaid season

Preparation of Cropping Systems Map

GIS technology has been employed to develop a cropping system analysis map of NARP zones by spatially integrated temporal crop inventory information of various crop seasons of that area (Mohan *et al*. 2005). A database was developed for analysis of cropping systems in Microsoft excel. All collected crop data entered in Microsoft Excel file were converted in. dbf format that file link with India digital map in ARC GIS and develop thematic maps using existing dataset. After linking database, major cropping systems maps were generated after overlaid district boundary that gives very clear view of the cropping systems of the different NARP zones of Uttar Pradesh. It has favourable and suitable climate, vast areas of fertile soils, sunshine and adequate water resources.

Analysis of Land Use Efficiency Indices, Indices for delineating efficient cropping zone and Production Efficiency (PE)

(i) Land Use Efficiency Indices

The cropping system approach is a holistic management of variant and invariant resources to optimize the food production. Various indices are used to assess and evaluate the efficiency and sustainability of the systems (Panigrahy *et al.* 2005). Cropping system indices are essential in the evaluation of performance of existing agricultural systems in an area, and for carrying out effective measures to achieved desired systems in the long run. The data are used in this study to derive cropping pattern, crop rotation and crop calendar. These were used as inputs to generate 6 cropping system performance indices. These were used to prioritize the districts for crop intensification and diversification. Several indices have been proposed to evaluate and compare the efficiencies of different cropping systems (Palaniappan, 1985). Characterization of cropping system is essential for studying the sustainability of a cropping system by knowing its benefits and losses (Panigrahy *et al.* 2009).

Different cropping system efficiency indices were computed for characterization the crops and cropping system of NARP zones of Uttar Pradesh. In the current study, indices are used for land use efficiencies analysis these are Multiple Cropping Index (MCI), Cultivated Land Utilization Index (CLUI) and Crop Intensity Index (CII) were computed (Ray *et al.* 2005).

MCI measures the cropping intensity (Dalrymple,1971); the MCI is indicator of crop intensification in time domain and quantifies vertical expansion of agricultural area. It is used to quantify intensity as single, double or triple cropping practice. Cultivated Land Utilization Index (CLUI) is indicator of land utilization efficiency, and indicates when and where the land lies unutilized. This index is useful in fine-tuning the cropping pattern to increase the total productivity. For a cropping pattern, where the land remains unutilized for a very short period, the CLUI attains a value near to 1.0, whereas for a completely unutilized land (throughout the year), the CLUI is 0.0. Crop Intensity Index indicates the number of times a field is grown with crops in a year. These three indices are useful to identify areas that need crop intensification, crop diversification or both.

(i.a) Multiple Cropping Index (MCI)

It is the ratio of total area cropped in a year to the total land area available for cultivation and expressed in percentage. (It measures the sum of areas planted to different crops and harvested in a single year divide by the total cultivated area times 100)

$$\text{Multiple Cropping Index (MCI)} = \frac{\sum_{i=1}^{n} \text{ai}}{\text{A}} \times 100$$

Where

i: 1,2,3........n,

n: Total number of crops

ai: Area occupied by the ith crop plant and harvested within one year

A: Total land area available for cultivation

(i.b) Cultivated Land Utilization Index (CLUI)

It is calculated by summing the products of land area planted to each crop, multiplied by the actual duration of that crop and divided by the total cultivated land area, times 365 days.

$$\text{Multiple Cropping Index (MCI)} = \frac{\sum_{i=1}^{n} \text{ai.di}}{\text{A} \times 365} \times 100$$

Where

i: 1,2,3........n,

n: Total number of crops

ai: Area occupied by the ith crop plant and harvested within one year

di: Days that the ith crop occupies; and

A: Total cultivated land area available for 365 days.

CLUI can be expressed as a percentage or fraction. This gives an idea about how the land area has been put into use. If the index is 1 (100%), it shows that the land has not been left fallow and more than 1, speaks about the specification of inter cropping and relay cropping. Limitation of CLUI is its inability to consider the land temporarily available to the farmer for cultivation.

(i.c) Crop Intensity Index (CII)

It is calculated by dividing gross cropped area with net area available in the farm, region or country multiplied by 100.

$$\text{Crop Intensity Index (CII)} = \frac{\text{Gross Cropped Area}}{\text{Net Area}} \times 100$$

When long duration crop grown, crop remains for a longer time in field. This is the drawback of CI. So time is not considered.

(ii) Indices for delineating efficient cropping zone

A particular crop in a specific zone used for alternation crop in the efficient cropping zone. It may alter the inefficient crops of particular region and it is used as to extend the area of efficient crops in a region. The Efficient cropping zone is derived from Relative Yield Index (RYI) and Relative Spread Index (RSI) used for implement to new technologies for the specific crops.

The uneconomical crops cultivated in an area will be replaced and introduction of most economic crops with reference to natural resources are the main objective of this indices. RYI and RSI are worked out as follows (Geethalakshmi, 2003) *(ii.a) Relative Spread Index (RSI)*

It is the ratio of the area of the particular crop in percentage to total cultivated area in the district to area of that crop in percentage of the total cultivable area in the state and expressed in percentage.

$$\text{Relative Spread Index (RSI)} = \frac{\text{Area of the crop expressed as percentage to total cultivable area of district}}{\text{Area of the crop expressed as percentage to total cultivable area of State}} \times 100$$

(ii.b) Relative Yield Index (RYI)

It is the ratio of the mean yield of a particular crop in a district to the yield of that crop in the state and expressed in percentage.

$$\text{Relative Yield Index (RYI)} = \frac{\text{Mean yield of a crop in a district}}{\text{Mean yield of a crop in a state/region}} \times 100$$

(iii) Production Efficiency (PE)

Many types of crops/cultivars are included in a multiple cropping sequences. It is very difficult to compare the economic produce of one crop to another (Verma and Modgal 1983) evolved the equation for calculating wheat equivalent yield (WEY).

(iii.a) Crop Equivalent Yield (CEY): Rice Equivalent Yield (REY)

The yields of different intercrops/crops are converted into equivalent yield of any one crop based on price of the produce. For easy comparison of different sequences, the economic produce of the individual crop was converted to rice equivalent yield based on the local market price as:

$$\text{Rice Equivalent Yield (REY)} = \text{Crop yield} \times \frac{\text{Price of unit wt. of the crop}}{\text{Price of unit wt.of the rice}}$$

All the inputs given in every sequence were well recoded to find out economics of the different sequences (Singh and Baruah 1992). This type of comparison is valid when considering the gross returns. However, it does not indicate the net gain obtained from a cropping system. This will not give any explanation about the land use pattern of the cropping system (Behera *et al.* 2007). The CEY give biological suitability of cropping system to an area. At the same time, cropping system should be economically viable and profitable.

RESULTS AND DISCUSSION

The triennium land use data of Uttar Pradesh state has total cultivated and cultivable area about 190mha and 177mha respectively. The central Plain region has highest geographical coverage 23.8% and Bhabar and Tarai zone has lowest 1.9% (Table 3.1) in terms of distribution of district geographical area. The crops are grown by farmers for cereal, pulses, oil seeds and vegetables which are used by human beings for food nutrition and its stored long time for future purpose. Crops are grown throughout year seasonal condition namely rabi (winter), kharif (autumn) and zaid. The dominant rabi season crops are wheat, sugarcane, Barely, Mustard, Potato, lentil and gram while kharif season crops are rice, maize, sorghum, pearl millet and pigeon pea. The zaid crops are growing for short period in between kharif and rabi season mainly vegetables, kharbooz and tarbooz (Table 3.2). But have not storage for long time as compare to other season crops and not have much economic value in term of cash crops. The South-west monsoon help for kharif crop coverage growth because water loving crops are grow more than rabi crops. The most of districts of Uttar Pradesh are covered maximum agricultural areas in rabi and kharif season rice and wheat crop. So rice-wheat system is pre-dominant cropping system.

Table 3.1. Land Use/Coverage of NARP Zone in Uttar Pradesh

NARP Zone	Geographical Area (ha)	Cultivable Area (ha)	Cultivated Area (ha)	Distribution of %GA
Bhabar and Tarai Zone	456100	349956	339427	1.9
Bundelkhand Zone	2941700	2348787	2143439	12.2
Central Plain Zone	5729400	4599607	4196218	23.8
Eastern Plain Zone	3850000	3134436	2891762	16
Mid Western Plain Zone	2569600	2134349	2070072	10.7
North Eastern Plain Zone	3317600	2614329	2504572	13.8
South Western Semi Arid Zone	2242400	1788734	1681277	9.3
Vindhyan Zone	1131000	575029	434106	4.7
Western Plain Zone	1855000	1508074	1463194	7.7
Total (9 Zones)	**24092800**	**19053302**	**17724066**	**100**

The dominant five cropping systems categories are observed namely CS1, CS2, CS3, CS4 & CS5 and crops *viz.* rice, maize, arhar, pearlmillet and sorghum based systems are observed. The eleven systems are Rice-wheat, Rice-Sugarcane, Rice-lentil, Maize-wheat, Maize-sugarcane, Arhar-wheat, Arhar-sugarcane Pearlmillet-wheat, Pearlmillet-sugarcane, Sorghum-sugarcane and Sorghum-wheat in NARP zone of Uttar Pradesh (Fig. 3.4). That system is distributed in different NARP zones; the four systems in CS1 category are Rice-wheat, rice-sugarcane, sorghum-wheat and pearl millet-wheat. The CS2, CS3, CS4 and CS5 categories observed six, five, seven and four cropping systems respectively (Table 3.3). These cropping systems are observed due to seasonal weather, soil variability and availability of resources. The cropping system is useful for sustainability of agricultural system.

Table 3.2: Major Crops Detail and Current Minimum Support Price of NARP Zones in Uttar Pradesh

Sl. No.	Crops	Common Name	Family	Scientific Name	Maturity Days	MSP (20013-14)* Price (Rs/q)
			Rabi season			
1.	Rice	Dhan/Chawal)	Poaceae (Gramineae)	*Oryza sativa*	125-130 Days	1310
2.	Maize	Makka	Poaceae (Gramineae)	*Zea mays*	95-100 Days	1310
3.	Sorghum	Jowar/Great millet	Poaceae (Gramineae)	*Sorghum bicolor*	105-110 Days	1500
4.	Pearl millet	Bajra/Bulrush millet/ Spiked millet	Poaceae (Gramineae)	*Pennisetum glaucum*	80-85 Days	1310
5.	Pigeon pea	Arhar/Toor/Red gram	Leguminosae	*Cajanus cajan*	260-270 Days	4300
			Kharif Season			
6.	Wheat	Gehu	Poaceae (Gramineae)	*Triticum aestivum*	125-130 Days	1350
7.	Sugarcane	Ganna	Poaceae (Gramineae)	*Saccharum officinarum*	270-280 Days	210
8.	Barley	Jau	Poaceae (Gramineae)	*Hordeum vulgare*	105-110 Days	980
9.	Rapeseed/ Mustard	Sarson	Brassicaceae	*Brassica juncea*	115-120 Days	3000
10.	Lentil	Massur	Leguminosae	*Lens culinaris*	65-70 Days	2900
11.	Gram	Channa/Bengal gram	Leguminosae	*Cicer arietinum*	115-120 Days	3000
12.	Pea	Matar	Leguminosae	*Pisum sativum*	130- 135 Days	2500
13.	Potato	Aalu	Solanaceae	*Solanum tuberosum*	90 -120 Days	1400
14.	Sunflower	Surajmukhi	Asteraceae	*Helianthus annuus*	75- 110 Days	3700
			Zaid Season			
15.	Muskmelon	Kharbooz	Cucurbitaceae	Cucumis melo	90-100 Days	Seasonal
16.	Watermelon	Tarbooz	Cucurbitaceae	Citrullus lanatus var. Lanatus	90-100 Days	Seasonal

* http://pib.nic.in/newsite/erelease.aspx?relid=100092 & http://pib.nic.in/newsite/erelease.aspx?relid=96854

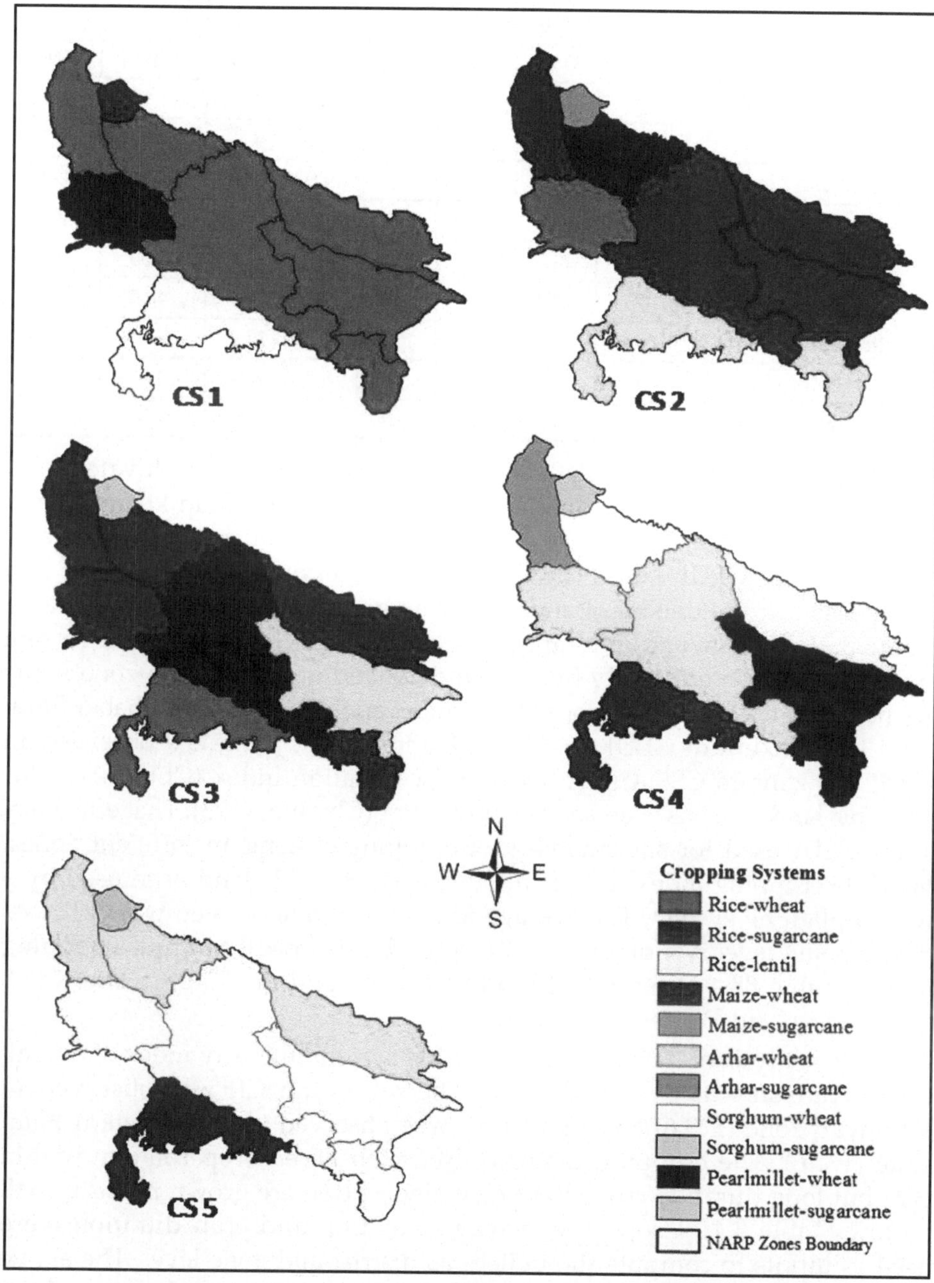

Fig. 3.4: Dominant Cropping Systems in NARP Zones of Uttar Pradesh

Table 3.3: Cultivated Land Utilization Index (CLUI) of Cropping Systems and Seasons Crops in NARP Zones of Uttar Pradesh

NARP Zone	Categories of Cropping Systems					Crop Season	
	CS1	CS2	CS3	CS4	CS5	Kharif	Rabi
Bhabar and Tarai Zone	26.3	23.5	23.5	23.5	23.5	1.14	6.51
Bundelkhand Zone	6.5	7.0	6.4	6.2	6.1	1.04	2.73
Central Plain Zone	14.1	9.9	9.6	9.9	9.5	2.78	3.19
Eastern Plain Zone	19.2	10.7	11.1	10.5	10.4	4.17	2.81
Mid Western Plain Zone	18.7	12.2	11.3	11.1	11.2	3.53	4.08
North Eastern Plain Zone	19.4	13.9	10.7	10.1	10.4	4.45	3.37
South Western Semi Arid Zone	13.4	13.1	11.5	11.3	10.7	2.61	2.92
Vindhyan Zone	10.1	7.7	6.3	6.1	6.0	2.87	1.82
Western Plain Zone	11.2	19.9	9.0	17.7	8.8	1.56	5.76

The analysis of data of Rabi and kharif season observed cultivated land utilization index (CLUI) for NARP zones of Uttar Pradesh, in kharif season North Eastern Plain Zone CLUI value 4.45 and in rabi season Bhabar and Tarai zone 6.51 CLUI value. The CLUI value observed lowest in Kharif and Rabi season in Bundelkhand and Vindhyan zone 1.04 and 1.82 CLUI value (Table 3.3). The Bhabar and Tarai zone agricultural lands are used in rabi and kharif season efficiently but in Bundelkhand and Vindhyan zone lands are not used efficient. The cropping systems analysis observed Bhabar Tarai zone has maximum CLUI 26.3 in CS1 and lowest value 6.0 observed in Vindhyan zone in CS5. Cultivated Land Utilization Index (CLUI) used for available land area has been used over the year (Chuang, 1973). That efficiency index CLUI used for sustainability of cropping systems in different zones. Multiple cropping index reflects the intensity of arable land been used by a certain planting system. The average MCI of the state derived was 121.3. At NARP zones level it varied from 88.4 to 145.8. The lowest Multiple Cropping System value 88.4 observed in Vindhyan zone and maximum value 145.8 observed in Mid Western Plain zone.

The analysis of database, the cropping system intensity index of overall Uttar Pradesh was observed 153.8. The minimum CII was observed in Vindhyan zone (129.6) and maximum was observed in Mid Western Plain zone (171.6). The cropping Intensity Index observed crop rotation within year but long duration crops like sugarcane, cotton are grown intensity will be low (Table 3.4). Crop type, acreage, rotation and crop duration were used as inputs to compute the indices as district and zone level. The above indices are give information of production performance and potential for developing resources and technologies. And also involved risk management strategies. The efficient cropping zone for a particular crop in a zone suggest for alter the inefficient crops. The every NARP Zone has maximum coverage area and production then other crops are grown in rabi and kharif season that zone is derived from Relative Yield Index and Relative Spread Index.

Table 3.4: Multiple Cropping Index & Cropping Intensity Index in NARP Zones of Uttar Pradesh

NARP Zone	MCI (Kharif & Rabi)	Cropping Intensity Index (Crops)
Bhabar and Tarai Zone	114.6	130.7
Bundelkhand Zone	91.2	130.0
Central Plain Zone	119.2	149.8
Eastern Plain Zone	133.1	163.0
Mid Western Plain Zone	145.8	171.6
North Eastern Plain Zone	143.1	153.8
South Western Semi Arid Zone	134.7	161.9
Vindhyan Zone	88.4	129.6
Western Plain Zone	122.0	156.5
Uttar Pradesh	121.3	153.8

The main role of this indices are the uneconomical crops cultivated in an area will be replaced and introduced of most economic crops with reference to natural resources (TNAU, 2003). That is useful for agriculture planning and management to implement to new technologies for the specified crops. Statistical indices are used for effective temporal data analysis of existing cropping pattern. The efficient crop and cropping system is depending on the available resources and emerging needs. In the rice-wheat system, the highest RSI values is in Mid Western Plain zone and North Eastern Plain zone 125.8 & 179.5 respectively. The lowest RSI value 9.1 and for 51.3 for Bundelkhand zone and Vindhyan zone. The sugarcane crop have maximum efficient zones are Bhabar Tarai Zone and Western Plain Zone but uneconomical zones are Bundelkhand and Vindhyan zone. The Pearlmillet, potato and mustard crops have maximum RSI value viz. 507.2, 394.4 and 287.6 respectively in South Western Semi Arid zone have most of the efficient zone. The sugarcane, gram, pea and pearlmillet crops have maximum RSI value 566.7,533, 530.3 and 507.2 respectively.

The overall data analysis of cropping pattern observed the Bhabar and Tarai zone has lowest RSI value 0.1 for maize and Pearlmillet, north eastern plain zone RSI value 0.6 for Pearlmillet and western plain zone has 0.5 for gram crop. Those crops are not good for growing season. The relative yield index value is 104.5 maximum for sunflower in Bhabar & Tarai zone. Arhar has maximum relative yield index value in Bundelkhand and North Eastern region 113.6 & 147.3 value respectively. The central Plain zone has value 129.3 for Pearlmillet, eastern plain zone for 107.4 of sunflower and north eastern plain zone 147.3 values for arhar crop. The Mid western plain zone and south western semi arid zone have 120.8 and 118 value for sugarcane crop. The two zones Vindhyan and Western Plain zones have 140 and 136 value for barley crop. The overall analysis of RYI data observed lowest value 44.4 and 56.1 in Eastern Plain zone and Bhabar and Tarai zone respectively.

The study of RSI and RYI data classified in four efficient zones are Most efficient cropping zones, Efficient cropping zones, Less efficient cropping zones and Not efficient cropping zones. The Bhabar and Tarai zone has most efficient zone for sugarcane crops but Bundelkhand region has not most efficient zone for rabi and kharif season due to weather and soil condition. The central region is most efficient zone for maize, sorghum, sunflower and mustard crops. The Eastern zone has most efficient zone for rice crop. The mid eastern zone is most efficient zone for rice, wheat and sugarcane crops. The North eastern plain zone rice is most efficient zone. The south western semi arid region has most efficient region for maize, pearl millet, barley, potato and mustard. This is most efficient for these crops due to less irrigation required. The Vindhyan region most efficient region for gram and western plain region for sugarcane is most efficient zone due to soil, agricultural machineries and irrigation facility (Table 3.5). Rice based cropping systems have maximum coverage area of all zones. Rice equivalent to all Rabi and kharif season crops are used for further analysis. The analysis of Rice Equivalent Yield observed potato crops has maximum value in all zones. The Bundelkhand and Vindhyan zone has lowest value 746 and 811 for Barley and pearlmillet. The Bundelkhand and Vindhyan zones are less and not efficient zones for pearlmillet and barley crops. Except sunflower REY value maximum 6134 in Bundelkhand zone rest of other zone has second most value sugarcane crop (Table 3.6).

CONCLUSION

The Uttar Pradesh is the main part of Indo- Gangetic Plain with river Ganges makes large fertile land of Gangetic land, having alluvial soil with rich quantity of an organic carbon. The mixed types of crops are grown in Rabi, Kharif and Zaid season in agricultural land. Every crop have key role in agriculture food market based on the requirement of healthy environment for human beings. The state receives rainfall from mid June to mid September the kharif crops covered most of the zones including Vindhyan and Bundelkhand zone. The dominant five cropping systems categories (CS1, CS2, CS3, CS4 & CS5) are observed. The main cropping systems are Rice-wheat, Rice-Sugarcane, Maize-wheat, Maize-sugarcane, Arhar Pearlmillet-wheat, and Sorghum-wheat. The crops and cropping system indices RSI, RYI, CII and REY are used for sustainable development and CLUI and MCI used for land use management. Indices are use for the dynamic analysis of distribution of crop coverage in land uses coverage. The different types of available lands are used for agriculture, forest, fallow land and population habitation (rural or urban) etc.

Table 3.5: Classification of Efficient Zone Based on RSI & RYI Value in Rabi and Kharif Season Crops in NARP Zones of Uttar Pradesh

Crops	Bhabar and Tarai Zone			Bundelkhand Zone			Central Plain Zone			Eastern Plain Zone			Mid Western Plain Zone			North Eastern Plain Zone			South Western Semi Arid Zone			Vindhyan Zone			Western Plain Zone		
	RSI	RYI	EZC	RSI	RYI	EZC	RSI	RYI	EZC	RSI	RYI	EZC	RSI	RYI	EZC	RSI	RYI	EZC	RSI	RYI	EZC	RSI	RYI	EZC	RSI	RYI	EZC
Rice	53.7	118.8	NECZ	9.1	56.1	NECZ	86.3	109.6	ECZ	159.7	104.7	MECZ	142.6	101.7	MECZ	179.5	103.7	MECZ	43.7	109.6	NECZ	63.4	79.8	NECZ	52.6	115.9	NECZ
Maize	0.1	98.7	NECZ	45.6	91.8	NECZ	125.8	102.5	MECZ	74.0	85.8	NECZ	26.4	116.3	NECZ	171.0	76.4	ECZ	153.8	149.8	MECZ	72.4	47.3	NECZ	111.0	131.6	ECZ
Sorghum	0.6	106.1	NECZ	351.6	90.0	ECZ	158.6	115.3	MECZ	80.7	105.6	ECZ	13.2	101.6	NECZ	1.3	108.0	NECZ	6.1	101.0	NECZ	92.5	100.2	ECZ	1.0	72.1	NECZ
Pearl millet	0.1	79.9	NECZ	27.5	58.4	NECZ	70.0	102.5	NECZ	36.4	94.9	NECZ	209.7	92.2	ECZ	0.6	129.3	NECZ	507.2	127.1	MECZ	38.8	86.9	NECZ	17.1	128.7	NECZ
Arhar	0.4	94.7	NECZ	162.6	99.3	ECZ	109.2	134.1	ECZ	119.3	113.6	ECZ	6.6	97.0	NECZ	88.0	79.8	LECZ	91.4	101.3	ECZ	235.7	84.6	ECZ	69.0	95.6	NECZ
Wheat	64.0	102.9	NECZ	63.2	77.9	NECZ	98.0	106.3	ECZ	110.7	95.8	LECZ	125.8	114.0	MECZ	109.4	96.2	LECZ	117.1	115.4	ECZ	51.3	65.8	NECZ	95.0	125.7	ECZ
Sugar-cane	566.7	109.7	MECZ	2.1	74.6	NECZ	80.5	97.4	LECZ	31.0	91.1	NECZ	152.3	110.6	MECZ	102.5	95.8	LECZ	9.2	98.9	NECZ	2.4	102.0	NECZ	413.5	120.0	MECZ
Barley	0.3	107.5	NECZ	160.6	79.1	ECZ	87.9	84.2	LECZ	80.7	89.3	LECZ	14.5	110.9	NECZ	18.7	106.3	NECZ	272.9	136.8	MECZ	315.4	44.4	LECZ	80.4	141.6	ECZ
Gram	0.7	92.5	NECZ	533.0	90.0	ECZ	94.8	115.4	ECZ	34.7	105.6	NECZ	1.6	93.1	NECZ	5.7	92.7	NECZ	6.1	114.3	NECZ	136.2	103.6	MECZ	0.5	92.8	NECZ
Pea	1.8	98.7	NECZ	530.3	86.5	ECZ	30.0	102.8	NECZ	92.3	98.3	LECZ	11.4	114.0	NECZ	55.4	98.7	NECZ	8.7	112.9	NECZ	71.0	89.6	NECZ	3.9	98.5	NECZ
Potato	9.6	103.1	NECZ	3.2	103.5	NECZ	130.1	97.1	ECZ	84.6	88.0	LECZ	73.3	93.1	NECZ	32.9	95.0	NECZ	394.4	117.7	MECZ	16.7	103.5	NECZ	48.5	99.0	NECZ
Sun-flower	1.8	86.6	NECZ	5.1	104.5	NECZ	298.2	102.3	MECZ	16.0	101.8	NECZ	64.3	96.7	NECZ	13.6	101.8	NECZ	157.9	97.6	NECZ	1.1	107.4	NECZ	10.0	101.2	NECZ
Mustard	22.7	109.9	NECZ	64.2	65.9	NECZ	128.4	108.7	MECZ	33.3	100.1	NECZ	125.4	99.9	ECZ	71.2	86.0	NECZ	287.6	151.5	MECZ	28.9	58.0	NECZ	44.3	120.1	NECZ
Lentil	13.0	101.4	NECZ	348.8	91.3	ECZ	50.2	107.0	NECZ	67.0	109.7	NECZ	63.9	106.9	NECZ	160.3	99.5	ECZ	8.1	108.0	NECZ	92.4	87.3	LECZ	11.6	88.9	NECZ

Note: EZC: Efficient Zone class; MECZ: Most Efficient Cropping Zones; ECZ: Efficient Cropping Zones; LECZ: Less Efficient Cropping Zones & NECZ: Not Efficient Cropping Zones.

(Contd...)

Classification of Efficient Zone based on RSI & RYI value

RSI	RYI	Efficient Zones
>125	>100	Most Efficient Cropping Zones (MECZ)
>125	75-100	Efficient Cropping Zones (ECZ)
>125	=<75	Less Efficient Cropping Zones (LECZ)
75-125	>100	Efficient Cropping Zones (ECZ)
75-125	75-100	Less Efficient Cropping Zones (LECZ)
75-125	=<75	Less Efficient Cropping Zones (LECZ)
<75	>100	Not Efficient Cropping Zones (NECZ)
<75	75-100	Not Efficient Cropping Zones (NECZ)
<75	=<75	Not Efficient Cropping Zones (NECZ)

Table 3.6: Rice Equivalent Yield value of different crops in NARP zone of Uttar Pradesh

NARP Zone	Bhabar and Tarai Zone	Bundelkhand Zone	Central Plain Zone	Eastern Plain Zone	Mid Western Plain Zone	North Eastern Plain Zone	South Western Semi Arid Zone	Vindhyan Zone	Western Plain Zone
Rice	1310	1310	1310	1310	1310	1310	1310	1310	1310
Maize	1384	1287	1437	1203	1631	1071	2101	663	1845
Sorghum	1213	1028	1318	1207	1161	1235	1154	1145	824
Pearl millet	1110	811	1422	1317	1279	1794	1764	1206	1787
Arhar	2407	2525	3410	2887	2466	2030	2575	2152	2431
Wheat	3057	2313	3158	2846	3386	2857	3429	1955	3733
Sugarcane	9010	6129	7998	7485	9082	7866	8123	8382	9855
Barley	1804	1327	1414	1500	1861	1784	2296	746	2377
Gram	2056	2000	2564	2347	2068	2059	2539	2301	2062
Pea	2337	2049	2435	2328	2701	2337	2674	2121	2332
Potato	24739	24825	23284	21116	22335	22777	28243	24825	23754
Sunflower	5080	6134	6005	5973	5672	5976	5729	6301	5941
Mustard	2490	1493	2462	2267	2263	1947	3430	1313	2720
Lentil	1785	1608	1884	1933	1883	1752	1902	1538	1565

The lands are alternate continuous use in agriculture purpose in three seasons. The cropping systems analysis observed Bhabar Tarai zone has maximum CLUI 26.3 in CS1 and lowest value 6.0 observed in Vindhyan zone in CS5. The average MCI and CII of the state derived was 121.3 and 153.8 observed. The Bhabar and Tarai zone has most efficient zone for sugarcane crops but Bundelkhand region has not most efficient zone for rabi and kharif season due to weather and soil condition. Rice based cropping systems have maximum coverage area of all zones. The analysis of Rice Equivalent Yield observed potato crops has maximum value in all zones. The Bundelkhand and Vindhyan zone has lowest value 746 and 811 for Barley and Pearlmillet. The Bundelkhand and Vindhyan zones are less and not efficient zones for Pearlmillet and barley crops. The indices give information of management and sustainability of crops and cropping system which growing from long time in a particular region.

REFERENCES

Ali, M., Joshi, P. K., Pande, S., Asokan, M., Virmani, S. M., Kumar, R. and Kandpal, B. K. (2000). *Legumes in the Indo-Gangetic Plain of India.* In: Legumes in Rice and Wheat Cropping Systems of the Indo-Gangetic Plain - Constraints and Opportunities. *International Crops Research Institute for the Semi-Arid Tropics,* Patancheru, Andhra Pradesh, India, pp. 35-70.

Behera, U.K., Sharma, A.R. and Pandey, H.N. (2007). Sustaining Productivity of Wheat-soybean Cropping System Through Integrated Nutrient Management Practices on the Vertisols of Central India. *Plant and Soil.* 297: 185-199.

Chuang, F.T. (1973). An Analysis of Change of Taiwan's Cultivated Land Utilization for Recent Years. *Rural Econ. Div., JCRR Rep.* 21, Taipei, Taiwan.

Census (2011). http://www.census2011.co.in/census/state/uttar+pradesh.html

Devasenapathy, P., Ramesh, T. & Gangwar, B. (2008). Efficiency Indices for Agriculture Management Research. *New India Publishing.* Pp. 162.

Dalrymple, D.F. (1971). Survey of Multiple Cropping in Less Developed Nations. United States Department of Agriculture, Washington D.C. *FEDS.* 108p.

Ghosh, S.P. (1991). Agroclimatic Zone Specific Research. Indian Perspective Under N.A.R.P. New Delhi, India: *Indian Council of Agricultural Research.* 539 pp.

Geethalakshmi,V., Balasubramanian,T.N., Karthikeyan, R., Huda, S. and Vasanthi, C. (2003). Probing the Association of Lunar Phases (Thithies) with Rainfall at Coimbatore. *Jour. of Agrometeorology.* 5(2): 27-36.

India Forest Report (2011). Forest Survey of India, Ministry of Environment & Forest, Govt. of India. pp. 230-235.

Mohan, B., Pandey, P.S. & Lavania, R.P. (2005). Temporal Change in Cropping Pattern in Western Plain Zone of U.P. *Jour. Farming Systems Research Development* 12(1&2): 54-58.

NRAA.(2012). Prioritization of Rainfed Areas in India, Study Report 4, *NRAA*, New Delhi, India. 100p.

Panigrahy, S., Manjunath, K.R., and Ray, S.S. (2005). Deriving Cropping System Performance Indices Using Remote Sensing Data and GIS. *Int. Jour. Remote Sensing.* 26(12): 2595-2606.

Panigrahy, S., Ray, S.S., Manjunath, K.R., Pandey, P.S., Sharma, S.K., Sood, A., Yadav, M., Gupta, P.C., Kundu, N. and Parihar, J.S. (2009). A Spatial Database of Cropping System and its Characteristics to AID Climate Change Impact Assessment Studies. *ISPRS Achieves XXXVIII-8/W3 workshop proc.:* Impact of Climate on Agriculture. pp. 150-155.

Palaniappan, S.P. (1985). Cropping Systems in the Tropics: Principles and Management. Longman, *Great Britain*. pp. 215.

Provisional Population Totals. Census of India (2011). Retrieved 23 July 2012. 1. Statistics of Uttar Pradesh". *Census of India 2011*. UP Government. 1 March 2011. Retrieved 31 July 2012.

Planning Commission Report (2005). Agro-climatic Zones of India, National Bureau of Soil Survey and Land use Planning.

Ray, S.S., Sood, A., Panigrahi, S., and Parihar, J. S. (2005). Derivation of Indices Using Remote Sensing Data to Evaluate Cropping System. *Jour. of the Indian Society of Remote Sensing,* 33(4): 475-480.

Subbian, P., Lal, R. and Subramainian. K.S. (2000). Cropping Systems Effects on Soil Quality in Semi arid Tropics. *Jour. of Sustainable Agrc.* 16: 7 - 38.

Singh, L.N. and Baruah, A.R. (1992). Rice Base Cropping System with the Inclusion of Fodder-legumes Under Rainfed Upland Conditions. *Manipur Jour. Agric. Sci.* 83-86.

Singh, N.J., Kudrat, M., Jain, K., Pandey, K.(2011). Cropping Pattern of Uttar Pradesh Using IRSP6 (AWiFS) data. *Int. Jour. of Remote Sensing.* 32(16): 4511-4526.

Upkar Prakashan. (2008). Uttar Pradesh General Knowledge. Upkar Prakashan. pp. 26. ISBN 978-81-7482-408-0.

Virmani, S.M. & Singh, G.B. (1997). Sustainable Agriculture Biophysical and Agro Ecological Indicators. *In Proceedings of the 3rd Agric. Science Congress*, M.S. Bajwa, et.al. (eds.), Punjab Agricultural University, Ludhiana, 12-15 March, Vol. 1 (New Delhi: National Academy of Agricultural Sciences). pp. 57-62.

Verma, S.P. and Modgal, S.C. (1983). Production Potential and Economics of Fertilizer Application as Resource Constraints in Maize-wheat Crop Sequence. *Himachal Jour. Agric. Res.*, 9: 89-92.

Willey, R.W. (1989). Intercropping its Importance and Research Needs. I. Competition and Yield Advantages. *Field Crop Abstr.* 32: 1-10.

Zandastra, H.G. (1977). Cropping System Research for the Asian Farmers. In Procesidings of the Symposium on Cropping Systems Research and Development for the Asian farmer, *IRRI, Manila*, 21-24 September 1976 (Manila: IRRI), pp. 10-29.

Pages: 60-77

CROP PRODUCTIVITY AND PLANT DISEASE MANAGEMENT
Edited by: Dr. Alka Chauhan; Dr. Pawan Kumar 'Bharti'; Ms. Deepti Sadana
ISBN: 978-93-5056-791-3
Edition: 2016
Published by: Discovery Publishing House Pvt. Ltd., New Delhi (India)

CHAPTER – 4

Analysis of Trends in Monsoon Rainfall and its Influence on Productivity of *Kharif* Rice

A District wise Latest Update

Jitendra Kumar Meher[1*]; Lalu Das[1]; Vikram Jeet Singh[2]

ABSTRACT

Monsoon rainfall plays an important role in the productivity of *Kharif* rice in India. Present study was attempted to explore the characteristics of monsoon rainfall in 55 districts spreading over five states in north Indian region for last 11-years. Three states belongs to the Western Himalayan region namely Uttarakhand, Himachal Pradesh and Jammu and Kashmir and the other two namely Punjab and Haryana falls under the fertile Indo-Gangetic plains. Mann-Kendall test was employed to find out monotonic trends in the rainfall pattern for all the districts in monthly and seasonal scale. Linear regression method of least square fit was used to find out any possible association between amount of rainfall and yield of *Kharif* rice. Results show that monsoon rainfall is scanty and not reliable for Haryana and Jammu and Kashmir while it's ample for Uttarakhand and can be dependable from an agricultural prospective. August

1 Department of Agricultural Meteorology and Physics, Bidhan Chandra Krishi Viswavidyalaya, Mohanpur, Nadia - 741 252, West Bengal (India)

2 Department of Seed Science and Technology, Bidhan Chandra Krishi Viswavidyalaya, Mohanpur, Nadia - 741 252 West Bengal (India)

rainfall is the major contributor to the total monsoon rainfall. Rainfall in August, September and monsoon season has a non-significant increasing trend in the study domain. Uttarakhand has shown a significant (95% level) increase of monsoon rainfall in the last decade. Yield of *Kharif* rice is found to be significantly influenced by rainfall climatology in August and September for all the states except Himachal Pradesh. Total monsoon rainfall is strongly related (R^2=0.67) to the yield of rice in Haryana as yield has shown a significant decrease for the monsoon rainfall of more than 550 mm.

Keywords: *Kharif* rice, Monsoon rain, North India, Trend.

INTRODUCTION

Mother earth is beautiful and beautiful are its resources. Biodiversity and geodiversity are the integral part of natural resources which are frequently challenged by climate change. As an inevitable consequence of anthropogenic activity, climate change can be a threat to food and water security in many regions across the globe. According to report produced by intergovernmental panel on climate change (IPCC, 2014) food production and food security are most vulnerable to rising air temperature. There is a general consensus among the scientific community that global surface temperature is increasing at a rate of 0.74±0.18 °C over 1906-2005 (IPCC, 2007). Such an increase in air temperature is causing global warming and increase in the atmospheric moisture content. One of the most significant consequences of increasing temperature could be an uncertainty of the precipitation distribution both spatially and temporally.

The behaviour, distribution and characteristics of long term seasonal rainfall over the Indian subcontinent is well documented in several studies (Guhathakurta and Rajeevan, 2008; Kumar *et al.*, 2010; Kumar and Jain, 2011; Krishnamurthy and Krishnamurthy, 2013). Starting from the erstwhile analysis of seasonal and annual rainfall (Parthasarathy and Dhar, 1978; Mooley and Parthsarathy, 1984) to contemporary years (Guhathakurta and Rajeevan, 2008; Krishnamurthy and Krishnamurthy, 2013) it is seen that annual and seasonal rainfall is free from any significant trend and typically random in nature. Monsoon season (Jun-September) which contribute 74.2% of the total annual rainfall in India (Guhathakurta and Rajeevan, 2008) has decreased non-significantly over the last century.

Northern region of India comprises of states Jammu & Kashmir, Himachal Pradesh, Uttarakhand, Punjab and Haryana. Major share of rice in these regions is cultivated during the monsoon season which is popularly known as *Kharif* rice. Agriculture in these regions is rain-fed as well as depends on irrigation. Rainfall during monsoon season plays a vital role for the yield of major crops like rice and wheat. Understanding rainfall distribution in the past and recent time will help the government for agricultural management as well as action plan for food and water security. Insight to rainfall trend in a regional scale sows that Punjab and Haryana has an non-significant increasing trend (i.e. 19.4 mm and 55.6 mm respectively) of monsoon rainfall from 1901-2003 as reported by Guhathakurta and Rajeevan (2008). Over the states of Uttarakhand and Himachal Pradesh same study has documented a non-significant decreasing trend of monsoon rainfall (i.e. -79.00 mm per year and -61.4 mm per 100 year respectively) while Jammu and Kashmir has a significant (90% level) increasing trend of 41.0 mm in 100 years. Interannual monsoon rainfall variability in India leads to large-scale droughts and floods, resulting in a major effect on Indian food grain production (Selvaraju, 2003; Kumar *et al.*, 2004).

More over studies related to precipitation in the Western Himalayan states, Punjab and Haryana are mostly limited to first decade of 21st century. Similarly studies related to productions of rice with monsoon rainfall variation are limited to last decade of 19th century only. Over the western Himalayan region scientific observations and its impacts on agriculture is poorly studied. A very recent study is missing in the literature which is necessary for short term agricultural and hydrological assessment. This study aimed at filling those gaps by analysing rainfall at district level for the regions mentioned above. This study also been attempted to find the association between the yields of *Kharif* rice with the monsoon rainfall in a state level.

STUDY REGION

Study region comprises of five meteorological subdivisions of India namely Uttarakhand, Haryana, Punjab, Himachal Pradesh and Jammu & Kashmir. Uttarakhand, Himachal Pradesh and Jammu & Kashmir falls under the western Himalayan region while Punjab and Haryana falls under the fertile Indo-Gangetic plain. Geographically the study region is located between 27.66 °N to 37.24 °N Latitude and 73.55 °E to 81.03 °E Longitude.

MATERIALS AND METHODS

District wise monthly rainfall data (June-September) for 55 districts (Table 4.1) over the states of Jammu & Kashmir, Himachal Pradesh, Uttarakhand, Punjab and Haryana were taken from the Indian meteorological department (IMD) for last 11 years (2004-2014). As IMD have only rainfall records from 2009-2014 so the previous year's (2004-2010) data was collected from India Water Portal. India Water portal and IMD made this data publicly available as an RTI filled by the South Asia Network on Dams, Rivers and People. Yield data of *Kharif* rice for the period of 2004-2012 were taken from the Directorate of Economics and Statstics (DES), Department of agriculture and cooperation, India. Advanced estimate of *Kharif* rice yield (State wise) for the year 2013-14 are not available in the DES archives so these years are excluded in the study. Only yield data of Haryana state for the year 2013 is taken from the Department of Agriculture, Haryana.

Table 4.1: Details of Districts taken over the Study Domain with Their Longitude and Latitude

Districts	Latitude (°N)	Longitude (°E)
Himachal Pradesh		
Bilaspur	31.33	76.75
Chamba	32.55	76.12
Hamirpur	31.63	76.51
Kangra	32.21	76.31
Kinnaur	31.58	78.41
Mandi	31.70	76.93
Solan	30.90	77.09
Una	31.47	76.27
Reg. avg#	32.40	76.89
Jammu and Kashmir		
Anantnag	33.43	75.17
Doda	33.14	75.54
Jammu	32.73	74.87
Kathua	32.58	75.50
Kupwara	34.52	74.25
Leh	34.16	77.58
Baramulla	34.10	74.30
Pulwama	33.87	74.89
Srinagar	34.08	74.83
Udhampur	33.00	75.16
Reg. avg#	34.33	76.40
Uttarakhand		
Almora	29.59	79.65
Chamoli	30.42	79.33
Champawat	29.33	80.10
Dehradun	30.19	78.40
Garhwal (Pauri)	30.15	79.30
Hardwar	29.96	78.16
Nainital	29.38	79.45
Rudra Prayag	30.28	78.98
Uttarkashi	30.73	78.45
Reg. avg.#	30.33	79.15

(Table Contd...)

Districts	Latitude (°N)	Longitude (°E)
Haryana		
Ambala	30.5	76.71
Bhiwani	28.78	76.13
Faridabad	28.43	77.24
Fatehabad	29.31	75.27
Gurgaon	28.37	77.40
Jhajjar	28.61	76.66
Jind	29.43	76.33
Kaithal	29.8	76.39
Kurukshetra	29.97	76.85
Mahendergarh	28.04	76.10
Panchkula	30.69	76.86
Panipat	29.43	76.93
Rewari	27.95	76.28
Rohtak	28.54	76.34
Sirsa	29.54	75.03
Sonepat	28.98	77.02
Yamuna Nagar	30.12	77.28
Reg. avg.#	29.33	76.23
Punjab		
Amritsar	31.64	74.86
Gurdaspur	31.96	75.25
Hoshiarpur	31.58	75.98
Jalandhar	31.33	75.57
Ludhiana	30.88	75.85
Moga	30.82	75.17
Muktsar	30.47	74.51
Nawan shehar	31.12	76.11
Patiala	30.34	76.38
Roop Nagar	30.97	76.51
Sangru	30.23	75.83
Reg. avg.#	30.53	75.15

Here Reg. avg. is used for the whole state

Time series analysis is carried out for each district and their regional average under a particular state. Statistics namely mean, Coefficient of

Variance (CV), Percentage contribution of each month rainfall to the monsoon rainfall are calculated for the rainfall data along with Mann Kendall trend test is employed to find out monotonic trend in the rainfall time series.

MANN-KENDALL TREND TEST

Mann-Kendall test, Here onwards MK test is a nonparametric test for detection of monotonic trend in the time series of any frequency distribution. It is based on the test statistics S defined as (Yue *et al.*, 2002a):

$$S=\sum_{i=1}^{N-1}\sum_{j=i+1}^{N}\mathrm{sign}(x_j - x_i)$$

Here, x_j are the sequential data values, N is the length of the data set (for our case N=11) and

$$\mathrm{sign}(y) = \begin{cases} 1 & \text{if } (y > 0) \\ 0 & \text{if} (y = 0) \\ -1 & \text{if} (y < 0) \end{cases}$$

For N > 8, the statistic S is approximately normally distributed with mean μ=0 and variance is

$$V(S) = \frac{N(N-1)(2N-5)-\sum_{i=1}^{M} t_i(t_i-1)(2t_i+5)}{18}$$

Where M is the number of tied groups and t_i is the size of the ith tied group. The standardized test statistic Z is computed by:

$$Z_{MK} = \begin{cases} \frac{S-1}{\sqrt{V(S)}} & \text{when } S > 0 \\ 0 & \text{when } S = 0 \\ \frac{S+1}{\sqrt{V(S)}} & \text{when } S < 0 \end{cases}$$

Sen's Slope Estimator Test:

The magnitude of trend is predicted by the Sen's estimator. Here, the slope (Ti) of all data pairs is computed as (Sen, 1968)

$$T_i = \frac{x_j - x_k}{j-k}, \text{ for } i = 1, 2 \ldots, N.$$

Here x_j and x_k are considered as data values at time j and k (j>k) correspondingly. The median of these N values of T_i is represented as Sen's estimator of slope which is given as Sen's estimator is computed as $Q_{med}=T_{(N+1)/}2$ if N appears odd, and it is considered as $Q_{me\,d}= [T_{N/2}+T_{(N+2)/2}]/2$ if N appears even. At the end, Q_{med} is computed by a two sided test at 100 (1-α) % confidence interval and then a true slope can be obtained by the non-parametric test. Positive value of Q_i indicates an upward or increasing trend and a negative value of Q_i gives a downward or decreasing trend in the time series.

ANALYSIS OF RAINFALL AND YIELD

To find out whether there is any linear association between the yield of *Kharif* rice and the monthly and/or seasonal rainfall, yield data for each state were compared with the rainfall in each month as well as with their possible combination of months. As the yield data were taken state wise hence regionally averaged rainfall time series were tested for their correlation with the yield for the period 2004-2012. Linear regression line with 95% confidence level is fitted for each of the possible correlation pair or scatter plot between the rainfall and yield.

RESULTS AND DISCUSSION

Data pertaining to mean, coefficient of variance, percentage contribution of each month rainfall to the total JJAS rainfall, trend and Sen slope of rainfall in all 55 districts for the period 2004-2014 was calculated and results on monthly and seasonal basis are presented as under:

JUNE MONTH

Rainfall climatology in June month has shown (Figure 4.1) a minimum rainfall of 11.4 mm in the Leh district of Jammu and Kashmir while the maximum rainfall is 261.5 mm in the Dehradun of Uttarakhand. Regional average rainfall over the 11-year period in Jammu and Kashmir, Himachal Pradesh, Uttarakhand, Punjab and Haryana is observed as 73.7 mm, 131.1 mm, 185.8 mm, 81.3 mm, and 60.1 mm respectively. June month has shown a high value of CV (0.60 to 0.95) for almost all the districts with some exception in Leh (2.74), Kinnaur (1.70), Moga (1.30), Anantnag (0.32), Baramulla (0.36). It is observed that June month has a contribution of 15-20 % to the total monsoon rainfall in almost all the districts with exception to Baramulla (27.1%), Sirsa (25.2%), Kupwara (23.0%), Faridabad (9.0 %), Sonipat (9.7%) and Panchkula (9.8%).

MK trend analysis of June month (Table 4.2) has a non-significant decreasing trend (slope between -0.9 and -6.9) of rainfall in nearly all the districts of Haryana except for Panchkula and Yamuna Nagar with a slope of 4.2 mm year^{-1} each. Similarly in the state of Punjab most of the districts have shown non-significant decreasing June month rainfall (slope between -0.5 to -3.0) except Ludhiana, Moga, Roop Nagar and Sangru (slope between 0.1 and 2.3). In Himachal Pradesh districts have shown an increasing trend (slope between 4.8 and 13.9) except for Hamripur (slope -0.3), Kangra (slope -0.4) and Una (slope -2.9). Kinnaur has shown a significant (90% level) increasing trend of 4.6 mm year^{-1}. In the state Jammu and Kashmir majority of districts have a non-significant increasing trend (slope between 0.1 and 5.7) except for Doda, Jammu, Pulwama, Udhampur. In the state of Uttarakhand except Pauri Garhwal (slope -4.0) all other districts have shown increasing trend of rainfall (slope between 2.2 to 22.9). Rudra Prayag has shown a significant

(90% level) increasing trend of 21.5 mm year^{-1}. Regionally averaged state wise rainfall trend shows that Himachal Pradesh and Uttarakhand has an increasing trend (slope 5.0 and 8.0 respectively) while the other states has a nominal decreasing trend that varies from -0.1 mm year^{-1} (Jammu and Kashmir) to -3.4 mm year^{-1} (Haryana)

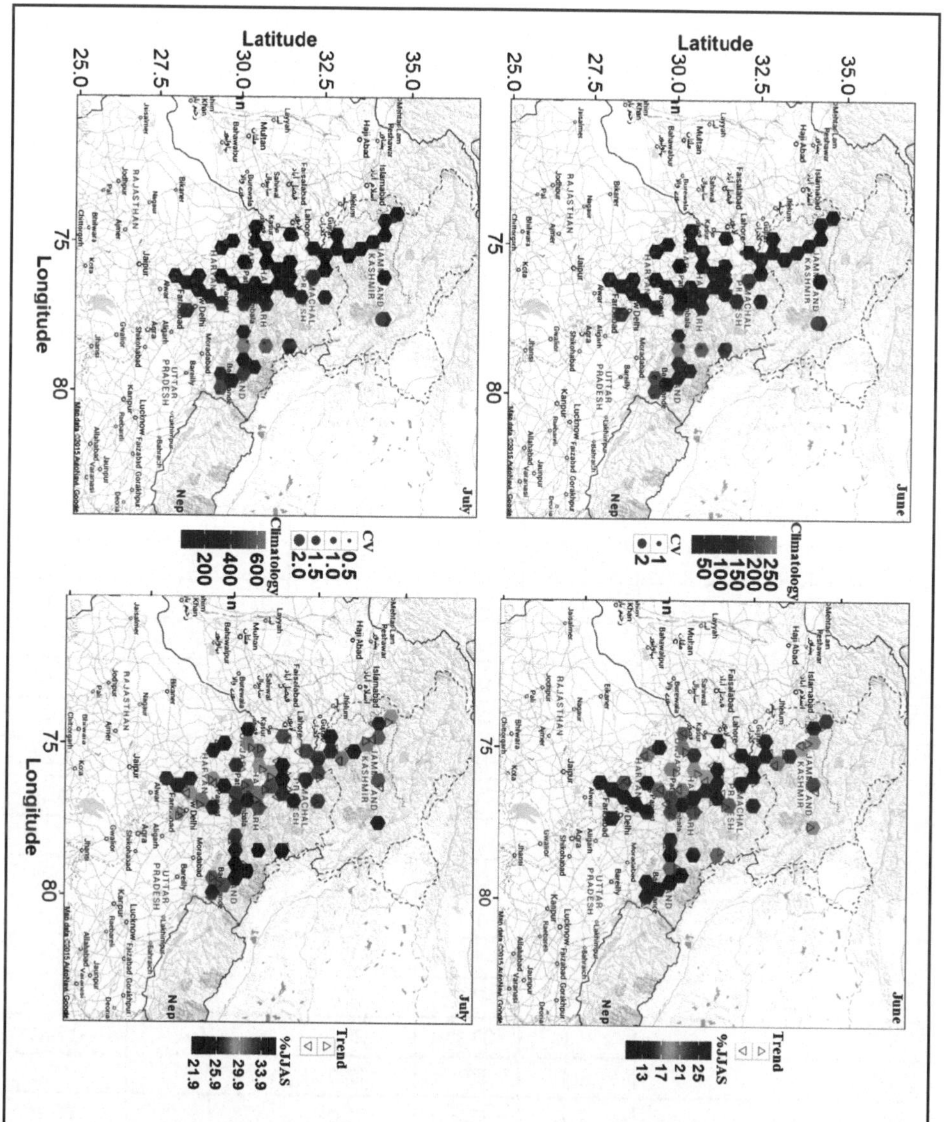

Fig. 4.1: Figure showing rainfall climatology at each districts and there corresponding coefficient of variation along with the Mann-Kendall trend result for June and July month. Where the symbol " shows increasing trend and ∇ shows decreasing trend

Table 4.2: Sen's Slope of Monthly and Seasonal Rainfall

Dist.	Sen's Slope (mm/year)				
	June	July	August	September	JJAS
Himachal Pradesh					
BIL	10.6	-8.8	-0.6	2.4	-2.9
CHA	4.8	6.1	22.2	**10.0**$^{+}$	**42.2***
HAM	-0.3	5.4	7.6	5.8	21.5
KAN	-0.4	17.4	**50.7***	9.8	**78.2***
KIN	**4.6***	-1.2	1.2	3.7	14.6
MAN	9.8	7.8	**20.1**$^{+}$	3.3	**30.6***
SOL	13.9	11.9	3.2	1.3	**31.7***
UNA	-2.9	-8.1	-15.8	4.1	6.3
REG	5.0	7.3	**14.9**$^{+}$	7.3	**23.7***
Jammu and Kashmir					
ANA	1.8	-1.7	3.1	3.1	5.0
DOD	-2.2	-5.7	4.6	**6.7**$^{+}$	4.8
JAM	-2.4	-1.9	**39.8***	**7.9**$^{+}$	**37.0**$^{+}$
KAT	4.2	-0.7	25.9	7.7	42.1
KUP	5.7	0.3	5.6	3.0	12.3
LAD	0.2	-0.03	**0.5**$^{+}$	0.4	1.7
BAR	0.1	-2.8	4.9	2.7	8.1
PUL	-0.1	0.3	2.6	2.5	1.8
SRI	0.1	-4.1	2.8	2.6	4.7
UDH	-1.3	-12.7	4.2	-1.7	-1.24
REG	-0.1	-4.3	9.8	3.3	9.4
Uttarakhand					
ALM	2.2	0.5	1.0	-1.5	-14.4
CHM	2.2	-1.1	10.2	1.9	17.5
CHP	22.9	-1.8	3.1	-7.4	8.3
DEH	2.2	-7.3	17.8	3.4	12.8
GAR	-4.0	**-35.1***	-20.5	-15.4	**-104.2**$^{+}$
HAR	6.4	5.6	17.0	0.4	15.8
NAI	16.8	25.2	21.0	1.9	**70.2**$^{+}$
RUD	**21.5**$^{+}$	13.0	**39.2***	6.1	**81.2***
UTT	12.6	**-44.2***	-0.4	0.1	**-53.7**$^{+}$
REG	8.0	-8.1	7.5	1.4	0.3

(Table Contd...)

Dist.	Sen's Slope (mm/year)				
	June	July	August	September	JJAS
Haryana					
AMB	-3.2	5.8	8.5	1.7	-1.4
BHI	-5.5	0.0	5.1	1.5	-4.1
FAR	-0.9	4.3	12.5	6.9	14.1
FAT	-3.8	-1.8	6.1	0.2	-5.5
GUR	-5.3	5.6	13.6	1.8	9.5
JHA	-6.9	-3.5	7.4	-1.8	-7.8
JIN	-0.9	-3.4	8.3	-4.8	-10.2
KAI	-6.0	2.1	6.3	-4.8	-9.3
KUR	-4.1	1.4	8.2	-2.4	0.4
MAH	-1.2	5.6	12.3	5.3	15.5
PAN	4.2	11.2	-1.7	5.0	-3.4
PAI	-1.2	1.5	11.9	-4.8	-11.3
REW	-0.2	-6.6	16.1	5.3	3.5
ROH	-2.0	-2.4	7.8	-2.2	-5.0
SIR	-8.0	3.1	**8.6+**	2.7	4.1
SON	-2.2	4.9	10.2	2.2	8.6
YAM	4.2	0.1	**24.0***	10.9	36.2
REG	-3.4	3.1	9.9	1.2	1.0
Punjab					
AMR	-3.0	-2.3	**13.8+**	1.5	10.9
GUD	-2.9	-1.3	**31.9+**	7.0	24.2
HAS	-0.5	3.1	12.0	**11.9***	32.0
JAL	-2.1	-4.1	-0.5	3.4	1.4
LUD	0.3	2.5	4.0	0.2	15.5
MOG	2.3	10.6	7.9	1.2	**35.7***
MUK	-2.1	2.1	11.2	-2.2	8.9
MAW	-1.9	4.2	5.1	5.9	15.6
PAT	-0.8	9.4	2.5	-2.9	-3.8
ROP	0.8	2.7	-7.4	3.4	0.8
SAN	0.1	2.6	3.2	**7.8***	23.3
REG	-0.8	2.6	6.7	4.1	9.7

Name of districts under each state is the abbreviated form of the actual names mentioned in table 4.1. Here bold numbers shows the trends are either significant at 0.05 level (*) or 0.1 level (+)

JULY MONTH

Rainfall climatology in July month has shown (Figure 4.1) a minimum rainfall of 12.7 mm in Leh and maximum rainfall of 672.6 mm in the Dehradun. Regional average rainfall over the 11-year period in Jammu and Kashmir, Himachal Pradesh, Uttarakhand, Punjab and Haryana is observed as 144.5 mm, 289.3 mm, 459.9 mm, 157.8 mm, and 124.6 mm respectively. It is merely twice the rainfall received during June for most of the states. This month has a relatively lower value of CV (0.30 to 0.65) for majority of districts as well as the regional average rainfall compared to June. There is some exception to this result for some districts like Leh (2.16), Sangru (0.96), Kupwara, Sirsa, Moga (0.94 each), Jammu (0.15), Dehradun (0.18), Hamripur, Kangra (0.2 each) and Chamoli (0.23). For the districts of Himachal Pradesh and Uttarakhand the CV values are low (0.2-0.4). July month has a contribution of 28-35 % to the total monsoon rainfall for almost all the districts with some exception in Chamoli (37.1%), Jammu (36.7%), Leh (21%), Kinnaur (22.2%), Mahendergarh (23.5%) and Muktsar (23.8%).

MK trend analysis of July month (Table 4.2) has a non-significant increasing trend (slope between 1.4 and 5.8) of rainfall in most of the districts of Haryana except for Fatehabad, Jhajjar, Jind, Rewari and Rohtak (slope between -1.8 and -6.6). In Punjab a group of district have shown non-significant increasing trend (slope between 2.1 and 9.4) with some exception to Amritsar, Gurdaspur and Jalandhar (slope between -1.3 and -4.1). In Himachal Pradesh greater part of the districts have shown an increasing trend (slope between 5.4 and 17.4) except for Bilaspur (slope -8.8), Kinnaur (slope -1.2) and Una (slope -8.1). In Jammu and Kashmir majority of districts have non-significant decreasing trend (slope between -12.7 and -1.7) except for Kupwara and Pulwama (slope 0.3 each). In Uttarakhand majority of the districts are showing decreasing trend. Pauri Garhwal and Uttarkashi have shown an exceptionally significant (95% level) decreasing trend of -35.1 mm year^{-1} and -44.2 mm year^{-1} respectively. Regionally averaged state wise rainfall trend shows that Jammu and Kashmir and Uttarakhand has a non-significant decreasing trend (slope -4.3 and -8.1 respectively) while the other states has an increasing trend which varies from 2.6 mm year^{-1} (Punjab) to 7.3 mm year^{-1} (Haryana).

AUGUST MONTH

Long-term average rainfall in August month has shown (Figure 4.2) a minimum of 18.9 mm in Leh and maximum 689.0 mm in the Dehradun. Regional average rainfall in Jammu and Kashmir, Himachal Pradesh, Uttarakhand, Punjab and Haryana is observed as 167.4 mm, 319.5 mm, 448.1 mm, 175.2 mm, and 142.9 mm respectively. The regional averaged rainfall received during this month is more than the rainfall received during July month except for the state of Uttarakhand. CV values in August month are closer to the CV value of July month for most of the districts. In Jammu and

Kashmir, Punjab and Uttarakhand majority of the districts have shown increased CV value from July to August but they have not shown any major changes in case of Uttarakhand while for Haryana they decreased from July to August with a nominal amount. August month has a contribution of 30% to 38% to the total monsoon rainfall for almost all the districts with some exception for Gurdaspur (42.5%), Kathua (42%), Jammu and Una (40.1% each), Kinnaur (23%), Baramulla (25%) and Sangru (26.5%).

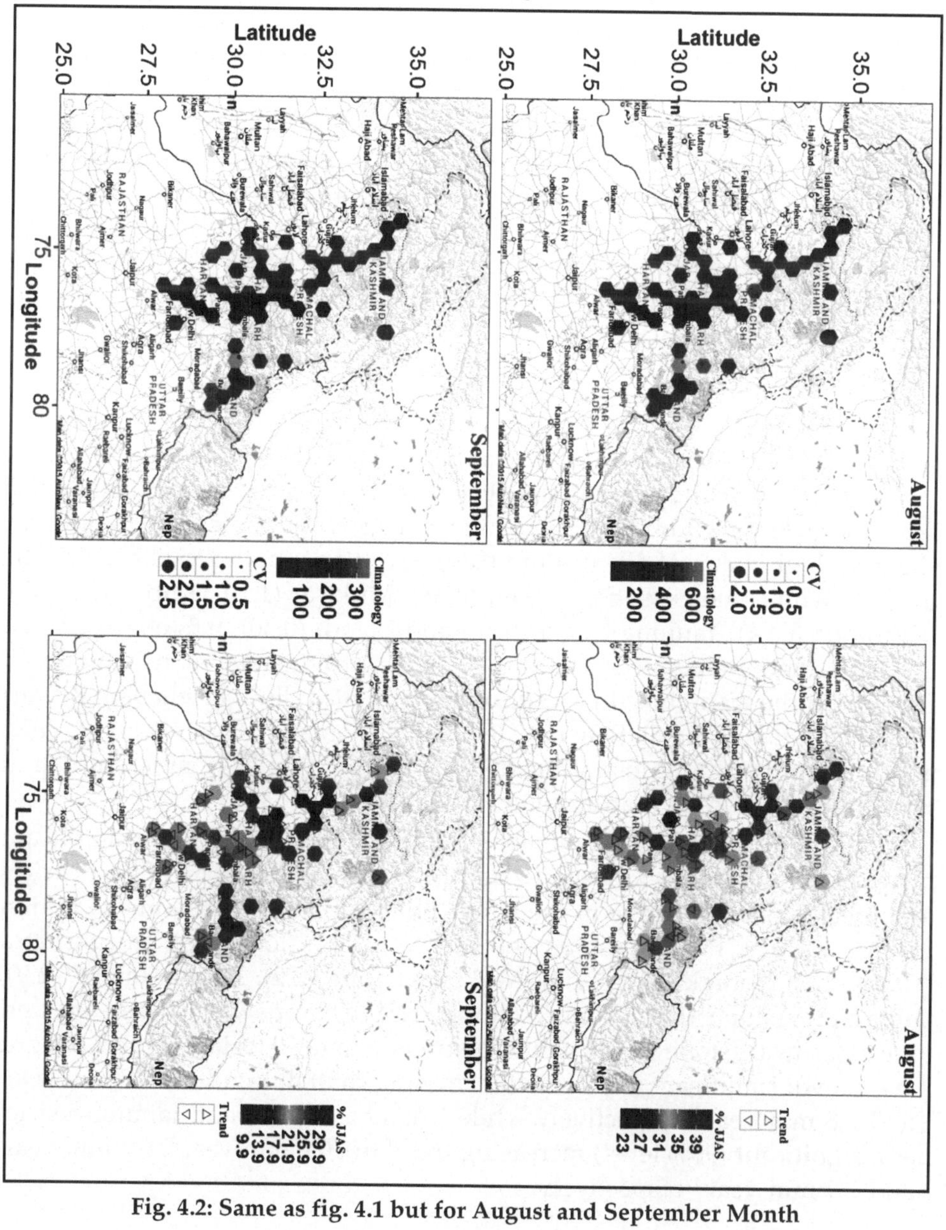

Fig. 4.2: Same as fig. 4.1 but for August and September Month

MK trend analysis has a non-significant increasing trend in greater number of districts and their regional average over the study domain. There are few districts namely Panchkula, Jalandhar, Roop Nagar, Bilaspur, Una, Pauri Garhwal, and Uttarkashi, they have shown a non-significant decreasing trend of -1.7 mm $year^{-1}$, -0.5 mm $year^{-1}$, -7.4 mm $year^{-1}$, -0.6 mm $year^{-1}$, -20.5 mm $year^{-1}$ and -0.4 mm $year^{-1}$ respectively. Kangra and Mandi districts of Himachal Pradesh have shown significant increasing trend of 50.7 mm $year^{-1}$ (95% level) and 20.1 mm $year^{-1}$ (90%) respectively. In Jammu and Kashmir two districts namely Jammu and Leh have significat increasing trend of 39.8 mm $year^{-1}$ (95% level) and 0.5 mm $year^{-1}$ (90% level). Rudra Prayag district under the state Uttarakhand has shown an exceptionally significant (95%) increasing trend of 39.2 mm $year^{-1}$. Similarly in Haryana, districts like Sirsa and Yamuna Nagar have significant increasing trend of 8.6 mm $year^{-1}$ (90% level) and 24.0 mm $year^{-1}$ (95% level) respectively. Amritsar and Gurdaspur districts under Punjab also have significant (90%) increasing trend of 13.8 mm $year^{-1}$ and 31.9 mm $year^{-1}$ respectively.

SEPTEMBER MONTH

Rainfall climatology in September month has shown (Figure 4.2) a minimum rainfall of 14.8 mm in the Leh while the maximum rainfall is 354.4 mm in Dehradun. Regional average rainfall in Jammu and Kashmir, Himachal Pradesh, Uttarakhand, Punjab and Haryana is observed as 68.5 mm, 143.5 mm, 236.7 mm, 83.5 mm, and 99.2 mm respectively. September month has shown a high value of CV (0.40 to 0.80) like June month for almost all the districts with some exception in Leh (2.68), Muktsar (1.20), Kupwara (0.97), Baramulla (0.94), Yamuna Nagar (0.90) and Mandi (0.30). It is observed that September month has a contribution of 14-20 % to the total monsoon rainfall for most of the districts with exception to Faridabad, Jind, Fatehabad, Rewari (25% each), Leh, Kaithal, Sonepat (26% each), Rohtak (28.3%), Panipat (30%) and Kinnaur (33.7%). Most of the districts of Haryana have more rainfall in September (22%-27%) than in June (13%-18%).

MK trend analysis of September (Table 4.2) month has a non-significant increasing trend (slope between 1.2 and 10.9) of rainfall in most of the districts and their regional average in the whole study domain with some exception to Jind, Kaithal, Panipat (slope -4.8 each), Jhajjar (slope -1.8), Kurukshetra (slope -2.4), Rohtak (slope 2.2), Muktsar (slope -2.2), Patiala (slope -2.9), Udhampur (slope -1.7), Almora (slope -1.5), Champawat (slope -7.4) and Pauri Garhwal (slope -15.4). Some districts namely Hosiarpur and Sangru have shown significant (95% level) increasing rainfall trend of 11.9 mm $year^{-1}$ and 7.8 mm $year^{-1}$ respectively while Chamba , Doda, and Jammu district has a significant (90% level) increasing trend of 10.0 mm $year^{-1}$, 6.7 mm $year^{-1}$ and 7.9 mm $year^{-1}$ respectively.

MONSOON SEASON (JUNE-SEPTEMBER)

Rainfall climatology in the whole monsoon season (Table 4.2) has a minimum of 57.8 mm in the Leh while the maximum of 1977.5 mm in Dehradun (Figure 4.3). Regional average rainfall in Jammu and Kashmir, Himachal Pradesh, Uttarakhand, Punjab and Haryana is observed as 454.1 mm, 883.4 mm, 1330.6 mm, 459.2 mm, and 444.8 mm respectively. Monsoon season have shown lower values of CV (0.25 to 0.40) in most of the districts over the study domain with some exception in Leh (2.46), Kinnaur, Moga, Kupwara (0.50 each), Muktsar (0.55), Hamirpur (0.10) and Ropar (0.16). CV value for entire of Himachal Pradesh (0.10) seems promising from an agricultural prospective.

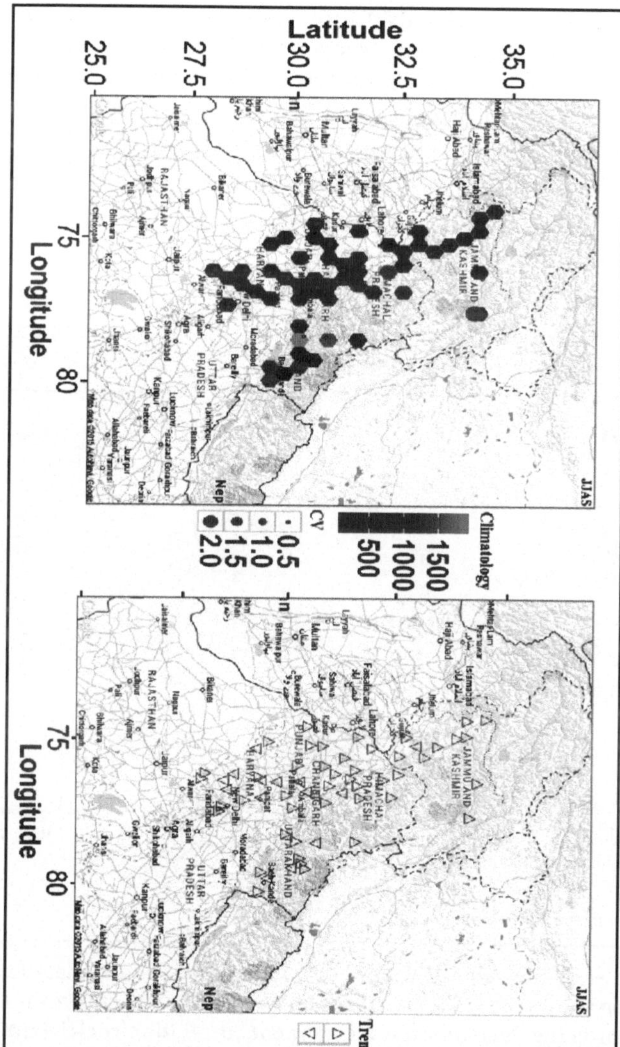

Fig. 4.3: Same as fig. 4.1 but for Whole Monsoon Season (JJAS)

MK trend analysis shows that four districts of the Himachal Pradesh and their regional average have an exceptionally significant (95% level) increasing trend which is not observed in any other regional averaged time series. The four districts are Chamba (slope 42.2), Kangra (slope 78.2), Mandi (slope 30.6) and Solan (23.7). In Uttarakhand there are also four such districts which are showing significant increasing and decreasing trend, the districts are Pauri Garhwal, Uttarkashi (slope -104.2 and -53.7 respectively, 90% level each), Nainital (slope 70.2, 90% level) and Rudra Prayag (slope 81.2, 95% level). In Jammu and Kashmir and Punjab nearly all the districts are showing non-significant increasing trend (slope between 1.4 and 42.1) with some exception to Udhampur (slope -1.24) and Patiala (slope -3.8). One district each in Jammu and Kahmir (Jammu, 90% level) and Punjab (Patiala, 95% level) has significant increasing trend of 37.0 mm year^{-1} and 35.7 mm year^{-1} respectively. In Haryana, both increasing and decreasing trends were found among the districts. In a regional context Haryana, Punjab, Jammu and Kahsmir, Uttarakhand has shown a non-significant increasing trend of 1.0 mm year^{-1}, 9.7 mm year^{-1}, 9.4 mm year^{-1} and 0.3 mm year^{-1} respectively.

State wise analysis of yield of *Kharif* rice and its association with the monsoon rainfall.

Scatter plots and the linear regressing model fit in between the rainfall time series (independent variable) and the yield data (dependent variable) shows (Figure 4.4) following results.

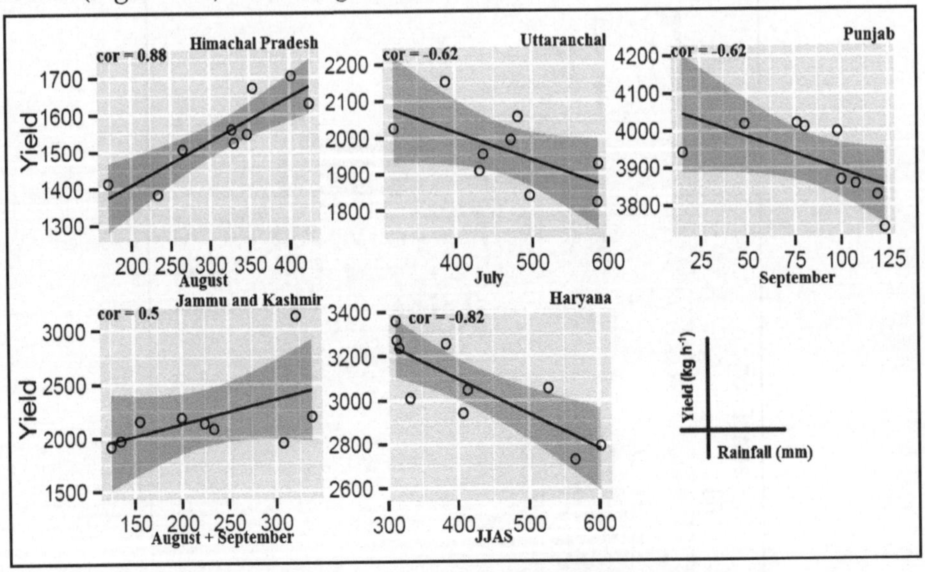

Fig. 4.4: Plots showing rainfall (mm) and Yield association at state level. The shaded region shows the 95% confidence level, Straight line shows the linear regression fit. cor is the Pearson product-moment correlation coefficient.

HIMACHAL PRADESH

August month rainfall in Himachal Pradesh is found out to be best correlated with the yield data of *Kharif* rice with a correlation of 0.88 (99% level). The linear regression line fit show that for the regional rainfall received during August month lies between 340 mm to 450 mm there is a significant (95%) rice yield of 1550 kg ha^{-1} to 1700 kg ha^{-1}. For a scanty august rainfall year of 150 mm to 275 mm the yield has reduced which varies between 1380-1500 kg ha^{-1}.

JAMMU AND KASHMIR

Total aggregate rainfall of August and September is found out to be correlated with the yield having a non-significant correlation of 0.5. The liner regression fit show that, for the regional total rainfall received during August and September lies between 150 mm to nearly 230 mm there have been a significant rice yield of 2000 to 2250 kg ha^{-1}. Above 300 mm rainfall the yield results are insignificant.

UTTARAKHAND

July month rainfall in Himachal Pradesh is found out to be best correlated with the yield having a correlation of -0.62 (90% level). The linear regression line fit show that, for the regional rainfall received during July month lies between 440 mm to 470 mm there is a significant (95%) rice yield of 1950 kg ha^{-1} to 2000 kg ha^{-1}. In a year with high august rainfall of 590 mm to 600 mm yield have shown a reduction which is below 1925 kg ha^{-1}.

HARYANA

Total monsoon rainfall in Haryana is found out to be highly correlated with the yield data of the state having a high correlation of -0.82 (99% level). The linear regression line fit show that, for regional rainfall received during monsoon season lies between 300 mm to 320 mm there is a high yield of 3200 kg ha^{-1} to 3400 kg ha^{-1}. For a high monsoon rainfall year of more than 400 mm the yield decreased significantly below 3100 kg ha^{-1} to even 2700 kg ha^{-1}.

PUNJAB

September month rainfall in Punjab is found out to be correlated with the yield data of the state with a correlation of -0.62 (90% level). The linear regression line fit shows that, for regional rainfall received during September month lies between 100 to 125 mm the yield has decreased significantly below 3900 kg ha^{-1}.

CONCLUSION

Following important conclusions can be made from the results discussed above:

- Out of all the districts taken for study Leh has experienced very less amount of rainfall during the monsoon season with high value of CV while Dehradun has experienced highest amount of rainfall. High value of CV in the study domain denotes that rainfall in the June and September months are not dependable for agricultural prospective as the farmer can't reliably use the average rainfall as an estimate of what might occur in the forthcoming years. In a state wise context rainfall climatology in the Jammu and Kashmir and Punjab is not reliable for agriculture while in Uttarakhand and Himachal Pradesh the monsoon rainfall can be dependable followed by Haryana. Overall monsoon rainfall is found out to be scanty for Haryana while it's very high for Uttarakhand. August month is found out to be the showery month in the whole study domain while June is relatively dry.

- Trend analysis of monthly and seasonal rainfall time series shows that rainfall has been decreased (nominal) non-significantly for the last 11-year for June month in Jammu and Kashmir, Punjab and Haryana while it's increasing in the Himachal Pradesh and Punjab. July month rainfall is observed to be decreasing non-significantly in Jammu and Kashmir while for other states it has an increasing trend. Over the whole study domain August, September rainfall has increased non-significantly except a significant increase is found in Himachal Pradesh. Rate of increase of August rainfall is found out to be more than in the September month. Total monsoon rainfall is found out to be significantly increasing for Himachal Pradesh. Non-significant and nominal increasing trends in the monsoon rainfall is observed in Uttarakhand and Haryana but for Jammu and Kashmir and Punjab the rate of this increment is found out to be equal.
- Productivity of *Kharif* rice in most of the states (except Uttarakhand) is found out to be highly influenced by the rainfall in August and September. For more than climatological rainfall in August and September, the yield is found out to be significantly reduced over all the states except Himachal Pradesh. In Himachal Pradesh higher value of August rainfall than the long term average has a positive impact on the yield of *Kharif* rice. Total monsoon rainfall is found out to be strongly related (R^2=0.67) to the yield of *Kharif* rice in Haryana. Yield has shown a significant decreasing trend for the monsoon rainfall of more than 550 mm.

The study finally come to terms with this remark that results and conclusions obtained from this study will be helpful for assessment of water resource and rainfall for developmental planning and economic growth in the study domain.

REFERENCES

Guhathakurta, P. and Rajeevan, M. (2008). Trends in the Rainfall Pattern Over India. *International Journal of Climatology,* 28: 1453-1469.

IPCC (2014). Climate Change 2014: Impacts, Adaptation, and Vulnerability. Contribution of Working Group II to the Fifth Assessment Report of Intergovernmental Panel on Climate Change, Cambridge University Press, Cambridge.

IPCC (2007). Climate Change 2007: Impacts, Adaptation and Vulnerability. Contribution of Working Group II to the Fifth Assessment Report of Intergovernmental Panel on Climate Change, Cambridge University Press, Cambridge.

Krishnamurthy, L. and Krishnamurthy, V. (2013). Decadal Scale Oscillations and Trend in the Indian Monsoon Rainfall. *Climate Dynamics,* 43: 319-331.

Kumar, V. Jain, S.K. and Singh, Y. (2010). Analysis of Long-term Rainfall Trends in India. *Hydrological Science Journal,* 55(4): 484-496.

Kumar, V. and Jain, S.K. (2011). Trends in Rainfall Amount and Number of Rainy Days in River Basins of India (1951-2004). *Hydrology Resesearch,* 42: 290-306.

Kumar, K.K., Kumar, K.R., Ashrit, R.G., Deshpande, N.R. and Hansen, J.W. (2004). Climate Impacts on Indian Agricutlure, *International Journal of Climatology* 24(11), 1375-1393.

Mooley, D.A. and Parthasarathy, B. (1984). Fluctuations in all-India Summer Monsoon Rainfall during 1871-1978. *Climate Change,* 6: 287-301.

Parthasarathy B., and Dhar ON. (1978). *Climate Fluctuations Over Indian Region–Rainfalt: A Review.* IITM, Pune. Research Report No. 31: RR-025.

Selvaraju, R. (2003). Impact of El Nino- Southern Oscillation on Indian Food Grain Production *International Journal of Climatology,* 23, 187-206.

Sen, P.K. 1968. Estimates of the Regression Coefficient Based on Kendall's Tau. *Journal of American Statistical Association.* 39, 1379-1389.

Yue, S., Pilon, P. and Cavadias, G. (2002). Power of the Mann–Kendall and Spearman's Rho Tests for Detecting Monotonic Trends in Hydrological Series. *Journal of Hydrology* 259: 254-271.

Pages: 78-96

CROP PRODUCTIVITY AND PLANT DISEASE MANAGEMENT

Edited by: Dr. Alka Chauhan; Dr. Pawan Kumar 'Bharti'; Ms. Deepti Sadana

ISBN: 978-93-5056-791-3

Edition: 2016

Published by: Discovery Publishing House Pvt. Ltd., New Delhi (India)

CHAPTER – 5

Ecology of Rice Blast (*Magnaporthe grisea*) Disease and its Management

Kadu Tanvi Pradeeprao[1*]; Kale Sonam Sureshrao[1]
Chavan Narendra Rameshsing[1], Vandana Shukla[2]

INTRODUCTION

Rice blast, caused by the phytopathogen Magnaporthe grisea (anamorph - Pyricularia grisea) has been reported in over 85 countries across the world. Blast generally considered as the most destructive disease of rice due to its widespread distribution and potential to cause up to 50% yield loss when conditions are favourable for its occurrence (Skamnioti and Gurr, 2009).The fungus infecting rice from seedling stage through maturity causes lesions on stems, leaves, panicles, peduncles, seeds, and even roots (Mithrasena *et al.*, 2012). Rice blast is controlled usually by use of fungicides that results in high production costs and environmental pollution (Ghazanfar *et al.*, 2009).To avoid chemical use for the control and management of rice blast, which are harmful to ecology plant breeders have achieved significant progress towards the enhancement of host plant resistance with limited success in the development

1 Department of Plant Molecular Biology and Biotechnology.

2 Department of Plant Pathology
College of Agriculture, Indira Gandhi Krishi Vishwavidyalaya, Raipur - 492 006 (Chhattisgarh) (India)

of cultivars with durable resistance (Jia 2003). Up to date more than 96 blast R genes (Sharma *et al.*, 2012) have been described and mapped but a limited number of reports are available on the genetics of blast resistance in rice. Mostly resistance to rice blast is governed by dominant genes,but in some cases recessive genes are also responsible (Padmanabhan *et al.*,1973; Marchetti *et al,* 1987). Both the major and minor genes can contribute to durable resistance (Wang *et al.,* 1994) against rice blast. Breeding of rice varieties with effective and sustained resistance to blast is considered as the most economical and environmentally sound strategy for management of rice blast (Mackill and Bonman, 1992). In rainfed, upland areas M. grisea is noted for expressing a large number of virulence forms or pathotypes due to, the most favourable environments for epidemic development (Ou, 1980). For most rice growing areas, rice blast disease management relies on the frequent introduction of resistant rice cultivars. However, blast resistance is rarely effective for more than 2-3 years (Barman *et al.*, 2005). Consequently, detailed genetic information on population structure is essential for understanding strategies to reduce the impact of rice blast disease.

The Biology of *M. oryzae*

The symptoms in rice fields induced by *M. oryzae* can be found on all the above ground parts of the rice plant at all growth stages. Seeds display brown spots after infection, infected roots have also been observed however, lesions on the sheaths were relatively rare. In young seedlings infections are initiated when the conidia are deposited on the surface of the leaves. For spores germination and attachment to the leaf surface water is most essential (Hamer J.E. *et al.*, 1988; Bourett T.M. *et al.*, 1990). Under optimal conditions, germination of spore occurs rapidly while within an hour's after landing of spore on the leaf polarized germ tubes are formed (Talbot N.J. *2003*). The secondary cycles are repeated many times through the growing season by initiating the spores produced by lesions on the young seedlings. Typically blast lesions are diamond shaped. Initially it appears dark green or grey with brown borders while, older lesions become light with necrotic borders. Under favourable conditions, lesions rapidly enlarge to several centimeters in length, eventually killing the leaf, and ultimately resulting in plant death. On resistant cultivars, lesions induced by *M. oryzae* usually remain small in size (1-2mm) and appear brown to dark brown in color. Disease severity of rice blast and the amount of spores produced on single lesion depends on temperature, field conditions, relative humidity, fertilization levels, and genotype of rice cultivars. In general, moderate temperatures (~24°C), high relative humidity (90-92%), and high moisture with at least a 12-hour period are advantageous for rice blast. The disease severity of the vegetative phase during the growing season highly influences the amount of disease during the reproductive phase. Spores produced at the end of the growing season may result in collar blast and neck blast; neck blast often causes direct crop losses.

Structure of *Magnaporthe grisea*

The perfect stage of the pathogen is *Magnaporthe grisea* (Hamer *et al.*, 1988) Barr. which belongs to ascomycotina. Perithecia of this fungus occur singly or in groups without apparent stroma. The asci are beak-shaped, cylindrical to subclavate containing fusiform hyaline four celled ascospores. The asci arose from the base of perithecium and measure 7-10 × 55-90 micron. Ascospores measure 4-7 × 17-24 micron. Hyaline, pyriform to obclavate, 1-3 septate, conidia with around base and a narrow apex, provided with a small basal appendage, having slightly constricted at septa, measuring 14-40 µm broad. Mycelium is septate, branched with multinucleate cells. From the mycelium conidiopores arise, which are simple, rarely branched, grayish, septate and slender, producing conidia at their apex. Conidia are produced singly, are ovate, 3- celled when mature with pointed blunt apex and multinucleate. Conidiophores are produced in clusters from each stoma (Fig. 5.1a). They are rarely solitary with 2-4 septa. The basal area of the conidiophores is swollen and tapers toward the lighter apex. The conidia of the fungus measure 20-22 × 10-12 µm. The conidia are 2-septate, translucent, and slightly darkened. They are obclavate and tapering at the apex. They are truncate or extended into a short tooth at the base.

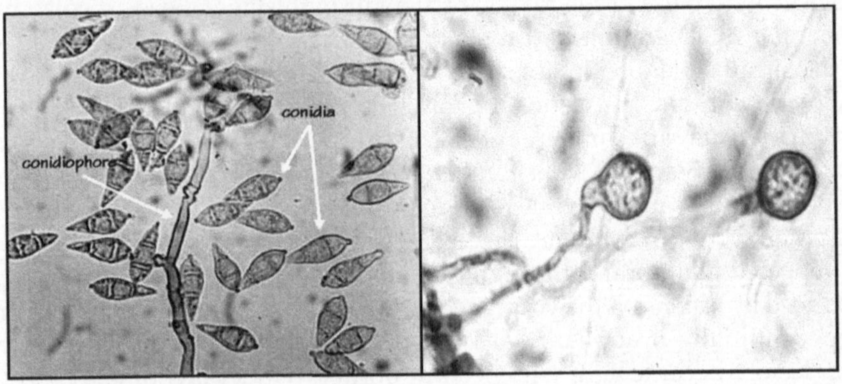

(a) (b)

Fig. 5.1: Conidia and Conidiophore (b) Appressoria

HOST RANGE

The fungus can infect rice plants at any growth stage. Although rice (*Oryza sativa*) is its main host, *M. grisea* can survive on the following plants: *Agropyron repens, Agrostis palustris, A. tenuis, Alopecurus pratensis, Andropogon* sp., *Anthoxanthum odoratum, Arundo donax, Avena byzantina, A. sterilis, A. sativa, Brachiaria mutica, Bromus catharticus, B. inermis, B. sitchensis, Canna indica, Chikushichloa aquatica, Costus speciosus, Curcuma aromatica, Cynodon dactylon, Cyperus rotundus, C. compressus, Dactylis glomerata, Digitaria sanguinalis,*

Echinochloa crus-galli, Eleusine indica, Eragrostis sp., Eremochloa ophiuroides, Eriochloa villosa, Festuca altaica, F. arundinacea, F. elatior, F. rubra, Fluminea sp., Glyceria leptolepis, Hierochloe odorata, Holcus lanatus, Hordeum vulgare, Hystrix patula, Leersia hexandra, L. japonica, L. oryzoides, Lolium italicum, L. multiflorum, L. perenne, Muhlenbergia sp., Musa sapientum, Oplismenus undulatifolius, Panicum miliaceum, P. ramosum, P. repens, Pennisetum typhoides, Phalaris arundinacea, P. canariensis, Phleum pratense, Poa annua, P. trivialis, Saccharum officinarum, Secale cereale, Setaria italica, S. viridis, Sorghum vulgare, Stenotaphrum secundatum, Triticum aestivum, Zea mays, Zingiber mioga, Z. officinale and *Zizania latifolia.* The role of these hosts in the rice blast disease cycle has been subject to controversy. Research indicates that although *M. grisea* can infect a wide range of plant hosts, some strains are very specific, and even sometimes cultivar, specific (Valent and Chumley 1991; Borromeo *et al.,* 1993).

MECHANISM OF PATHOGENESIS

Rice infection by *M. grisea* is initiated when three-celled, teardrop - shaped conidia land on the surface of a rice leaf. These spores germinate within 0-2hr on contact with the rice leaf, and adhere tightly to the hydrophobic surface by means of spore tip mucilage that is released from the apex of the spore (Hamer *et al.,* 1988). The formation of a specialized cell, the appressorium (Fig. 5.1b) that mediates the penetration of the fungus into host plant tissues. These cells bring about plant infection primarily by physical breakage of the leaf cuticle shown in figure 5.2. Experiments performed in the early 1990s demonstrated that appressoria of the rice blast fungus generate substantial turgor (Howard *et al.,* 1991). As a result of this enormous turgor, the appressorium produces a narrow penetration hypha at the base of the cell, which is forced through the underlying cuticle and later develops into invasive hyphae that fill the epidermal cells of the leaf. Rice blast symptoms become apparent 4-5 days after initial infection (Talbot, 2003; Valent *et al.*,1991; Howard *et al.,* 1991).

DISEASE CYCLE

Plant diseases are often severe during periods of warm temperatures and high moisture, the Spores do not germinate in direct sun light. The pathogen over seasons as mycelium and conidia on rice straw and seed from contaminated crops. The disease cycle shown in figure 5.3, the pathogen produces and releases conidia in abundance at a favourable temperature and relative humidity. The blast pathogen may go through several disease cycles in a single season. Each begins when a blast spores (conidium) infects and produces a lesions on the rice plant, produces new spores on the lesions and they are dispersed to another area on that plants or other plants. Most dispersions and spread of spores is through the air. As a result, rice in a field without leaf blast may develop collar and neck blast from air borne spores.

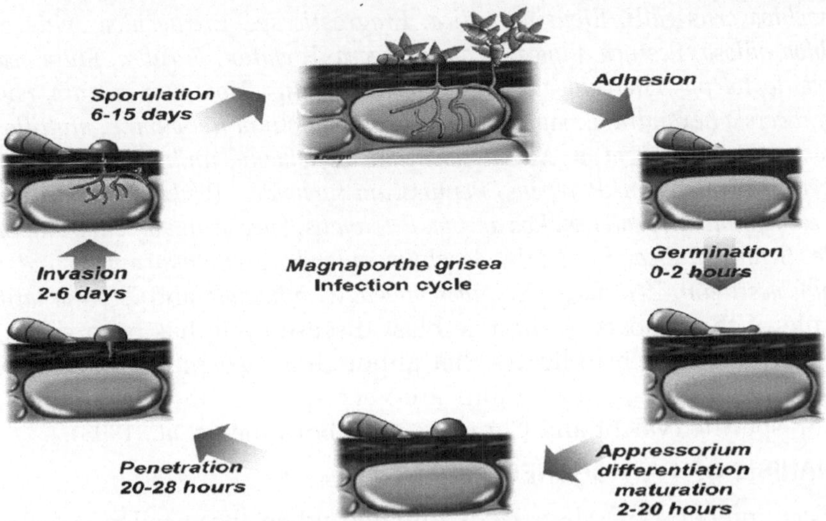

Fig. 5.2: Infection cycle of the rice blast pathogen, *M. oryzae*. Within 4-5 days after penetration, the fungus destroys the colonized tissues, leading to necrotic sporulating lesions spreading the disease.(Ribot C. *et al.*, 2008)

When environmental conditions are favourable for sporulation and infection, a single cycle of disease may occur within 7-10 days with individual lesions producing thousand of spores (Supriya Devi *et al.*, 2010).

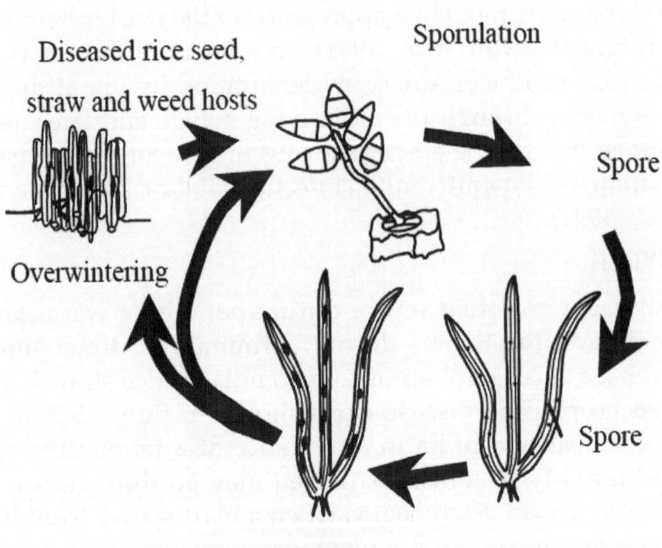

Fig. 5.3: Disease Cycle of the Rice Blast (Cother E. *et al.*, 2009)

ENVIRONMENTAL CONDITION FAVOURING BLAST

Environmental condition that favour the occurrence of the blast disease includes extended periods of free moisture on plant surfaces and temperatures at night between 63 to 73 °F with little or no wind high relative humidity. Conidia are produced and released under high RH with no spore production below 89% RH. Leaf wetness or free moisture form dew or other sources is required for infection to occur. Optimum temperatures for germination, infection, lesion formation and sporulation are 77 to 82 °F.

SYMPTOMS

Identification/Symptoms

Rice blast infected plant symptoms can be either lesions or spots. Lesions/ spots shape, colour and size vary depending on varietal resistance, environmental conditions and the age of the lesions (Ou 1985).The blast symptoms appear on leaves and other above ground parts of rice plants although leaves and the neck of the panicle are more commonly affected.

Leaf blast: The affected leaves developed water soaked, boat shaped white to grey lesions. Initial lesions/spots are white to gray-green with darker borders (Fig. 5.4a). Older lesions are white-grey, surrounded with a red-brown margin and are diamond shaped (wide centre and pointed toward either end). It may be from 0.5 cm to several centimeters in size and they are surrounded by a yellowish halo. The lesions enlarge and coalesce with each other covering the whole leaf surface and the leaves subsequently die off. Lesion size is commonly 1-1.5 cm long and 0.3-0.5 cm wide. Under favourable conditions, lesions can coalesce and kill the entire leaf.

Collar rot: Lesion is located the junction of the leaf blade and leaf sheath and can kill the entire leaf show in fig 5.4c.

Neck rot: On stem nodes, brown to black lesions (fig 5.4b) are formed and cover 1 to 2 cm on both sides. After the heads are emerged, the fungus attacks the peduncle neck node, which is girdled. This stage is known as neck infection which is most destructive. Symptoms (rotten neck) appear at the base of the panicle. Such attack often results with the killing of the entire panicle. Infected panicles appear white and are partly or completely unfilled. However, in such a situation the panicle base is broken due to grain weight and weaking of neck tissue. Such panicles hang down and are visible in a rice field even from distances. The whitehead symptoms can easily be confused with a stem borer attack which also results in a white and dead panicle.

Panicle blast: In this case the panicle appears brown or back in colour.

Node infection: Infected nodes appear black-brown and dry and often occur in a banded pattern. This kind of infection often causes the culm to break, resulting with the death of the rice plant.

Fig 5.4: Symptom of Rice Blast on Different Plant Parts: (a) Leaf Blast, (b) Neck Rot, (c) Collar Rot, (d) Panicle Blast

DISEASE MANAGEMENT

Burning or composting of diseased tissues, straw and stubble must be burned or composted, otherwise they can become inoculum sources for the next crop season. For reducing the severity of disease, different management strategies have to be initiated that are not only environmentally-friendly but also cost effective. Blast disease can be managed either through different methods includes using Cultural practices, biological control, chemical protection, Fertilizer managements or by introducing genetic resistance through either plant breeding or biotechnological methods.

CULTURAL PRACTICES

Cultural practices such as cultivation techniques, mulching, intercropping, plant density, planting date, crop rotation, strip farming, timing of harvest, barrier crops, crop mixtures, roguing, healthy planting material, soil solarization, soil amendments and fertilizer management, and water management have been used singly and in combination as tools for disease management. For some crops in developing countries, such control practices may be the only economically viable method available (Palti 1981; Thurston 1992). Cultural control methods not only serve in promoting the healthy growth of the crop, but are also effective in directly reducing inoculum potential (pruning, roguing, crop rotation, ploughing, etc.) and in enhancing the biological activities of antagonists in the soil (solarization, crop rotation, mulching, etc.).

BIOLOGICAL CONTROL

The search for the biological agents which can control the rice blast started in end of 1980's. The first report of a biological agent found effective in control of blast was of *Chaetomium cochliodes*. When the rice seeds were coated with spore suspension of *C. cochlioides* the early infection by blast was controlled and seedlings were healthy and taller than the control. It has been found that rice blast incidence can be reduced by mass vaccination method with avirulent isolates of *P. oryzae*. In India the studies on bacterial agents for the control of rice blast were conducted at "Center for Advanced Studies in Botany, University of Madras", and it was found that among the 400 bacterial isolates collected from rice fields of IRRI, 3 strains of *Pseudomonas fluorescens*, 5 of *Bacillus spp.*, and one of *Enterobacter spp.*, were inhibitory under in vitro conditions. Microbes have also been engineered to control rice blast. An epiphytic bacterium *Erwinia ananas* transformed with the chitinolytic enzyme gene (Chi A) from an antagonistic bacterium *Serratia marcescens* strain B2, a tomato epiphytic bacterium, was found inhibitory against *P. oryzae*. (Someya *et al.*, 2004). Recent studies on biocontrol of rice blast showed that *Bacillus subtillis* strain B-332 (Mu *et al.*, 2007), 1Pe2, 2R37 and 1Re14 (Yang *et al.*, 2008) and *Streptomyces sindenius* isolate 263 have good antagonistic activity against *P. oryzae*. However, biological control appears to be a suitable environment-friendly strategy for disease control and management. Due to rapid pathogen variation biological control for Blast has not received much attention thus preventing the development of suitable biological agents for disease control.

FERTILIZER MANAGEMENT

In case of rice blast, two nutrients viz. Nitrogen and Silicon have been found to affect the disease occurrence and development significantly. Since long time back, studies have shown that high N supply always induces heavy incidence of rice blast (Hori, 1898). Delayed or large top dressings are often responsible for severe disease. (Murata *et al.*,1933; Ikeda, 1933). A limit of 15 kg N/ha is recommended for upland rice in Brazil, specifically to reduce vulnerability to blast (Prabhu & Morais, 1986). Plant receiving large amount of N are found to have fewer silicated epidermal cells and thus have lower resistance (Miyake & Ikeda, 1932) The correlation between silica content and disease incidence was also studied on different cultivars of rice and it was observed that plants with high silica content or large number of silicated epidermal cells had slight damage from blast disease (Onodera, 1917). So it is suggested that resistance of rice to blast can be increased by applying silica slag in the field (Kawashima, 1927). Studies conducted at University of Florida USA, showed that reduction in the rice blast with the application of silica (calcium silicate slag) was comparable to that of fungicide (Benomyl) and now silicon fertilization has become a routine practice in Florida rice production (Datnoff *et al.*, 1997). In 1980, Singh & Singh reported that application of water hyacinth compost to soil reduces the rice blast disease.

CHEMICAL CONTROL

There is a wide range of chemicals/fungicides available, which can moderately control the growth of *M. grisea*. Their efficacy is determined by the time of application, quantity of application, stage of the pathogen and their chemical nature. Many fungicides act in different ways and target different stages of the pathogen. For example, melanin biosynthetic inhibitors inhibit the formation of the appressorium, while the choline biosynthesis fungicides affect the synthesis of phosphatidylcholine, which is the component of the fungal cell wall. Other than the fungicide alone, plant defense activators also being used against this disease. These chemicals will induce the systemic acquired resistance and these chemicals provide resistance not only to the fungal pathogens but also to bacteria and viruses also (Skamnioti and Gurr, 2009). However, pathogen evolves against this kind of chemicals (Suzuki and Arai, 2007) and these chemicals are not affordable and economic to the poor farmers. These chemicals are not eco-friendly and they are hazardous to the environment and leads to the land, air and water pollution. Hence, these fungicides are not suitable for the long term usage.

GENETIC RESISTANCE

Race-specific and race-nonspecific resistant cultivars have been bred all over the world. Based on the information of distribution of races, these cultivars can be selected. As various techniques have been used to control blast disease, including chemical and biological method, but these measures is not long lasting .while the chemical use is not only costly, but also hazardous to the environment. Introgression of resistant genes into rice cultivars is a very effective and safe option for controlling blast disease. Genetic studies related to blast resistance started a long time ago (Takahashi V. 1965), Breeders have identified more than 100 Pi loci and 350 QTL in rice genome responsible for blast disease. These Pi genes and QTLs can be introgressed into a blast - susceptible cultivar through different molecular breeding and biotechnological methods. These molecular techniques provide time saving, environment friendly and labour-cost-saving ways to control blast disease. But few cultivars have been developed with durable resistance (S.H. Ou 1985) mainly due to the pathogen's variability towards virulence. Therefore, breeders recently focused on combining genes with the help of molecular markers to get partial and complete resistance against blast (Wang M. *et al.*, 2000). At present, the blast is spreading in major rice-growing areas of the world; therefore, there is an urgent need for rice varieties having high and durable resistance against blast to assure food security in the developing countries. Considering the importance of resistance development among rice cultivars against blast (Fatah A. T. *et al.*, 2015). The pyramiding of resistant genes or providing them with multigenic resistance is an efficient way to manage blast disease. New information and knowledge gained from molecular biology research on disease resistance gene-mediated defense responses will undoubtedly provide new insights into the nature of rice disease resistance, which is convenience for developing new rice varieties with high blast disease resistance (Table 5.1). So, understanding and application of molecular biology and biotechnology is a prerequisite for accelerating the development of blast resistance rice.

Table 5.1: List of Blast Resistant Cultivar/variety Developed Using Molecular Breeding Methods

Disease	Gene/QTL	Type/Name of Marker Used	Method Used	Targeted Variety	Reference
Blast resistance	Pi1 and Pi2	Xa21(pT248) SSR Marker	MABB	Ronfeng B hybrid rice	Fu C. *et al.*, 2012
	Pi1, Piz-5, Pi2, Pita	RFLP, SSR, ISSR	MAS	C039	Hittalmani S. *et al.*, 2000
	Pi1	SSR and ISSR markers	MABB	Zhenshan 97A	Liu D.W. *et al.*,2003
	Pi5 and Pi54	Xa21 (pT248) SSR Marker	MABB	PRR 78, Basmati rice	Singh V.K. *et al.*, 2012
	Pi-9 (t)	pB8 (gene specific marker)	MABB	Luhui17	Wen S. *et al.*, 2011
	Pi2	SSR	MAS	Zhenshan 97B	Chen X. *et al.*, 2004
	Pi1, Pi2, Pi33	SSR	MABB	Jin23B	Chen H. *et al.*, 2008
	Pid1, Pib, Pita	–	–	Target genes were pyramided to G46B variety	Chen X.W. *et.,al* (2004)
	Pi-ta	Gene specific marker	MAS		Wang Z. *et al.*, 2007
	Pi-1, Pi-2 and Pi-33		Backcrossing and Multi-crossing combined with MAS	Jin 23B	Chen H.Q. *et al.*, 2008

(Table Contd...)

Disease	Gene/QTL	Type/Name of Marker Used	Method Used	Targeted Variety	Reference
Blast resistance +BB	Pi genes, *xa5*	Xa21(pT248) SSR Marker	MABB	–	Pinta W. *et al.*, 2013
	Pi1 and Pi2, *Xa23*	SSR	MABB	Rongfeng B	Fu C. *et al.*, 2012
	Xa21 & Piz	STS for Piz, transgene specific marker for Xa21	MAS applied for pyramiding of target traits. Xa21 gene originally introduced intodonor lines through genetic engineering	IR50	Narayanan N.N. *et al.*, (2002)
Submergence Tolerance + BPHResistance+ Bacterial blightresistance + Blastresistance + quality	Subchr9 QTL, Xa21, Bph and blast QTLs and quality loci	SSR and STS	MABB	–	Toojinda T. *et al.*, (2005)

A. Molecular breeding methods

1. *Marker-assisted selection:*

The continued development of molecular markers promises to overcome most of the existing limitations associated with morphological markers. In particular, the tight linkage of a molecular marker to a gene can be exploited for indirect selection of traits in a breeding programme, which is also referred to as MAS. Advances in the development of molecular markers and their implementation in cereal breeding programmes have led to a greater understanding of rice genetics and genomes. Disease assays to evaluate resistance to rice blast are time-consuming and laborious procedures that require specialized facilities. However, PCR-based analyses promise to significantly reduce the amount of labor needed for evaluating phenotypes by prescreening with MAS. To accelerate the effectiveness of MAS, the map locations of target gene/QTL must first be precisely determined, and several flanking markers must be developed. Four QTLs derived from upland rice cultivars that control partial resistance to rice blast have been successfully pyramidized into lowland rice cultivars using MAS (Yamamoto, T. *et al.*, 2009). However, the successful application of MAS requires extremely tight linkages between markers and phenotypic traits. Compared with previously reported RFLP markers linked to the *Pi-1(t)* gene (Hittalmani S. *et al.*, 2000; Yu, Y.G 1996), microsatellite markers are potentially more useful in developing countries where financial support is the principal limiting factor to establishing MAS rice breeding programmes. PCR-based allele-specific markers provide an efficient system for MAS in blast resistance breeding programmes (Hayashi K. *et al.*, 2006). However, the importance of using DNA markers within or flanking genes of interest during MAS strategies in rice should be stressed (Fjellstrom, R. *et al.*, 2004). It is possible that several blast resistance genes could be combined using MAS in a single genetic background to develop rice cultivars with broad-spectrum durable resistance to blast (Jena K.K. 2008). The application of marker-assisted selection is very powerful in case of blast resistance breeding because single or a few genes are involved in the resistance mechanism (Semagn K *et al.*, 2006). The development of durable blast-resistant rice varieties against the different strains of M. oryzae progressed through the availability of different molecular markers applied for marker-assisted selection (Jia Y. *et al.*, 2002). A dominant marker specific for the particular blast resistance gene has been developed, it can be used in a marker-assisted selection programme for the development of an improved blast-resistant rice cultivar.Several blast resistance genes Pi-z, Pi-ta Pi-b, Pi-k and Pi-I have been introgressed through marker-assisted selection into susceptible varieties (Nakamura S. *et al.*,1997 ;Monna L. *et al.*,1997).

2. Pyramiding

Pyramiding is the most common application of MAS in rice for resistance to diseases. The process of accumulating more genes together from more than two parents into a single genotype is known as pyramiding. Pyramiding may be possible through conventional breeding but it is usually not easy to identify the plants containing more than one gene. However, many researchers have postulated a pyramid of major genes to constitute a stable basis for blast resistance. Incorporation of genes with different resistance spectra into a single plant variety will reduce the selection pressure of the pathogen. For example, the gene combinations of *Pik* and *Piz* genes gave high degree of resistance in the rice variety, Jefferson ever since from its release in 1997 (McClung *et al.*, 1997; Fjellstrom *et al.*, 2004). The combination of *Pi*1+*Piz*-5 and *Pi*1+*Piz*-5+*Pita* also showed higher resistance in the background of CO39 than the individual resistance of the genes (Hittalmani S. *et al.*, 2000).

3. Marker-assisted backcrossing

For blast resistance Marker-assisted backcross breeding has received attention for the introgression of blast resistance genes into the genomic background of the susceptible varieties of rice. The main objective of this method is to reduce the donor genome content into the target varieties. Mainly, two steps i.e., foreground selection and background selection, are applied in backcrossing. Fore-ground selection is done by selecting a specific marker near the target genome, whereas background selection is applied by dispersing markers throughout the genome for the recovery of the recurrent parent (Charcosset A. *et al.*,1997). Backcross breeding has been widely used for the introgression of qualitative characters such as resistance against specific pathotype disease controlled by a single dominant gene (Allard I. 1960). The main purpose of MABC is to transfer the desired character along with recovering the recurrent parent characters. Marker-assisted back - crossing is currently playing an important role in plant breeding and genetic engineering for the development of blast-resistant cultivars (Sundaram R.M. *et al.*, 2009). Recently, blast resistance genes Piz5 and Pi54 have been introgressed into the genetic background of PRR78 rice variety from donor parent C101A51 and Tetep, and blast-resistant lines have been developed with the application of marker-assisted backcross breeding (Singh V.K. *et al.*, 2012). The selection was based on foreground markers RM287 and RM206 by following repetitive backcrossing. Pi1 leaf blast resistance gene has been introgressed into D521 line derived from donor line BL122 (Fu C. *et al.*, 2012)

Breeding for broad spectrum resistance is necessary to improve blast resistance in rice. Resistance genes can be specific for different causal pathogens. Pyramiding disease resistant genes into a single genetic background might be expected to give more durable disease resistance, as more resistant genes are incorporated into single genotypes (Koide *et al.*, 2010). The long history of rice cultivation and favourable climatic factors in tropical Asia are conducive to many diseases (including BB, blast and ShB) that pose a constant threat to rice production (Khush 1989). Consequently, breeding cultivars with multiple disease resistance would help sustain rice productivity. Diverse sources of resistance to major diseases and insects have been identified and rice varieties with multiple resistance have been developed.

B. Biotechnological approach

For the shortening of breeding process various tissue-culture methods and gene-transfer techniques used which significantly overcome some of the substantial agronomic and environmental problems that have not been solved using conventional methods. (Zapata-Arias F.J. *et al,* 1995).

Tissue culture: In crop science research tissue culture is one of the fundamental tools. For inducing resistance to diseases in susceptible cultivars which are well adapted to local soil and climatic conditions cell culture is one of the alternative methods. Genetic variation produced in tissue culture, termed as somaclonal variation has been reported in many crop species (Larkin P. J. *et al.,* 1981). Fortunately during the last 30 years, extensive work has been done on selecting the disease resistant plants against different pathogens. For the selection of novel disease resistant plants, the cell free culture filtrate (CF) or the pure toxins of the pathogens and direct infection by the pathogen or all of them together could be used (El-Kazzaz A.A 2001; El-Kazzaz A.A. *et al.,* 2004).

De Arau´jo G.L. *et al.,* (2002) was conducted an experiment on Basmati-370 rice which was susceptible to some pathotypes of *P. grisea* in Brazil, to assess the degree of blast resistance and some agronomic characteristics in the advanced generations of its somaclones. These evaluations were carried out in R5 to R9 generations, in field trials, in rice blast nursery and greenhouse. Significant variations in grain quality and other agronomic characteristics were not observed. However, some of the somaclones showed higher degree of blast resistance. The degree of blast resistance of upland rice (*Oryza sativa* L.) cultivar Araguaia has decreased significantly due to yield loss obtained from resistant somaclones, adaptation to greenhouse and field selection procedures (Arau´jo G.L. *et al.,* 2000).

Gene Transformation

Transgenic technologies allow multiple genes insertion simultaneously into genome to obtain broad-spectrum resistant lines. It's an important approach in the management of fungi diseases by introducing and overexpressing of genes that encode proteins involved in the synthesis of compounds toxic to fungi and with direct inhibitory effect on the growth of fungi (Cornelissen B.J.C.*et al.,* 1993). Several transformation methods including Agrobacterium, biolistic, and DNA uptake by protoplasts, have been employed to produce transgenic rice Some transgenic strategies for improving blast resistance based on the host–pathogen gene-for-gene interaction system and antifungal protein genes have been developed (Campbell M.A. *et al.*, 2002; Tan Y.N. *et al.*, 2004). Up till now, some reports have been on increasing rice blast resistance through transformation of plant antitoxin gene (Stark-Lorenzen P. *et al.*, 1997), chitinase gene (Nishizawa Y. *et al.*,1999), chitinase–glucanase gene (Feng D.R. *et al.*,1999), trichosanthin gene (Ming X.T. *et al.*, 2000) and rice blast resistance genes Pi-ta, Pi-9, Pi-2 etc. (Wang Z.X. *et al.*,1999; Bryan G.T. *et al.*, 2000 ; Qu S.H. *et al.*, 2006; Chen J. *et al.*, 2006, Zhou B. *et al.*, 2006). Transgenic approach has been used as an attractive alternative to conventional techniques for the genetic improvement of Basmati rice (Jain R.K. *et al.*, 2000).

REFERANCES

1. Allard I., (1960). Principles of Plant Breeding, John Wiley & Sons, New York, (Chapters 6-9).
2. Arau´jo G.L., Prabhu A.S., Freire A.B. (2000). Development of Blastresistant Somaclones of the Upland Rice Cultivar Araguaia. Pesq Agropec Bras Brasý´lia 35(2): 357-367. doi:10.1590/ S0100-204X 2000000200015.
3. Barman S.R. and Chattoo B.B. (2005). Rice Blast Fungus Sequenced. *Curr. Sci.* 89, 930-931.
4. Borromeo E.S., Nelson R.J., Bonman J.M., Leung H. (1993). Genetic Differentiation Among Isolates of *Magnaporthe grisea* Infecting Rice and Weed Hosts. *Phythopathology* 83, 393-399.
5. Bourett T.M., Howard R.J. (1990). In vitro Development of Penetration Structures in the Rice Blast Fungus Magnaporthe grisea. Canadian Journal of Botany; 68(2) 329-432.
6. Bryan G.T., Wu K.S., Farrall L., Hershey H.P., McAdams S.A., Faulk K.N., Donaldson G.K., Tarchini R., Valent B. (2000). A Single Amino Acid Difference Distinguishes Resistant and Susceptible Alleles of the Rice Blast Resistance Gene Pi-ta. Plant Cell 12(11): 2033-2046. doi:10.1105/tpc.12.11.2033.
7. Campbell M.A., Heather A.F., Pamela C.R. (2002) .Engineering Pathogen Resistance in Crop Plants. Transgenic Res 11(6): 599-613. doi:10.1023/A:1021109509953.
8. Charcosset A. (1997). Marker-assisted Introgression of Quantitative Trait loci, Genetics 147 (3) 1469-1485.
9. Chen H.Q., Chen Z.X., Ni S., Zuo S.M., Pan X.B., Zhu X.D. (2008) Pyramiding Three Genes with Resistance to Blast by Marker Assisted Selection to Improve Rice Blast Resistance of Jin 23B, Application, Zhongguo Shuidao Kexue. Chin J Rice Sci 22(1): 23-27.
10. Chen J., Henny R., Devanand P., Chao C. (2006). AFLP Analysis of Nephthytis (Syngonium Podophyllum Schott) Selected from Somaclonal Variants. Plant Cell Rep 24(12): 743-749. doi: 10.1007/s00299-005-0032-2.
11. Chen, X.W., S.G. Li, J.C. Xu, W.X. Zhai, Z.Z. Ling(2004). Identification of Two Blast Resistance Genes in a Rice Variety, Digu. J. Phytopathol. 152 77-85.
12. Cornelissen B.J.C, Melchers L.S. (1993). Strategies for Control of Fungi Diseases with Transgenic Plants. Plant Physiol 101: 709-712.
13. Cother E., Lanoiselet V. (2002). Crop Nutrition. In 'Production of Quality Rice in South-eastern Australia'. (Eds LM Keaky and WS Clampett) (RIRDC: Kingston, ACT, Australia).
14. Datnoff, L., Deren, C., & Snyder, G. (1997). Silicon Fertilization for Disease Management of Rice in Florida. Crop protection, 16(6), 525-531. http://dx.doi.org/10.1016/j.bbr.2011.03.031.

15. De Arau´jo G.L., Prabhu A.S. (2002). Blast Resistant Somaclones of Aromatic Rice Cultivar Basmati-370. Pesq Agropec Bras Brasý´lia 37(8):1127–1135. doi:10.1590/S0100-204X2002000800010.

16. El-Kazzaz A.A. (2001). Inheritance of Resistance to Fusarium Oxysporum f.sp. lycopersici in F2 Tomato Plants Via Tissue Culture. Egypt J Genet Cytol 30: 51-59.

17. El-Kazzaz A.A., Ashour A.M.A. (2004). Genetically Resistant Cucumber Plants to Wilt Pathogen via Tissue Cultures. Egypt J Phytopathol 32: 1-10.

18. Fatah A.Tanweer, Mohd Y., Rafii, Kamaruzaman Sijam, Harun A.R., Fahim Ahmeda, Mohammad A. L. (2015). Current Advance Methods for the Identification of Blast Resistance Genes in Rice, C.R. Biologies 338 321-334.

19. Feng D.R., Wei J.W., Xu X.P., Xu Y., Li B.J. (1999) Introduction of Multiple Antifungal Protein Genes into Rice and Preliminary Study on Resistance to Pyricularia Oryzae of Transgenic Rices. Acta Sci Nat Univ Sunyatsen 38(4): 62-66 (in Chinese with English abstract).

20. Fjellstrom, R.,Conaway-Bormans, C.A., McClung, A.M., Marchetti, M.A., Shank, A.R., Park, W.D.(2004). Development of DNA Markers Suitable for Marker Assisted Selection of Three *Pi* Genes Conferring Resistance to Multiple *Pyricularia grisea* Pathotypes. *Crop Sci.*, *44*, 1790-1798.

21. Fu C., Wu T., Liu W., Wang F., Li J., Zhu X., Huang H., Liu Z.R., Liao Y., Zhu M., Chen J., Huang Y. (2012). Genetic Improvement of Resistance to Blast and Bacterial Blight of the Elite Maintainer Line Rongfeng B in Hybrid rice (Oryza Sativa L.) by Using Marker-assisted Selection. Afr J Biotechnol 11(67): 13104-13124. doi: 10.5897/AJB12.1465.

22. Ghazanfar, M.K., Wakil, W. and Sahi, S.T. (2009). Influence of Various Fungicides on the Management of Rice Blast Disease. Myco. Path. *7*, 29-34.

23. Hamer J.E., Howard R.J., Chumley F.G., Valent B. (1988). A Mechanism for Surface Attachment in Spores of a Plant Pathogenic Fungus. Science; 239(4837) 288-290.

24. Hayashi K., Yoshida H., Ashikawa I. (2006). Development of PCR-based Allele-specific and InDel Marker Sets for Nine Rice Blast Resistance Genes. *Theor. Appl. Genet.*, *113*, 251-260.

25. Hittalmani S., Parco A., Mew T., Zeigler R., Huang N. (2000). Fine Mapping and DNA Marker-assisted Pyramiding of the Three Major Genes for Blast Resistance in Rice, Theor. Appl. Genet. 100 (7) 1121-1128.

26. Hori, S. (1898). Blast Disease of Rice Plants. Special Report, Imperial Agricultural Experimental Station, Tokyo. 1, 1-36.

27. Howard R.J., Ferrari,M., Roach,D.H. and Money,N.P. (1991). Penetration of Hard Substrates by a Fungus Employing Enormous Turgor Pressures. Proc. Natl Acad. Sci. USA, 88, 11281-11284.

28. Ikeda M. (1933). Influence of Application of Various Nitrogenous Fertilizers on Silica Content of Rice Plants. Tottori Society of Agricultural Sciences 4, 23-33.

29. Jain R.K., Jain S. (2000). Transgenic Strategies for Genetic Improvement of Basmati Rice. Indian J Exp Biol 38(1): 6-17.

30. Jena K.K., Mackill D.J. (2008). Molecular Markers and Their Use in Marker-assisted Selection in Rice.*Crop Sci.*, *48*, 1266-1276.

31. Jia Y. (2003). Marker Assisted Selection for the Control of Rice Blast Disease. *Pesticide Outlook* 14, 150-152.

32. Jia, Y.,Wang, Z., Singh, P. (2002). Development of Dominant Rice Blast *Pi-ta* Resistance Gene Markers. *Crop Sci*, *42*, 2145-2149.

33. Kawashima R. (1927). Influence of Silica on Rice Blast Disease. Japanese Journal of Soil Science and Plant Nutrition, 1, 86-91.

34. Khush G.S., Mackill D.J. and Sidhu G.S., (1989). Breeding Rice for Resistance to Bacterial Blight. In: Pages 207-217, Proc. International Workshop on Bacterial Blight of Rice, International Rice Research Institute, Los Banos, Philippines.

35. Koide Y., Kawasaki A, Yanoria M.J., Hairmansis T., Nguyet A., Bigirimana N.T.M., Fujita J. D., Kobayashi N., Fukuta Y. (2010). Development of Pyramided Lines with Two Resistance Genes, Pish and Pib, for Blast Disease (Magnaporthe oryzae B. Couch) in Rice (Oryza sativa L.). Plant Breed. 129: 670-675.

36. Larkin P.J., Scowcroft W.R. (1981). Somaclonal Variation-a Novel Source of Variability from Cell Cultures for Plant Improvement. Theor Appl Genet 60(4): 197-214. doi:10.1007/BF02342540

37. Liu D.W., Oard S.V., Oard J.H. (2003). High Transgene Expression Levels in Sugarcane (Saccharum officinarurn L) Driven by Rice Ubiquitin Promoter RUBQ2. Plant Sci 165: 743-750.

38. Mackill D.J. and Bonman J.M. (1992). Inheritance of Blast Resistance in Near Isogenic Lines of Rice. J. Phytopathology. *82*, 746-749.

39. Marchetti M.A., Lai X. and Bollich C.N. (1987) Inheritance of Resistance to *P. oryzae* in Rice Cultivars Grown in United States. *Genetics* 77, 799-804.

40. McClung, A.M., M.A. Marchetti, B.D. Webb, and C.N. Bollich. (1997). Registration of 'Jefferson' Rice. Crop Sci. 37: 629-630.

41. Mithrasena, J.Y., Wijesundera, W.S.S., Wijesundera, R.L.C., Wimalasiri, D.C. and Priyanti, R.P. (2012). Pathogenic and Genetic Diversity of *Magnaporthe oryzae* Population from Sri Lanka. Rice Science. *19(3)*, 241-246.

42. Miyake K., & Ikeda M. (1932). Influence of Silica Application on Rice Blast. Japanese.

43. Monna L., Miyao, A., Zhong H.S., Yano M., Iwamoto M., Umehara Y., Kurata N., Haysaka H., Sasaki T. (1997) Saturation Mapping with Subclones of YACs: DNA Marker Production Targeting the Rice Blast Disease Resistance Gene, *Pi-b. Theor. Appl. Genet.*, *94*, 170-176.

44. Mu C., Liu, X., Lu Q., Jiang X., & Zh, C. (2007). Biological Control of Rice Blast by Bacillus Subtilis B-332 Strain. Acta Phytophylacica Sinica, 34(2): 123-128.

45. Murata J., Kuribayashi K. & Kawai I. (1933). Studies on the Control of Rice Blast III. Influence of Homemade Manure on Blast Disease. Nogi Kairyo Shiryo 64, 1-138.

46. Nakamura S.; Asakawa S.; Ohmido N.; Fukui K.; Shimizu N.; Kawasaki S. (1997). Construction of an 800-kb Contig in the Near Centromeric Region of the Rice Blast Resistance Gene *Pi-ta2* Using a Highly Representative Rice BAC Library. *Mol. Gen. Genet 254*, 611-620.

47. Narayanan N.N., Baisakh N., Vera Cruz C.M., Gnanamanickam S.S., Datta K., Datta S.K. (2002). Molecular Breeding for the Development of Blast and Bacterial Blight Resistance in Rice cv. IR50. Crop Sci 42(6): 2072-2079. doi:10.2135/cropsci2002.2072

48. Nishizawa Y., Nishio Z., Nakazono K., Soma M., Nakajima E., Ugaki M., Hibi T. (1999). Enhanced Resistance to Blast (Magnaporthe grisea) in Transgenic Japonica Rice by Constitutive Expression of Rice Chitinase. Theor Appl Genet 99(3-4): 383-390. doi:10.1007/s001220051248

49. Onodera, I. (1917). Chemical Studies on Rice Blast (Dactylaria Parasitance Cavara). Journal of Scientific Agricultural Society 180, 606-617.

50. Ou S.H. (1980). A Look at Worldwide Rice Blast Disease Control. Plant Disease .Annu Rev. Phytopathol. 18: 167-187.

51. Ou S.H., (1985). Rice Diseases, Second ed., Commonwealth Mycological Institute, Kew, Surrey, England.

52. Padmanabhan S.Y., Mathur S.C. and Mishra R.K. (1973). Inheritance of Resistance to *Pyricularia oryzae. Oryza* 10, 45-53.

53. Palti J., (1981). Cultural Practices and Infectious Crop Diseases. Springer-Verlag, Beriln, Germany.

54. Pinta W., Toojinda T., Thummabenjapone P., Sanitchon J. (2013). Pyramiding of Blast and Bacterial Leaf Blight Resistance Genes into Rice Cultivar RD6 Using Marker Assisted Selection. Afr J Biotechnol; 12(28): 4432-4438.

55. Prabhu A., & Morais O. (1986). Blast Disease Management in Upland Rice in Brazil. In Proceedings of Symposium on Progress in Upland Rice Research, International Rice Research Institute, Manila, Philippines.

56. Qu S.H., Liu G.F., Zhou B., Bellizzi M., Zeng L.R., Dai L.Y., Han B., Wang G.L. (2006). The Broad-spectrum Blast Resistance Gene Pi9 Encodes an NBS-LRR Protein and is a Member of a Multigene Family in Rice. Genetics 172(3): 1901-1914. doi:10.1534/genetics. 105.044891

57. Ribota C., Hirsch J., Balzerguec S., Tharreaub D., Notte´ghembJ., Lebruna M., Morel j., (2008). Susceptibility of Rice to the Blast Fungus, Magnaporthe Grisea, Journal of Plant Physiology 165: 114-124.

58. Semagn K., Bjornstad A., Ndjiondjop M.N. (2006). An Overview of Molecular Marker Methods for Plants. *Afr. J. Biotechnol., 5,* 2540-2568.

59. Sharma, T.R., Rai, A.K., Guptha, S.K., Vijayanan, T., Devanna, B.N. and Ray, S. (2012). Rice Blast Management Through Plant Resistance: Retrospect and Prospect. Rev.Agri Res. DOI 10. 1007/S40003-011-0003-5.

60. Singh N. & Singh R.S. (1980). Lysis of Fusarium Oxysporium f.udum Caused by Soil Amended with Organic Matter. Journal of Mycology and Plant Pathology, 10, 146-150.

61. Singh V.K, Singh A., Singh S.P., Ellur R.K., Choudhary V., Sarkel S., Singh D., Krishnan S.G., Nagarajan M., Vinod K.K., Singh U.D., Rathore R., Prashanthi S.K., Agrawal P.K., Bhatt J.C., Mohapatra T., Prabhu K.V., Singh A.K.B. (2012). Incorporation of Blast Resistance into "PRR78", An Elite Basmati Rice Restorer Line, Through Marker Assisted Backcross Breeding. Field Crops Res.128: 8-16.

62. Skamnioti P., Gurr S.J. (2009). Against the Grain: Safeguarding Rice from Rice Blast Disease. Trends Biotechnol 27: 141-150.

63. Someya N., Numata S., Nakajima M., Hasebe A., Akutsu K. (2004). Influence of Rice-isolated Bacteria on Chitinase Production by the Biocontrol Bacterium Serratia Marcescens Strain B2 and the Genetically Modified Rice Epiphytic Bacterium. J Gen Plant Pathol 70: 371-375. DOI 10.1007/s10327-004-0141-8.

64. Stark-Lorenzen P., Nelke B., HanBler G., Muhlbach H.P., Thomzik J.E. (1997). Transfer of a Grapevine Stilbene Synthase Gene to Rice (Oryza sativa L). Plant Cell Rep 16(10): 668-673. doi: 10.1007/s002990050299

65. Sundaram R.M., Vishnupriya M., Laha G.S, Rani N.S., Rao P.S., Balachandran S.M., Sonti R.V., (2009). Introduction of Bacterial Blight Resistance into Triguna, a High Yielding, Mid-early Duration Rice Variety, Bio-technol. J. 4 (3) 400-407.

66. Supriya Devi and Sharma 1. G.D. (2010). Blast Disease of Rice Caused by Magnaporthe Grisea: A Review. Assam University Journal of Science & Technology: Biological and Environmental Sciences Vol. 6 Number I: 144-154.

67. Suzuki F. and Arai M. (2007) Genetic Analysis of *Pyricularia grisea* Population by Rep-PCR during Development of Resistance to Scytalone Dehydratase Inhibitors of Melanin Biosynthesis. Plant Dis. 91: 176-184.

68. Takahashi V, (1965). Studies on the Mechanism of the Resistance of Rice Plant to Piricularia Oryzae, in: The Rice Blast Diseases, John Hopkins Press, Baltimore, MA, pp. 303-329.

69. Talbot N.J. (2003). On the Trail of a Cereal Killer: Exploring the Biology of Magnaporthe Grisea. Annual Review of Microbiology; 57(1) 177-202.

70. Tan Y.N., Yi Z.L., Jiang J.X., Qin J.P., Xiao L. (2004). Strategies and Advnces in Improving Resistance to Rice Blast by Transgenic Approaches. Mol Plant Breed 2(6): 847-852 (in Chinese with English abstract)

71. Thurston H.D., 1992. Sustainable Practices for Plant Disease Management in Traditional Farming Systems. Western Press, Boulder, CO, USA.

72. Toojinda T., Tragoonrung S., Vanavichit A., Siangliw J.L., Pa-In N., Jantaboon J., Siangliw M., Fukai S. (2005). Molecular Breeding for Rainfed Low Land Rice in the Mekong Region. Plant Prod Sci8(3): 330-333.

73. Valent B., Chumley F.G. (1991). Molecular Genetic Analysis of the Rice Blast Fungus *Magnaporthe grisea.* Annu. Rev. Phytopathol., 29, 443-467.

74. Valent B., Farrall, L. and Chumley F.G. (1986). *Magnaporthe grisea* Genes for Pathogenicity and Virulence Identified Through a Series of Backcross. Genetics, 127, 87-101.

75. Wang G.L., Mackill D.J., Bonman J.M., McCouch S.R., Champoux M.C. and Nelson R.J. (1994) RFLP Mapping of Genes Conferring Complete and Partial Resistance to Blast in a Durably Resistant Rice Cultivar. *Genetics* 136, 1421-1434.

76. Wang S.M., Van Bergen B., Duijn V. (2000). Insights into a Key Developmental Switch and its Importance for Efficient Plant Breeding, Plant Physiol. 124 (2) 523-530.

77. Wang Z., Jia V, Rutger V, Xia Y., (2007). Rapid Survey for Presence of a Blast Resistance Gene Pi-ta in Rice Cultivars Using the Dominant DNA Markers Derived from Portions of the Pi-ta gene, Plant Breed. 126 (1) 36-42.

78. Wang Z.X., Yano M., Yamanouchi U., Iwamoto M., Monna L., Hayasaka H., Katayose Y., Sasaki T. (1999). The Pib Gene for Rice Blast Resistance Belongs to the Nucleotide Binding and Leucinerice Repeat Class of Plant Disease Resistance Genes. Plant J 19(1): 55-64. doi:10.1046/j.1365-313X.1999.00498.x

79. Wen S., Gao B. (2011). Introgressing Blast Resistant Gene Pi-9(t) into Elite Rice Restorer Luhui17 by Marker-assisted Selection. Rice Genomics Genet 2(4): 31-36. doi:10.5376/rgg.2011.02.0004

80. Yamamoto T., Yonemaru J., Yano M. (2009). Towards the Understanding of Complex Traits in Rice: Substantially or Superficially? *DNA Res., 16*, 141-154.

81. Yang J.H., Liu H.X., Zhu G.M., Pan Y.L., Xu L.P., & Guo, J.H. (2008). Diversity Analysis of Antagonists from Rice-associated Bacteria and Their Application in Biocontrol of Rice Diseases. Journal of Applied Microbiology, 104(1), 91-104. PMid: 17850318 http://dx.doi.org/10.1111/j.1365-2672.2007.03534.

82. Yu Y.G.; Saghai-Maroof M.A.; Buss G.R. (1996). Divergence and Allelomorphic Relationship of a Soybean Virus Resistance Gene Based on Tightly Linked DNA Microsatellite and RFLP Markers. *Theor. Appl. Genet, 92*, 64-69.

83. Zapata-Arias F.J., Torrizo L.B., Ando A. (1995). Current Developments in Plant Biotechnology for Genetic Improvement: The Case of Rice (Oryza sativa L.). World J Microbiol Biotechnol 11(4): 393-399. doi:10.1007/BF00364614

84. Zhou B., Qu S., Liu G., Dolan M., Sakai H., Lu G., Bellizzi M., Wang G.L. (2006). The Eight Amino-acid Differences Within Three Leucine-rich Repeats Between Pi2 and Piz-t Resistance Proteins Determine the Resistance Specificity to Magnaporthe Grisea. Mol Plant-Microbe Interact 19(11): 1216-1228. doi: 10.1094/MPMI- 19-1216.

Pages: 97-117

CROP PRODUCTIVITY AND PLANT DISEASE MANAGEMENT

Edited by: Dr. Alka Chauhan; Dr. Pawan Kumar 'Bharti'; Ms. Deepti Sadana

ISBN: 978-93-5056-791-3

Edition: 2016

Published by: Discovery Publishing House Pvt. Ltd., New Delhi (India)

CHAPTER – 6

Plant Quarantine
The First Line of Defense

Sanjeev Kumar[1*] and **Archana Rani**[2]

INTRODUCTION

The current state of affairs in our agricultural scenario is not a very remarkable one. The grain imports are bound to raise a big question mark on the progress we, as an agriculture oriented nation have made till date. The current food crisis has put the agriculture production on a tight leash, not allowing the producers any lassitude whatsoever. The reality is that the fundamental objectives will continue to remain focused on enhancing yields across crops and raising the food grain production in the country in new levels. It has been anticipated that we need to double our food grain production by 2015 to meet basic needs of our mounting population. The yield improvement is possible if we encourage farmers to use quality inputs like seeds, fertilizers, agrochemicals and micronutrients in adequate measures. Coupled with IPM and ICM practices and with adoption of new technologies,

1 Office of Dean, Faculty of Agriculture, Jawaharlal Nehru Krishi Vishwa Vidyalaya, Krishi Nagar, Adhartal, Jabalpur - 482 004 (MP), (India)

2 Ph.D, Department of Agricultural Biotechnology and Molecular Biology, (FBS & H), Rajendra Agricultural University, Pusa - 848 125, Bihar (India)

we can easily achieve the agriculture production goals, to be able to feed our increasing population- adequately and nutritionally.

Unfortunately our plant protection regime begins and ends with pesticides. It is the default option in the plant protection menu and all the other options more or less remain defunct and unused. Even though our major thrust areas of plant protection are promotion of Integrated Pest Management (IPM): ensuring availability of safe and quality pesticides for sustaining crop production from the ravages of pests and diseases, streamlining the quarantine measures for accelerating the introduction of new high yielding varieties, besides eliminating the chances of entry of exotic pests; we remain largely insulated from the these aspects in IPM. The chemicals in its myriad forms – fungicides, insecticides, weedicides, nematicides and many more have always been a true friends of the farmers as their effects are the most apparent and quick, salvaging the crops from 'dire consequences'. The agrochemicals industry undeniably has to play a proactive role, partnering with the government, in our national mission to produce quality food for all, at affordable prices. At this stage, our least negligence can torpedo our efforts to maintain the steady state of progress achieved in food grain production. Around 35% of what is produced is lost due to diseases and pest. In this state of affairs, plant protection measures assume significance.

With the globalization and liberalization in International trade of plants and plant material in the wake of Sanitary and Phytosanitory (SPS) Agreement under WTO, the plant quarantine measures are becomes more imperative. Liberalization in trade policies have helped the world agriculture trade to prosper which is key to sector for many countries like India whose economies are very much dependent on agrarian industry. But the likelihood of the presence of diseases/pest inherent in the import material can very well jeopardize the trade. It needs coherence from the participatory member countries. The phenomenon success of Indian Agriculture has been mainly due to the introduction of valuable germplasm. The tempo of agrarian industry can only be maintained if this flow of germplasm is continued. But the threat of accompanying pest/pathogen/weeds continues to overshadow this import. Domestic quarantine is also vital as the international quarantine and therefore, planting material should be moved from one state to another or from one place to another under strict phytosanitory conditions. Too much conservation on the part of plant quarantine officials and too liberal attitude on the part of plant introduction officials/breeders would be detrimental. Plant genetic stocks are a global resource meant for the welfare of humanity. For the success of agriculture as a whole, introduction of valuable germplasm is very important. Plant quarantine services are charged with the accountability of preventing the entry of hazardous pests, pathogens and weeds, but to deny entry to the valuable genetic resources would be against national interest.

These activities are meant to help agricultural development and they are complementary to each other and therefore necessary and we on our parts need to be fairly vigilant. As has been very truly said 'An ounce of prevention is worth a pound of cure'

The term 'Quarantine' is derived from the Latin word *quarantum,* meaning 40. It refers to the 40 days period of detention of ships from countries with bubonic plague and cholera in the Middle Ages. The first such quarantine was imposed in Venice in 1374. Present quarantine laws now include plants. Plant quarantine , restrict entry of plants, plant products, soil, cultures of living organisms, packing materials, and commodities, as well as their containers and means of conveyance to protect agriculture and the environment from avoidable damage by hazardous organisms. They exclude dangerous organisms while permitting plants and plant products to enter. The term *exclusion* conveys this objective more clearly than *plant quarantine.* Exclusion relates to keeping organisms out; plant quarantine relates to keeping plants out.

DEFINITION OF PLANT QUARANTINE

'Plant Quarantine' refers to the holding of plants in isolation until they are believed to be healthy. Now, broader meaning of the plant quarantine covers all aspects of the regulation of the movement of living plants, living plant parts/plant products between politically defined territories or ecologically distinct parts of them. Intermediate quarantine and post entry quarantine are used respectively to denote the detention of plants in isolation for inspection during or after arrival at their final destination.

The term frequently used in plant quarantine are *hazard, risk,* and *safeguards.*

Hazard: is the danger that a specified pathogen is known or perceived to present to the agriculture of the importing country should the pathogen is known or perceived to present to the agriculture of the importing country should the pathogen gain entr on imported items and subsequently become established.

Risks: is the chance that a hazardous organism will enter and become established.Since quarantine risks often have not been quantified, quarantine officers generally refer to the risk level as low, medium, or high. Risks associatd with germplasm vary with the collection site. For instance, rice seeds collected from the wild are of greater risk than those collected from the research station. Whole plants may be a greater risk than seeds, since not all pathogens are seed borne.

Safeguards: are action taken to reduce the risk of introducing hazardous organisms. Safeguards include rules and regulations, permits, phytosanitory certificate, insection treatment, isolation, passage through a quarantine green house, seed health testing, and other measures.

IMPORTANCE

The importance of plant quarantine has increased because of the increase in exchange of seeds or grains for consumption along with better means of transportation. The international exchange of plants or their parts is practiced widely to improve crops of a country and their genetic base. In addition, shiploads of grains for consumption or large quantities of seeds for direct sowing are imported in many countries. Even minute quantities of soil and plant debris contaminating true seeds can disseminate pathogens.

The entry of a single exotic insect or disease and its establishment in the new environment continues to cause great, national loss (Table 6.1) till such time it is brought under effective control. In certain cases a country has to spend a few million rupees before success in controlling the introduced insect pest or disease is achieved.

Table 6.1

Disease	Host	Country	Introduced From	Losses Caused
Bunchy top	Banana	India	Sri Lanka	Rs. 4 crores
Wart	Potato	India	Netherlands	2500acres infected
Canker	Citrus	U.S.A	Japan	$ 13 million; 19.5 milliontrees destroyed
Dutch elm	Elm	U.S.A.	Holland	$ 25 million -$ 50,000disease million
Powdery mildew	Grapevine	France	U.S.A	80% in wineproduction
Downy mildew	Grapevine	France	U.S.A	$ 50,000 million
Bunchy top	Banana	India	Sri Lanka	Rs. 4 crores
Wart	Potato	India	Netherlands	2500acres infected
Blue mould	Tobacco	Europe	U.K	$ 50 million

COMPONENT OF PLANT QUARANTINE

A. National and International Regulations

The first plant quarantine law was passed in 1873 in Germany to prohibit importation of plants and plant products from the United States to prevent the introduction of the Colorado potato beetle. In 1975, France imposed measures against the American pest. In 1877, United Kingdom Destructive Insects Act prevented the introduction and spread of this beetle. In 1891, first plant quarantine measure was initiated in the United States by setting up a seaport inspection station at San Pedro, CA. First U.S. quarantine law was passed in 1912. The Federal Plant Quarantine Service was established in Australia in 1909. In 1914, Destructive Insects and pest Act was passed in India.

On a global basis, the first International Plant Protection Convention (the Phyllozera Convention) was signed in 1881 with the objective of preventing the spread of severe pests. This convention was amended in 1889,

1929 and 1951. The International Plant Protection Convention (IPPC or Rome Convention) under the Food and Agriculture Organisation was established to prevent the introduction and spread of diseases and pests through legislation and organisations across international boundaries. This convention provided a model phytosanitary certificate (Rome certificate) to be adopted by member countries. Within this convention, ten regional plant protection organisations have been established on the basis of bio geographical areas:

1. The European and Mediterranean Plant Protection Organisation (EPPO)
2. The Inter-African Phytosanitary Council (IAPSC)
3. Organismo International Regional de Sanidad Agropecnario (OIRSA)
4. The Plant Protection Committee for, the South East Asia and Pacific region. (SEAPPC)
5. Near East Plant Protection Commission (NEPPC)
6. Comit'e Interamericano de Protection Agricola. (CIPA)
7. The Caribbean Plant Protection Commission (CPPC)
8. The North American Plant Protection Organisation (NAPPO).
9. Organismo Bolivariano de Sanidad Agropecuria (OBSA)
10. Association of South East Asian Countries (ASEAN)

Many countries are aided in their efforts to develop national germplasm systems by the International Board of Plant Genetic Resources (IBPGR), which was established in 1974 with head quarters in FAO/UN Rome. The IBPGR strives to build a world network of institutions to collect, conserve, evaluate, document and distribute germplasm of economic plants and their wild relatives. The IBPGR is one of 13 International Agricultural Research Centers, an informal consortium of governments , international and regional organisations, and private foundations established to promote agricultural research for the benefit of developing countries. The principles set forth in the General Agreement on Tariffs and Trade (GATT) Uruguay Round of the Multilateral Trade Negotiations are discussed in relation to the International Plant Protection Convention (IPPC) by Hedley.

B. Component of Plant Quarantine

Plant protection and quarantine (PPQ) programmes, or the plant health or quarantine services in most countries, usually have three components

1. Exclusion of pathogens and pests of quarantine and economic significance that might unintentionally be moved along manmade pathways when articles are imported, or induction of the risk of introducing such hazardous organisms to an acceptance level.
2. Containment, suppression, and eradication of exotic pathogens and pests recently introduced on natural and manmade pathways.
3. Assistance to exporters of plant products, such as fruits, vegetables, plants, cut flowers, commodities, etc., in meeting the quarantine or exclusion requirements of importing countries and, therefore, based on plant health, biologically facilitating the acceptance of imports.

Table 6.2: Examples of Pests and Diseases Introduced in India from Other Countries

Sl. No.	Pests	Causal Organism	Year of Introduction	Native Place
1.	Coffee rust	*Hemileia vastatrix*	1879	Srilanka
2.	Late blight of potato	*Phytophthora infestans*	1883	England
3.	Flag smut of wheat	*Urocystis tritici*	1906	Australia
4.	Downey mildew of grapes	*Plasmopara viticola*	1910	Europe
5.	Rust of chrysanthemum	*Puccinia carthami*	1904	Japan/Europe
6.	Downey mildew of cucurbits	*Pseudoperonospora. cubensis*	1918	Srilanka
7.	Downey mildew of maize	*S. philippinensis*	1912	1912
8.	Foot rot of Rice	*Fusarium moniliforme*	1930	South East Asia
9.	Black rot of crucifers	*Xanthomonas campestris*	1929	Java
10.	Leaf spot of sorghum		1934	South Africa
11.	Powdery mildew of rubber	*Oidium heveae*	1938	Malaya
12.	Blank Shank of Tobacco	*P. nicotianae*	1938	Holland
13.	Fire blight of pear		1940	England
14.	Crown gall of Apple/pear	*Agrobacterium tumefaciens*	1940	England
15.	Bunchy top virus		1940	Srilanka
16.	Canker of apple	*Sphaeropsis* spp.	1943	Australia
17.	Wart of potato	*Synchytrium endobioticum*	1953	Netherlands
18.	Bacterial blight of paddy	*X. oryzae*	1959	Philippine
19.	Golden Nematode ofpotato	*Heterodera avenae*	1961	Europe
20.	San Jose scale of apple	*Quadraspidiotus perniciosus*	1900	Italy
21.	Wooly aphid of apple		1928	Australia
22.	Sunflower downey mildew		1985	Australia

1. Pest Risk Analysis (PRA)

In view of manifold increase in the quantum of import and export of the plant commodities during the current years, the existing plant quarantine process seem to be far from being satisfactorily equipped. To cope with these difficulties, there hamper free market accessibility to the plant commodities and the quarantine should be based on the PRA (Rajak et al 1999). Risk can be defined as expected magnitude of loss. Hence, pest risk analysis aimed at identifying, quantifying and reporting of the possible management options on account of probable, introduction of a pest along with an imported plant commodity. Analysis of pest risk while introducing seeds planting materials is essential to determine the potential of a pest to cause damage. In general, risks are more with the introduction vegetative propagules than true seed. In case of true seed, risks are more with deep seated infections than surface contaminated seed. Further, risks are more with virus, viroid smuts, downy mildew etc. Risk increases with size of import. Bulk import creates more quarantine problems (Gupta and Khetarpal 2004).

(a) **Complete prohibition**: When the pest risk is high and safeguard against it is not available in the country, hence import should be prohibited.

(b) **High risk** - adequate safeguard: The pest risk is very high but adequate safe guard in the form of post entry isolation facilities or salvaging techniques are available.

(c) **Restricted:** Pest risk is not very high and import permit is require indicating condition for entry, inspection and treatment.

2. Movement of Pests and pathogens

Pests and plant pathogens of quarantine importance can move along natural and human made pathways, depending upon the life cycle of the organism, the environment through which it moves, and human activities. At the end of a pathway, the establishment of a pathogen or pest in a new area depends on the level of inoculums or pest carried by seeds, the susceptibility of host crop and the environment. Quarantine regulations to prevent movement of potential pests and plant pathogens source of introduction should be considered.

3. Legal basis for plant quarantine

The legal basis of plant quarantine comprises

- Legislation enacted by national and sometimes state or provincial governments.
- Enabling legislation that directs the Minister of Agriculture to issue necessary rules, orders or directives, or
- Legislation by a regional parliament representing groups of countries such as the EEC or Andean Pact Nations.

Table 6.3: Examples of Pests and Diseases which have been Introduced World Wise

Sl. No.	Pests	Causal Organism	Introduced from	Introduced in	Year
1.	Powdery mildew of grape	*Uncinula necator*	USA	England	1845
2.	Downy mildewof grape	*Plasmopara viticola*	USA	France	1878
3.	Golden nematode of potato	*Heterodera rostochinensis*	Europe	USA, Mexica	1881
4.	Citrus canker	*Xanthomonas citri*	Asia	USA	1907
5.	Blister rust ofpine	*Cronartium ribicola*	Europe	USA	1910
6.	Fire blight ofapple	*Erwinia amylovora*	America	Newzealand	1919
7.	Onion smut	*Urocystis cepulae*	France	Switzerland	1924
8.	Dutch elm	*Ceratostomellaulmi*	Holland	USA	1928-1930
9.	Coffee rust	*Hemilia vastatrix*	Africa andAsia	Brazil	1970
10.	Grape	*Phylloxera vitifoliae*	USA	France	1845
11.	Mexican bollweevil	*Anthonomusgrandis*	Mexica &C-America	USA	1892

Table 6.4: List of Fungal Pathogens Intercepted in germplasm importing

Fungal pathogen	Host	Origin
Septoria gladioli	*Gladiolus sp. (s)*	Europe
Puccinia helianthi	*Helianthus annus (s)*	Africa
Phoma coccoicola	*Cocos nucifera*	Asia
Phoma chrysanthemicola	*Chrysanthemum sp.*	Europe
Fusarium oxysporum f.sp.gladioli	*Gladiolus sp. (b)*	Europe
Drechslera maydis	*Sorghum sp. (s), Spinauaoleracea (s) Zea mays (s)*	Europe,North America,South America
Coniothyrium fuckelii	*Rosa spp*	Asia, Europe
Fusarium avenaceum	*Celosia sp.*	North America
Drecheslera spicifera	*Thugaplicatu (s)*	NorthAmerica
Cercospora dolichi	*Betal leaf*	North America
Botrytis fabae Vicia	*Viciafaba (s)*	Asia
Ascochyta rabiei	*Arachia hypogeal (s)*	Africa
Ascochyta gossypii	*Gossypium sp. (s)*	Africa
Alternaria helianth	*Helianthus annus*(S), *Sorghum* sp	North America

Table 6.5: List of Bacterial Pathogens Intercepted in Germplasm Importing

Bacterial Pathogen	Host	Origin
Agrobacterium tumefaciens	*Rosa sp (p)*	Europe
Corynebacterium michiganense	*Lycopersicon esculentum (s)*	North America
Erwinia carotovora	*Solanum tuberosum(t)*	Europe, North America
Erwinia herbicola	*Helianthus annus(s)*	Europe
Pseudomonas maculicola	*Brassica oleracea var. capitata (s)*	Europe, North America
Pseudomonas marginatum	*Gladiolus sp. (b)*	Europe
Pseudomonas pisi	*Pisum sativum (s)*	Europe, North America
Pseudomonas syringae	*Cucumis sativus (s)*	North America
Xanthomonas Campestris pv citri	*Citrus sp. (f)*	Asia

F= flowers, s=seeds, t=tubers, p=plant

Table 6.6: List of Viral Pathogens Intercepted in Germplasm Importing

Virus	Host	Geographical Distribution
Tobacco mosaicvirus	*Dahelia variabilis(t)*	Europe, North America
Spotted wilt virus	*Chrysanthemum sp. (p)*	Europe
Orchid virus	*Orchid (p)*	Asia
Pea mosaic virus	*Pisum sativum(s)*	South pacific Asia
Mosaic virus	*Jasminum sp, Hibiscus cooperi* (p)	Asia, Europe
Grape fan leaf virus	*Vitis vinifera*(p)	South pacific Asia
Ficus mosaic virus	*Ficus sp.* (p)	North America

s=seeds, t=tubers, p=plants

4. Requirement for a Quarantine programme

1. A phytosanitory certificate that attests to the inspection, origin and identification of the seeds.
2. A permit requirement for added declaration on the phytosanitory certificate that the mother plants were inspected during the growing season.
3. A requirement for treatment at origin.
4. The acceptance of a special certification or safe guarding programme at origin, such as may be practiced at International Agricultural Research Centers (IARC)
5. Inspection and treatment , if necessary ,upon arrival at port of entry; and
6. Isolation, special testing, or additional quarantine after entry.

C. Basic Principles of Plant Quarantine

Plant quarantine regulations have certain prerequisites. They must be

- Based on sound biological grounds. Only pests that pose a threat to major crops or forest should be taken into consideration.
- Formulated to control or prevent the entry of pests and not to hinder trade or attainment of other objectives. Quarantine measures are for crop and not trade protection.
- Derived from adequate legislation and operated solely under the law.
- Modified as conditions change or further facts become available.

D. Criteria for Determining Organisms for Quarantine Significance

1. General criteria

The following are general criteria considered for an organism of plant quarantine significance:

- The organism does not occur in the country but is known to cause economic damage elsewhere.
- The organism occurs in the country but is not extensively spread in the ecological range of its host in that country; is under a national domestic suppression or eradication programme; has exotic strains of quarantine importance that do not occur in the country; and/or causes economic damage or has a potential to cause such damage on economically important crops.
- The organism is a general pathogens established in the importing country. But government regulations require that commercial growers use pathogen-tested seed stocks so that imported stocks meet domestic standards.

2. Criteria based primarily on Pathogen Characteristics

The criteria are based on the general characteristics of a pathogen.

- Able to survive and move easily in international trade.
- Capable of developing a high population in a short time.
- Difficult to detect by general inspection or field survey.
- Capable of damaging and/or reproducing on many hosts.
- Has a potential for rapid dispersal , especially along manmade pathways.
- Has a potential for significant reduction in the quality and quantity of crop yields.
- Capable of adversely affecting the environment.

Neegard proposed that quarantine objects could be placed into three categories based on the following criteria.

Category A: Notorious pathogens are are not present in a region of introduction and have a high or considerable epidemic potential. Pathogens belonging to this category usually occur in only trace amount in seeds. Quarantine measures should prohibit introduction of such seeds from infested areas. Valuable seed material from infested area must be filtered through post entry control measures by growing plants in special glasshouses under closed quarantine. Viruses and viroids belonging to this category include Arabis mosaic, Pea seed borne mosaic, Stone fruit viruses, Avocado sun blotch.

Barley stripe mosaic, Broad bean true mosaic, Peanut stunt.

Category B: Dangerous plant pathogens that are not present in the region of introduction or present in restricted areas under effective control. Such pathogens have a moderated epidemic value. For instance. Bean common mosaic virus, Lettuce mosaic virus, and Pea early browning virus.

Category C: These pathogens are not strict quarantine objects but may be important to the field planting value of seeds. For instance, Alfalfa mosaic virus, Soybean mosaic virus and Cucumber mosaic virus.

PLANT QUARANTINE IN INDIA

History

The quarantine measures are of almost relevance to a country like India whose economy is largely Agriculture based. The awareness to quarantine measures in India started in early 20th century when the Indian Government in 1906, ordered compulsory fumigation of imported cotton bales to prevent the introduction of the dreaded Mexican cotton boll weevil (*Antonymous grandis*). On February 3, 1914 Comprehensive Plant Quarantine Act, known as Destructive Insects and Pests Act, (DIP Act) become operative. Over the years the DIP Act was revised and amended several times. However it needs to be periodically reviewed and amended to meet the growing requirements of liberalized trade under the WTO. In 1946, the Directorate of Plant Protection, Quarantine and Storage, under the ministry of Food and Agriculture were set up. In 1946, Plant quarantine activity stared with the initiation of plant introduction scheme in the Botany Division at Indian Agricultural Research Institute (IARI) New Delhi. In October 1949, the Directorate started its quarantine activities at Bombay seaport. On December 25, 1951 the first plant Quarantine and Fumigation station in India was formally inaugurated. In August, 1976 the National Bureau of Plant Genetic Resource (NBPGR) was created. In 1978, the Division of Plant Quarantine was created with Entomology, Plant Pathology and Nematology sections. In October, 1988, the Plants, Fruits and seeds (Regulation of Import into India) order, 1989 popularly known as PFS order came into force.

PLANT QUARANTINE SYSTEM IN INDIA

With a View to provide the farmers the best planting materials available in the world for maximizing productivity per unit area and to encourage the private seed industry in India not only to meet the internal requirements but also to develop export potential for high quality planting materials. The Government of Indian announced a new policy on seed development in September 1988. The main features of the existing plant quarantine regulations in India are as follows.

1. No consignment of seeds/planting materials shall be imported into India without a valid 'import permit ' which is to be issued by a competent authority to be noticed by the central Government from time to time in the official Gazette.
2. No consignment of seeds/planting materials shall be imported into India unless accompanied by a phytosanitary Certificate' issued for the official plant quarantine service of the source country.
3. All consignments of Plants and seeds for sowing propagation/planting purposes shall be imported into India through land customs station, seaport import and such other entry points as may be specifically notified by the central Government from time to time where there shall be inspected by and if necessary, fumigated disinfected by authorized plant quarantine official before quarantine clear once.
4. Seeds/Planting materials requiring isolation grow under deflection shall be grown in post entry quarantine facility approved and certified by the designated inspection Authority (DTP) to conform to the conditions laid down by the plant protection advises to the Govt. of India.
5. Hay, straw or any other material of plant origin shall not be used as packing material.
6. Import of soil, earth, sand, compost, and plant deters is accompanying seeds/planting material shall not be permitted. However, soil can be imported for research purpose under a special permit issued by the plant protection advises to the Gov to India. The DIP Act empowers the central Govt. to make rules for regulating the import of seeds/planting materials into India, & also the movements of the material form one state Govt. are also empowered to enact rules/regulation to regular the movement of materials from one region to another with in state.

INSPECTION PROCEDURES FOLLOWED IN QUARANTINE STATION

Inspection method:

1. *Visual inspection* - To detect sclerotia, nematode galls, bunt galls, smuts, insect infestations, weed seeds insect eggs, inert mater etc.
2. *X-ray test* - Insect infestation (hidden).
3. *Washing test* - Spores of fungus eggs of insect adhering to seeds, nematode galls.
4. *Sedimentation test* – Stem eel warm (*Ditylenchus dipsaci*) (Baerman Funnel Test).
5. Incubation test - Seed borne fungi/ bacteria (Blotter/agar test),

6. Grow out test - Seed borne bacteria/viruses/downy mildews,
7. Electron microscopy - Potentially used for identification and characterization of all plant viruses.
8. Serological methods:
   (a) ELISA (Enzyme Linked Immuno sorbant Assay)
   (b) DIBA (Dot Immuno-binding Assay)
   (c) ISEM (Immuno sorbant Electron Micro Scopy)
   (d) Latex agglutination test.
9. Nucleic acid hybridization,
   10 Polymarised chain reaction (PCR)

Plant quarantine measures

The measures suggested for effective plant quarantine are as follows:

Import control: Regulations of importing country:

1. **Embargoes**: Total prohibition of import of certain kind of infected material from particular region/country. This is most effective measure to exclude infected plant material.
2. **Inspection of seed lots:** The examination of seed samples must be by the most sensitive and reliable method for detection of dangerous pathogens. A sample may subject to more than one method.
3. **Post Entry Quarantine (PEQ):** because it is difficult to detect all types of seed born pathogens by simple tests, it may be necessary to subject seeds to PEQ. Seeds are subjected to a period of grow in quarantine station under strict supervision in importing countries.

Export control: Regulations of the exporting country:

1. **Field inspection of field crops**: The seed crop is inspected regularly for diseases, infected plants are rouged. The crop should meet requirements of the importing country.
2. **Inspection of seed lots:** The seed lot is thoroughly examined for the presence or absence of the microorganisms before export. The sample should meet the importing country.
3. **Seed treatment**: The seed lot should be treated as per the requirements of the exporting country. However the treatment should confine to regulations of the importing country.
4. **Phytosanitary certificate:** Phytosanitary certificates are issued by the exporting country along with the seed as per the international plant protection convention of 1951.

Intermediate Quarantine

This is an international cooperative effort to lower the risk of introducing a pathogen to one country with the germplasm from other by passing this germplasm.

Agencies Involved in Plant Quarantine

The authority to implement the quarantine rules and regulation formed under DIP Act rest basically with the Directorate of Plant Protection, Quarantine and Storage, under the ministry of Agriculture. The organisation handles bulk import and export of seed and planting material for Commercial purposes. Presently there are total '26'different quarantine stations located 10 at Airports, 9 at Seaports and 7 at Land Frontiers are functioning. These are the recognized ports for entries for import of plant and plant material. The names and places of the ports and stations are as follows.

A. Airports

1. Amritsar - Punjab
2. Calcutta - West Bengal
3. Chennai - Tamil Nadu
4. Hyderabad - Andhra Pradesh
5. Mumbai - Maharashtra
6. New Delhi - New Delhi
7. Patna - Bihar
8. Tiruchirappalli - Tamil Nadu
9. Trivandrum - Kerala
10. Varanasi - Uttar Pradesh

B. Seaports - Place State/Union territory

1. Bhavnagar - Gujarat
2. Calcutta - West Bengal
3. Chennai - Tamil Nadu
4. Cochin - Kerala
5. Mumbai - Maharashtra
6. Nagapattinam - Tamil Nadu
7. Rameswaram - Tamil Nadu
8. Tuticorin - Tamil Nadu
9. Visakhapatnam - Andhra Pradesh

C. Land frontiers

1. Amritsar Railway Station - Punjab
2. Attari Railway Station - Punjab
3. Attari-Wagah Border- Punjab
4. Bangaon Benapol Border - West Bengal
5. Gede Road Railway Station - West Bengal
6. Kalimpong - West Bengal
7. Sukhia Pokhri - West Bengal

The Government of India has also approved three other national institutions to act as official quarantine agencies, especially for research material.

1. **National Bureau of Plant Genetic Resources (NBPGR)**

The NBPGR in New Delhi and its regional station at Hyderabad in the agency involved in processing of germplasm, seed, plant material of agricultural, horticultural, and silvicultural crops of all the institutions of Indian Council of Agricultural Research (ICAR) functioning in the country. It is also responsible for quarantine clearance of seed and plant material received from International Agricultural Research Centers *viz.*, ICRISAT, ICARDA, CIMMYT, etc. ICRISAT was established in 1972 at Patancheru (near Hyderabad) to work on improvement of sorghum, pearlmillet, chickpea, pigeonpea and groundnut. The quarantine clearance of all its exchanges was handled by Central Plant Protection Training Institute of Directorate of Plant Protection, Quarantine & Storage, until July 1986. This authority was later passed on to NBPGR in August 1986.

2. **Forest Research Institute (FRI), Dehra Dun,** for forestry plants; and
3. **Botanical Survey of India (BSI)** for other plants.

Domestic Quarantine

Domestic Quarantine may be defined as the restriction imposed by Plant Quarantine authorities in association with State machinery on the production, movement and existence of plants and planting material and is brought under regulation in order to prevent the introduction or spread of a pest. The legislature measures to prevent the introduction and spread of destructive pests of crops are operative through the "Destructive insect and pest act, 1914". The domestic quarantine regulations are operative by the central government through powers vested under section 4A, B & D and section 5 authorizes the state government to enact similar regulations and section 5A provides for the penalties. Under the DIP Act, the Directorate of Plant Protection, Quarantine and storage has the responsibility to take the necessary steps and regulate the inter-state movement of plants and plant material in order to prevent the further spread of destructive insects and diseases that have already entered the country. The sole object of enforcing domestic quarantine is to prevent the spread of these diseases from infected to non-infected areas. The first domestic quarantine notification was issued by central, government in 1944 against fluted scale (*Icerya purchasi*) and San Jose scale (*Quadraspidiotus perniciosus*) in 1953. Under the DIP Act, 1914 there have been different notifications from time to time restricting the movement of plant and planting material due to the introduction & partial establishment of invasive pests in certain areas of the state. Some of such notifications issued under section 4A of this Act-Domestic Quarantine are given below:

Table 6.7: Notifications Issued Under Section 4A of DIP Act, 1914 - Domestic Quarantine

Pest/Disease	Notification No/date	Host Plant Material	Restricted		
			From	To	Requirement
Fluted Scale (*Icerya purchasi*)	(i) 22-1/46-PPS/16.2.1946 (ii) 3-5(1)/46-PPS/ 27-2-48 & 27-12-48	Many host plant species	Mysore (Karnataka), Madras (Tamil Nadu) & Kerala St	To any other state or place	Transport of the host plant material of this pest is permitted only with a certificate of freedom issued by the Director of Agriculture Movement of propagating plant material is prohibited except by a certificate issued by authorized Entomologist Plant pathologist
San Jose Scale (*Aspidiotus perniciosus)*	6-7/52- Dte.I/5.2.53.	Many host plant species	Punjab, UP, Madras (Tamil Nadu), WB, Assam, Orissa, HP, Jammu & Kashmir States	Any other part of India	Movement of plant material including packaging & wrapping material likely to carry this pest is prohibited unless accompanied by a certificate issued by authorized Entomologist/Plant Pathologists
Bananana bunchy top (virus)	6-5/59- PPS/25.9.59	Banana planting material	Assam, Kerala, Orissa, Tamil Nadu, & West Bengal states	Any other State & UT	Complete prohibition of transport of banana planting material
Potato Wart (*Synchytrium endobioticum)*	-11/59-PPS/ 8.10.59.	Potato	West Bengal	Any other State & UT	Movement of Potato prohibited
	6-7/62-PPS/ 10.5.63	Potato	Nepal	West Bengal (transit)	Transit permit issued by PPA
	8-26/75-PPS/ 14.6.76	Potato	Nepal	West Bengal (transit)	Phytosanitary Certificate with additional declarations
	8-26/75-PPS/ 31.10.77	Potato	Nepal	West Bengal (transit)	Same as above
	GSR.451 (E)/ 5.8.1997	Potato	Darjeeling Dt. of West Bengal	Any other State or place in India	Transport or export of potato tubers p

(Table Contd...)

Pest/Disease	Notification No/date	Host Plant Material	Restricted		
			From	To	Requirement
Apple Scab *(Venturia inaequalis)*	8-21/74-PPS/ 28.8.78	Apple planting material	Jammu & Kashmir	Any other State	Transport of planting material prohibited
	8-13/77-PPS/ 12.12.77	Apple planting material	Himachal Pradesh	Any other State	Export of planting material prohibited
	NIC20/76 Dt.28.12. 78	Apple planting material	Himachal Pradesh		Movement restricted within H.P.
	8-21/74-PPS/ 28.8.78	Apple planting material	Jammu & Kashmir	Any other State	Transport of planting material prohibited
Potato Cyst Nematodes (*Globodera rostochiensis & G. pallida)*	8-18/82-PPS/ 18.2.83	Potato	Tamil Nadu	Any other State & UT	Movement of seed potato prohibited. Movement of table potato permitted if accompanied with special permit
Coffee Berry Borer (*Hypothenamus hampei*)	S.O. 843 (E)/ 18.11.1992	Coffee seeds/ plants/powder	Nilagiri Dt (T.N), Kodagu Dt (Karnataka) & Wynad Dt (Kerala)	Any other parts of the Indian Union	Movement of coffee seeds, plants & powder is prohibited
	SRO. No. 548/96 dt. 29.6.96 issued by State Govt. of Kerala	Coffee beans	Kerala	Any other state	Movement or transport of any articles capable of carrying coffee berry borer is prohibited except authorized certificate issued by the Director of Agriculture/Horticulture, Kerala State or Chairman Coffee Board

Problems in Plant Quarantines

Quarantine serves as a filter against the introduction of dangerous pathogens, however pathogens are still introduced. Probable reasons are that:

- Difficult to detect all types of infectious pathogens by conventional methods.
- Methods may not be sensitive enough to detect traces of infection.
- Latent infections may pass undetected under post entry quarantine.
- Destruction of all infected or suspected material and Sensitive methods for testing fungicide treated seeds may be lacking

Plant Quarantine and Fumigation Stations in India

The list of plant quarantine and fumigation stations in India is given below:

New Delhi

1. Plant Quarantine and Fumigation Station, Palam Airport, New Delhi - 10.
2. Plant Quarantine and Fumigation Station, Garden Reach Road, Calcutta - 24.
3. Plant Quarantine and Fumigation Station Sukhiapokri, Darjeeling District.

Tamil Nadu

1. Plant Quarantine and Fumigation Station, 6, Clive Battery, Chennai - 1.
2. Plant Quarantine and Fumigation Station, 335, Beach Road, Tuticorin - 1.
3. Plant Quarantine and Fumigation Station, Tiruchirappalli Airport, Tiruchirappalli.
4. Plant Quarantine and Fumigation Station, 110, Railway Feeder Road, Rameswaram.

Punjab

1. Plant Quarantine and Fumigation Station, Hussainiwala, Ferozepur District.
2. Plant Quarantine and Fumigation Station, Attari – Wagah Border, near Attari Bus Stand, Attari, Ferozepur District.
3. Plant Quarantine and Fumigation Station, Civil Aerodrome, Rajasansi, Amritsar.

Gujarat

1. Plant Quarantine and Fumigation Station, Haryana Plot No.75, Behind Yusuf Bagh, Bhavnagar.

Maharashtra

1. Plant Quarantine and Fumigation Station, Haji Bunder Road, Sewri, Mumbai.

Andhra Pradesh

1. Plant Quarantine and Fumigation Station, The Harbour, Visakhapatnam - 1.

Kerala

1. Plant Quarantine and Fumigation Station, Willingdon Island, Cochin - 3.

REFERENCES

Agarwal, V.K., (1983). Quality Seed Production at Pantnagar, Seed Science Technology, 11, 1071.

Agarwal V.K. and Sinclair J.B. (1987), Principles of Seed Pathology, Vol. II, CRC Press, 168.

Anonymous, (1980) Plant Quarantine Information, Govt. of India, Ministry of Agriculture, Deptt. Of Agril. and Cooperation, Directorate of Plant Protection, Quarantine and Storage, Faridabad, 18pp.

Anonymous. (2007). "Flu Facts", Sunday Hindustan Times, 18 Febraury, 2007. pp. 17.

Baker, R.F., (1972). Seed Pathology, in Seed Biology, Vol. 2. Kozlowsk, T.T., Ed., Academic Press, New York, 317.

Bhalla, Shashi, Kapur M.L., La B.,. Verma, B.R and Singh, C. (2002). "Quarantine Risk Associated with Exchange of Plant Genera Carrying Hidden Infestation". Indian Journal of Plant Genetic Resources, 15(2): 160-163.

Chakrabarty, S.K., Anitha. K, Girish, A.G, Sarath Babu, B., Prasada Rao, R.D.V. J., Varaprasad, K.S., R.K. Khetarpal, R.K., and R.P. Thakur, R.P. 2005. Germplasm Exchange and Plant Quarantine of ICRISAT Mandate Crops. ICRISAT, Patencheru, Hyderabad.

Dev, U., R.K. Khetarpal, P.C. Agarwal, A. Lal, M.L. Kapur, Kavita Gupta and D. B. Parakh (eds.). 2005. Potential Quarantine Pests for India: Cereals. National Bureau of Plant Genetic Resources, New Delhi. Gupta, Kavita and R.K. Khetarpal. 2004. "Concept of Regulated Pests, Their Risk Analysis and the Indian Scenario". Annual Review of Plant Pathology, 3: 409-441.

Dickens, J.S.W. and Pemberton, A.W., Quarantine Measures for Seed in the United Kingdom, Seed Science Technology., 11, 1175.

Gabrielson, R.L.,(1983). Black Leg Disease of Cricufers Caused by Leptosphaeria Maculans and its Control. Seed Science Technology, 11, 479.

Gabrielson, R.L., (1980). Disease Problems in Cabbage Seeds, Iowa Seed Science., 2. 12.

Gupta, Kavita, Gaur, Ashok and Khetarpal, R.K. (2005). "Role of Regulatory Measures in Controlling Spread of Plant Pests," in Amerika Singh, O.P. Sharma and D.K. Garg (eds.): Integrated Pest Management: Principles and Application Vol. I. pp. 48-69. New Delhi: CBS Publishers and Distributors.

Gupta, Kavita,. Pande, B. M . and Khetarpal R.K. (2002). "Pest Risk Analysis and its Significance to India in WTO Regime". Seed Tech News, 32 (2&3): 266-69.

Gupta K. and Khetarpal R.K. (2004), Concept of Regulation Pests Their Risk Analysis and Indian Scenario, *Annual Review of Plant Pathology*, 4, 409-441.

Hewett, P.D., (1979). Regulating Seed Borne Disease by Certification, in Plant Health, the Scientific Basis for Administrative Control of Plant Diseases and Pests, Ebbels, D.L. and King, J.E., Eds., Blackewell Scientific, Oxford, 163.

Jordon, E.G., Manandhar, J.B., Thapliyal, P.N., and Sinclair, J.B.(1986)., Factors Affecting Soybean Seed Quality in Illinois. Plant Disease., 70, 246.

Khetarpal, R.K. and Pandey B.M. (2001). "Plant Quarantine and Safe Exchange of Transgenics," in G.J. Randhawa, R.K. Khetarpal, R.K. Tyagi and B.S. Dhillon (eds.): Transgenic Crops and Biosafety Concerns, pp. 101-109. New Delhi: National Bureau of Plant Genetic Resources.

Khetarpal, R.K., Varaprasad K.S., Lal A., Agarwal P.C ., and Lal, B. (2001). "Plant Quarantine of Germplasm Under Exchange," in B.S. Dhillon, K.S. Varaprasad, K. Srinivasan, M. Singh, S.

Archak, U. Srivastava and G. D. Sharma (eds.): National Bureau of Plant Genetic Resources: A Compendium of Achievements. pp. 90-115. New Delhi: NBPGR.

Khetarpal, R.K. and Gupta Kavita. (2002). "Implications of Sanitary and Phytosanitary Agreement of WTO on Plant Protection in India". Annual Review of Plant Pathology, 1: 1-26.

Khetarpal, R.K.(2004). "A Critical Appraisal of Seed Health Certification and Transboundary Movement of Seeds Under WTO Regime". Indian Phytopathology, 57(4): 408-427.

Khetarpal, R.K., Ram Nath and Raghunathan, V. (2004). "Safe Movement of Plant Germplasm," in B.S. Dhillon, R.K. Tyagi, Arjun Lal and S. Saxena (eds.): Plant Genetic Resource Management. Narosa Publishing House. New Delhi: 172-178 pp.

Khetarpal, R.K., Sankaran ,V., Chalam, V.C. and Gupta Kavita. (2005). "Seed Health Testing Standards in the Context of WTO/SPS Agreement," in: H.S. Prakash, S.R. Niranjana, K. Ramachandra Kini (eds.): Vistas in Applied Botany, pp. 1-30. Department of Applied Botany and Biotechnology, University of Mysore, Mysore, India. Khetarpal.

Khetarpal, R.K. and. Taneja ,V.K. (2006). "India's Preparedness for Pandemics". Discussion Paper submitted to Director General, ICAR, Krishi Bhawan, New Delhi in March, 2006.107.

Khetarpal R.K. and Gupta K (2002). Implication of Sanitary and Phytosanitary Agreement of Seeds Under WTO on Plant Protection in India, *Annual Review of Plant Pathology*, 1, 1-26.

Khetarpal R.K. and Gupta K (2005). Status of Plant Protection in India in the Wake of International Agreements, *Indian Journal of Plant Protection*, 33, 153-163.

Laxmi R.V, Geetanjaly and Sharma P. (2014) Plant Quarantine: An Effective Strategy of Pest Management in India Vol. 2(1), 11-16, January.

Lele, Ajay and Khetarpal, R.K. (2005). "Agro-terrorism and Threats in Indian Context". Abstracts of Second Global Conference on Plant Health – Global Wealth, 25-29 November 25-29, 2005, Maharana Pratap University of Agriculture and Technology, Udaipur, India, pp. 210.

Liew, R.S.S and Gaunt, R.E. (1981) Disease Problems in the Production of Broad Bean Seed. 34th N.Z. Weed Pest Control Conference., 55.

http://india.gov.in/sectors/agriculture/plant_protection.php

http://ppqs.gov.in/Ipmplant.htm

Rajak R.L., Radhey Shyam, Kumar U. and Chattargee G (1999)., PRA - amilstone in Plant Quarantine Functioning of India, *Plant Protection Bulletin,* 51, 1-2 7.

Ram Asre and Diwakar M.C., (1999) Role of Pest Surveillance in Plant Quarantine, *Plant Protection Bulletin,* 51, 32-34.

Rana, R.S., Dhillon B.S. and Khetarpal R.K.(2004). "Invasive Alien Species: The Indian Scene". Indian Journal of Plant Genetic Resources, 16(3): 190-213.

Shamsher Singh (1999), Management of Seed Borne Pathogens Through Quarantine Activities at NBPGR. *Proceedings of Training Course on Recent Advances in Detection and Management of Seed Borne Plant Pathogen* 85-90.

Singh, B. and Khetarpal, R.K. (eds.). 2005. Methods of Salvaging Germplasm Infected with Plant Pathogens. New Delhi: NBPGR.

Walker, J.C., (1922) Seed Treatment and Rainfall in Relation to the Control of Cabbage Black Leg. U.S. Dep. Agric. Bull., 1029, 26.

Webster, D.M., Atkin, J.D., and Cross, J.E., Bacterial Blights of Snap Beans and Their Control. Plant Disease., 67.935.

Pages: 118-145

CROP PRODUCTIVITY AND PLANT DISEASE MANAGEMENT

Edited by: Dr. Alka Chauhan; Dr. Pawan Kumar 'Bharti'; Ms. Deepti Sadana

ISBN: 978-93-5056-791-3

Edition: 2016

Published by: Discovery Publishing House Pvt. Ltd., New Delhi (India)

CHAPTER – 7

Piper nigrum L. as a Natural Biopesticide A Field Experiment on Growth, Yield and Diseases of *Solanum melongena* L.

Gayatri Nahak and **Rajani Kanta Sahu***

ABSTRACT

Piper nigrum L. is considered the king of spices of family Piperaceae throughout the world due to its pungent principle piperine. Different parts of *Piper nigrum* L. including secondary metabolites are also used as drug, preservative, insecticidal and larvicidal control agents. Biologically *Piper nigrum* L. is very important specie. The biological role of this specie is explained in different experiments that peppercorn and secondary metabolites of *Piper nigrum* L. can be used as Antiapoptotic, Antibacterial, Anticolon toxin, Antidepressant, Antifungal, Antidiarrhoeal, Anti-inflammatory, Antimutagenic, Anti-metastatic activity, Antioxidative, Antiriyretic, Antispasmodic, Antispermatogenic, Antitumor, Antithyroid, Ciprofloxacin potentiator, Cold extremities, Gastric ailments, Hepatoprotective, Insecticidal activity, Intermittent fever and Larvisidal activity.

The current investigation was to assess the effects of water leaf extract of *Piper nigrum* L. plant on growth parameters and diseases like Wilt, leaf spot in *Solanum melongena* L. To understand the mechanism, the phytochemical

KIIT School of Biotechnology, KIIT University, Bhubaneswar, Odisha, (India)

analysis of plants and its effect on bacteria and fungi were studied. The *Piper nigrum* L. treatment showed significant increase in number of flowers, buds, leaves, fruits on 10 to 70 days observation over untreated control at various significant levels and also a very much effective in reducing growth of leaf spot and Wilt diseases on all days of observations. This approach can contribute in reducing the amount applied of fungicides and subsequently minimize its hazards to the environment and human health. Work in this regards should continuing on other invasive species on isolating antifungal compounds and on field trials with promising extracts or compounds. Also, further research is needed in order to obtain information regarding the practical effectiveness of essential oils to protect the plants or the plant products without toxic effects.

Keywords: Growth parameters, Plant diseases, Aqueous extract, *Solanum melongena* L., *Piper nigrum* L.

INTRODUCTION

Agriculture has had to face the destructive activities of numerous pests like fungi, weeds and insects from time immemorial, leading to radical decrease in yields. With the advent of chemical pesticides, this crisis was resolved to a great extent. But the over dependence on chemical pesticides and eventual uninhibited use of them has necessitated for alternatives mainly for environmental concerns. Degraded soils and groundwater pollution has resulted in nutritionally imbalanced and unproductive lands. Volatile pesticide residues also sometimes raise food safety concerns among domestic consumers and pose trade impediments for export crops. Therefore an eco-friendly alternative is the end of the hour. Biopesticides or biological pesticides based on pathogenic microorganisms specific to a target pest offer an ecologically sound and effective solution to pest problems. They pose less threat to the environment and to human health.

In very general terms, biopesticides are pesticides derived from natural materials such as animals, plants, bacteria, and minerals. The two key categories focused on in this report include biochemical and microbial pesticides (reviewing the third category of biopesticides, transgenic crops, was outside the scope of this report). The subcategories of biochemical pesticides introduced in this report include insect pheromones, plant extracts and oils, plant growth regulators and insect growth regulators (Steinwand, 2008). Microbial pesticide subcategories discussed include bacteria, virus, fungus, and other less common microorganisms (Montesinos, 2003). Knowledge of the pests to which the secondary compounds produced in the plants are resistant may provide useful leads in predicting which pests may be controlled by compounds from a particular plant species. This approach has led to the discovery of different botanical pesticides. The most commonly used biopesticides are living organisms, which are pathogenic for the pest of interest. These include biofungicides (Trichoderma), bioherbicides (Phytopthora) and bioinsecticides (*Bacillus thuringiensis*).

The potential benefits to agriculture and public health programmes through the use of biopesticides are considerable. The interest in biopesticides is based on the advantages associated with such products which are: (i) inherently less harmful and less environmental load, (ii) designed to affect only one specific pest or, in some cases, a few target organisms, (iii) often effective in very small quantities and often decompose quickly, thereby resulting in lower exposures and largely avoiding the pollution problems and (iv) when used as a component of Integrated Pest Management (IPM) programmes, biopesticides can contribute greatly.

OPPORTUNITIES AND CHALLENGES FOR BIOPESTICIDES

The field of biopesticides is deep; consequently they are a source of both optimism and concern. There is a tremendous amount of work and research occurring in this field, but like other green chemistry solutions, developing safe, effective biopesticide products requires holistic thinking and multi-disciplinary approaches to establishing safety, which is a challenge for the biopesticide industry. Turning lab discoveries into profitable business products is also daunting. This mirrors what other inventors face when implementing green chemistry solutions in other sectors. Also, it is important to note that biopesticides fall along a spectrum of toxicity. At one end are products that are extremely narrow in focus (e.g. targeting a single species in a specific window of its life cycle). At the opposite end are biopesticide products that are wider in effect (pyrethroids for example, derived from chrysanthemums, affect a relatively wide range of species and can have unintended toxic collateral effects). When highly specified, biopesticides can be almost utterly benign in their human and environmental effects. When their impact is broader, however, biopesticides raise some of the same human and ecosystem impact concerns that conventional pesticides do (Desai, 1997).

CATEGORIES AND FORMULATIONS

Biopesticides are certain types of pesticides derived from such natural materials as animals, plants, bacteria, and certain minerals (US EPA Pesticides, 2008). The EPA separates biopesticides into three major classes based on the type of active ingredient used, namely microbial, biochemical, or plant incorporated protectants (GMOs). The active ingredient of a microbial pesticide is typically a microorganism such as a bacteria or fungus. A microbial active ingredient can be either the spores or the organism itself. Biochemical pesticides are chemicals either extracted from natural sources or synthesized to have the same structure and function as the naturally occurring chemicals. Biochemical pesticides are distinguished from conventional pesticides both by their structure (source) and by their mode of action (mechanism by which they kill or control pests). Plant incorporated protectants are substances produced by plants from genetic material that has been added to the plant.

The resultant plant is commonly known as a transgenic crop or a genetically modified organism. The topic of genetically modified organisms is a broad topic that warrants its own investigation, and will not be covered in this report. The US EPA has specific definitions that apply to biopesticides in a regulatory context. However, within the agricultural community, common use definitions of the term "biopesticide" can vary significantly. In addition there are related and overlapping terms that can create misunderstandings with terminology. For example, the term "biorational pesticide" also refers to natural organisms or plant-derived products (Krischik, 2008).

BIOPESTICIDE CATEGORIES

This section defines each key category of biopesticides, offer illustrative examples, and discuss formulation issues and biopesticide products. Advantages and disadvantages of biopesticides are summarized and discussed here are:

BIOCHEMICAL PESTICIDES

Biochemical pesticides are the most closely related category to conventional chemical pesticides. Biochemical pesticides are distinguished from conventional pesticides by their non-toxic mode of action toward target organisms (usually species specific) and their natural occurrence (Steinwand, 2008). The active ingredient can be a single molecule or a mixture of molecules, such as a naturally occurring mixture comprising a plant essential oil, or a mixture of very structurally similar molecules called isomers in the case of insect pheromones. While all active ingredients of biochemical pesticides occur in nature, the active ingredient in the product may be a synthetic analogue to the naturally occurring substance. This is often necessary to make a viable product and/or process, such as with insect pheromones. As many of the active ingredients in this category of biopesticides are synthetic, the full range of Green Chemistry principles should be applied to the development of the active ingredient and the biochemical pesticide product.

Not all naturally occurring chemicals are regulated as biopesticides, and some are quite toxic. For example, d-limonene is a component of several citrus essential oils. The concentrated extract of d-limonene is regulated as a conventional insecticide due to its toxic mode of action. In contrast, the oils from which d-limonene may be derived, when used as a pesticide, normally have a non-toxic mode of action and are regulated as biopesticides. Depending on the product and what it is used against, a classic mode of action for these types of oils is suffocation. Some essential oils work as repellents, and their mode of action would be as a fragrance (Steinwand, 2008). In practical terms, a non-toxic mode of action typically means that there is a delay between contact with the substance and death (Mandula, 2008).

Some examples of non-toxic modes of action include suffocation or starvation. Distinguishing between biochemical and conventional pesticides can be complex, and is determined by an EPA committee on a case by-case basis. Biochemical pesticides typically fall into distinct biologically functional classes, including semiochemicals, plant extracts, natural plant growth regulators, and natural insect growth regulators. These classes of biochemical pesticides are described below with examples provided for each category. There are almost 122 biochemical pesticide active ingredients registered with the EPA, which include 18 floral attractants, 20 plant growth regulators, 6 insect growth regulators, 19 repellents, and 36 pheromones (Steinwand, 2008).

MICROBIAL PESTICIDES

Microbial pesticides come from naturally occurring or genetically altered bacteria, fungi, algae, viruses or protozoans. They suppress pests either by producing a toxin specific to the pest, causing disease, preventing establishment of other microorganisms through competition, or various other modes of action (Clemson HGIC, 2007). For all crop types, bacterial biopesticides claim about 74% of the market; fungal biopesticides, about 10%; viral biopesticides, 5%; predator biopesticides, 8%; and "other" biopesticides, 3% (Thakore, 2006). At present there are approximately 73 microbial active ingredients that have been registered by the US EPA. The registered microbial biopesticides include 35 bacterial products, 15 fungi, 6 non-viable (genetically engineered) microbial pesticides, 8 plant incorporated protectants, 1 protozoa, 1 yeast, and 6 viruses (Steinwand, 2008). Microbial biopesticides may be delivered to crops in many forms including live organisms, dead organisms, and spores. The manufacture, regulation and use of microbial biopesticides differ most significantly from conventional chemical pesticides. To be effectively culture the organism, either in the field or during manufacture, requires an understanding of a broad range of ecological considerations. While microbial pesticides control a diverse array of pests, each specific microbial pesticide active ingredient is relatively specific to its target pest.

Bacterial bio-pesticides are probably the most widely used and cheaper than the other methods of pest bioregulation. Insects can be infected with many species of bacteria but those belonging to the genus *Bacillus* are most widely used as pesticides. One of the *Bacillus* species, *Bacillus thuringiensis,* has developed many molecular mechanisms to produce pesticidal toxins; most of toxins are coded for by several *cry* genes (Schnepf *et al.*, 1998). Since its discovery in 1901 as a microbial insecticide, *Bacillus thuringiensis* has been widely used to control insect pests important in agriculture, forestry and medicine. Its principal characteristic is the synthesis, during sporulation, of a crystalline inclusion containing proteins known as dendotoxins or Cry proteins, which have insecticidal properties. To date, over one hundred

B. thuringiensis-based bioinsecticides have been developed, which are mostly used against lepidopteran, dipteran and coleopteran larvae.

In addition, the genes that code for the insecticidal crystal proteins have been successfully transferred into different crops plants, which have led to significant economic benefits. Because of their high specificity and their safety in the environment, *B. thuringiensis* and Cry proteins are efficient, safe and sustainable alternatives to chemical pesticides for the control of insect pests (Roh *et al.*, 2007; Kumar *et al.*, 2008). The toxicity of the Cry proteins have traditionally been explained by the formation of transmembrane pores or ion channels that lead to osmotic cell lysis (Roh *et al.*, 2007). In addition to this, Cry toxin monomers also seem to promote cell death in insect cells through a mechanism involving an adenylyl cyclase/ PKA signalling pathway (Zhang *et al.*, 2006). However, despite this entomopathogenic potential, controversy has arisen regarding the pathogenic lifestyle of *B. thuringiensis*.

Recent reports claim that *B. thuringiensis* requires the co-operation of commensal bacteria within the insect gut to be fully pathogenic (Broderick *et al.*, 2006, Broderick et al., 2009). In clear opposition, genomic and proteomic studies have been argued as the most solid data to convincingly demonstrate that *B. thuringiensis* is a primary pathogen rather than a soil-dwelling saprophyte. In any case, what is certainly not doubtful is that *B. thuringiensis* is one of the most successful examples of the use of microorganisms in agricultural biotechnology, with about 70% of the global biopesticide market involving products based on *B. thuringiensis* (Thakore, 2006), and will continue to be one of the most important microbial weapons to defend our crops from insect pests. At the end of the twentieth century worldwide sales of bacterial pesticides amounted to about 2% of the total global insecticide market but their share in pesticide market steadily increases.

FUNGAL BIOPESTICIDES

Fungal biopesticides can be used to control insects, plant diseases including other fungi or bacteria, nematodes, and weeds (Milner, 1997). They are often parasitic or produce bioactive metabolites such as enzymes that dissolve plant walls. The mode of action is varied and depends on both the pesticidal fungus and the target pest. *Beauveria bassiana* spores germinate, grow, and proliferate in the insect's body, producing toxins and draining nutrients to cause insect death. Trichoderma is a fungal antagonist that grows into the main tissue of a disease-causing fungus and secretes enzymes that degrade the cell walls of the other fungus, then consumes the contents of the cells of the target fungus and multiplies its own spores. *Muscodor albus*, is a candidate to replace the problematic pesticide, methyl bromide in particular applications.

As shall be discussed below, *Muscador albus* releases gaseous toxins into the soil which can eradicate soil-borne pests and bacteria affecting major commercial crops. One advantage of fungal biopesticides in comparison with many of the bacterial and all of the viral biopesticides is that they do not need to be eaten to be effective. However, they are living organisms that often require a narrow range of conditions including moist soil and cool & temperatures to proliferate (Sosa-Goméz and Moscardi, 1998).

VIRAL BIOPESTICIDES

Baculoviruses (viral biopesticides) are pathogens that attack insects and other arthropods. Unlike other members of this category, they are not considered living organisms, but rather parasitically replicating microscopic elements (US e-CFR, 2008). Baculoviruses are extremely small and are composed primarily of double-stranded DNA required for the virus to establish itself and reproduce. Because this genetic material is easily destroyed by exposure to sunlight or by conditions in the host's gut, an infective baculovirus particle (virion) is protected by protein coat called a polyhedron (D'Amico, 2007).

Two main families of baculoviruses include Granulosis virus and Nucleopolyhedrosis virus. They differ in the number and structure of the protective protein coat and are both relatively large and complex in structure in comparison to many other types of viruses. All types of baculoviruses must be eaten by the host to produce an infection. The resulting infection is typically fatal to the insect host. Each strain of baculovirus is targeted for a specific insect species. The Nucleopolyhedrosis viruses have a relatively wide range of target pests among three different insect orders, including butterflies and moths (Lepidoptera), ants, bees, and wasps (Hymenoptera), and flies (Diptera). Target pests for Granulosis viruses are limited to species of Lepidoptera. Baculoviruses develop in the nuclei of the host insect cells.

When ingested by the host insect, infectious virus particles are liberated internally and become active. Once in the larval gut, the virus's protein overcoat quickly disintegrates, and the viral DNA proceeds to infect digestive cells. Within a few days, the host larvae become unable to digest food, and so weaken and die (Thakore, 2006).

Baculoviruses are particularly attractive for use as biopesticides due to their high host specificity. Each virus only attacks particular species of insects, and they have been shown to have no negative impacts on plants, mammals, birds, fish, or non-target insects (D'Amico, 2007). This specificity is useful in preservation of natural predators when used in Integrated Pest Management systems. Baculoviruses can also cause sudden and severe outbreaks within the host population for complete control. Another chief advantage of baculoviruses is that in some cases they replace antibiotics in agricultural use. Disadvantages of baculoviruses include the need for the virus to be ingested, resulting in lower efficacy, and their traditionally high cost of production. The lower efficacy resulting from the need to be ingested is partially counterbalanced by the mode of action. When the target insect dies, the dead insect host's body is spread on the foliage. The location and form of the infected insect carcass increases the probability the infected carcass will be eaten by another larval host. Historically the production of baculoviruses has required live hosts (*in vivo* production), making it costly.

OTHER BIOPESTICIDES

Various other organisms are also used as biological controls in integrated pest management systems. Protozoa are microscopic single-celled animal like organisms rarely used as biopesticides. Use of macroscopic predators such as live insect releases is also a common biological control strategy that can be very effective, but must be well managed to prevent ecological imbalances that can result from introducing insects into areas where they may have no natural predators. Macroscopic predators are not regulated as biopesticides, and are outside the scope of this study. Nematodes are microscopic worms that are typically parasitic and commonly used as insecticides. Although the EPA does not regulate them as biopesticides, they are often considered part of this category of control agents.

PLANT-INCORPORATED-PROTECTANTS (PIPS)

One approach, to reduce destruction of crops by phytophagous arthropod pests, is to genetically modify plants to express genes encoding insecticidal toxins. The adoption of genetically modified (GM) crops has increased in the last 11 years. Genetically modified (GM) plants possess a gene or genes that have been transferred from a different species. The production of transgenic plants that express insecticidal ä-endotoxins derived from the soil bacterium *Bacillus thuringiensis* (*Bt* plants) were first commercialized in the US in 1996. The expression of these toxins confers protection against insect crop destruction (Shelton *et al.*, 2000).

The lethality of *Bt* endotoxins is highly dependent upon the alkaline environment of the insect gut, a feature that assures these toxins are not active in vertebrates, especially in humans. These proteins have been commercially produced, targeting the major pests of cotton, tobacco, tomato, potato, corn, maize and rice, notably allowing greater coverage by reaching locations on plants which are inaccessible to foliar sprays (Shelton *et al.*, 2000). There are numerous strains of *Bt*, each with different Cry proteins, and more than 60 Cry proteins have been identified (Icoz and Stotzky, 2007). Most *Bt* maize hybrids express the Cry1Ab protein, and a few express the Cry1Ac or the Cry9C protein, all of which are targeted against the European corn borer (*Ostrinia nubilalis* Hubner) (Lepidoptera), a major pest of maize in North America and Europe.

Some recent maize hybrids express the Cry3Bb1 protein, which is targeted against the corn rootworm complex (*Diabrotica spp.*). Cotton expressing the Cry1Ac protein is targeted against the cotton bollworm (*Helicoverpa zea* Boddie) (Lepidoptera), which is a major pest of cotton; potato expressing the Cry3A or Cry3C is targeted against the Colorado potato beetle (*Leptinotarsa decemlineata* Say) (Coleoptera), which is a major pest of potato; and Cry4 proteins are targeted against some Diptera, such as certain flies (e.g., *Lycoriella castanescens* Lengersdorf) and mosquitoes (e.g., *Culex pipiens* L.).

EFFICACY

Biopesticides have an image problem. As is the case with many "greener" products, biopesticides suffer from user (in this case, grower) doubt about their effectiveness. Many growers do not trust biopesticides to work as well as traditional chemical pesticides, and indeed, in a head-to-head contest, some may not. But as noted throughout this study, biopesticides are not designed to be one-for-one replacements of existing, broad-spectrum, pesticides. They are best used as part of a systemic, integrated pest management strategy, and sometimes require more skill and understanding to use effectively. When used in the manner intended, however, biopesticides can be very effective and can not only help growers control pests, but can restore natural predators, protect workers' health, and provide consumers with chemical-free produce and clean water.

Opportunities to improve and/or promote awareness of the efficacy of biopesticides include expanding field trials, and deliberately fostering research and development collaborations between developers, growers, and agricultural experts. Biopesticides would benefit from broader and deeper testing of (and reporting on) how well they perform, how best to ensure optimal performance, and how differing conditions affect these outcomes. Expanding the resources available for field trials is essential. Engaging local agricultural colleges, universities and field extensions in these trials is also very important. Bringing in these partners not only improves the final product, but broadens the base of information resources available to farmers on how to best use them.

SAFETY

At their best, biopesticides are targeted exclusively on a particular pest, are non-toxic to humans and other species, and are environmentally benign. They allow growers and farm workers to enter fields immediately after usage, saving time, crops and money. Biopesticides can be, at the greenest end of the spectrum, among the least toxic means of managing pests. But this is not always the case. Some biopesticides are more broad-spectrum than others. Some, like pyrethroids, can affect human health in unexpected ways. Others, while benign to humans, can negatively impact non-target organisms, including beneficial insects and pollinators. The challenge of establishing the safety of biopesticides lies in their diversity. The wide spectrum of biopesticides available makes generalizations - and regulations - difficult.

While accelerating the review process for biopesticides is more efficient in bringing them to market, the predominant focus of the EPA pesticide registration process is on human health and safety. This is a serious challenge to biopesticides. Currently there are no adequate regulations to provide meaningful ecosystem-level protection, such as protection of birds, pollinators, and aquatic systems (Benbrook, 2008). While speed to market is an economically important goal, these environment and health data gaps must be addressed. The absence of regulations addressing these issues for biopesticides may lead to serious surprises followed by backlash against them. Speed to market is a real concern for biopesticide producers and consumers. Registration is a key cost in commercializing any new pesticide product.

For biopesticides, the regulatory process can dominate this cost of bringing a new product to market. The toxicological studies that must be performed for data submission to the EPA are very expensive. The testing requirements place a proportionately larger burden on small companies such as many of the biopesticide manufacturers. Separate registration is required for each designated product (e.g. soy or tomatoes). To recoup the costs of registration, most large chemical companies focus on registering pesticide products only for very high volume crops such as wheat and corn. Biopesticides are typically niche products used on lower volume crops such as fruits and vegetables. Thus it is often more difficult for biopesticide companies to recoup the cost and time of the regulatory process. In addition, small biopesticide companies often lack the experience and expertise to navigate the regulatory process.

There are opportunities to mitigate the high costs and time investments for biopesticide testing and registration. A governmental programme that should be expanded is the Interregional Research Project No. 4 (IR-4). IR-4 is a programme funded by the USDA to support registration of products used for specialty crops (low volume crops). The programme provides expert assistance to help companies through the regulatory process, and funds grants for research to promote reduced risk and biopesticide development. The IR-4 Project has been a key support to the growth of the Biopesticides Industry Alliance (BPIA). In addition to working with the EPA to register biopesticides, the BPIA has also worked with the EPA to educate growers on these products. An IR-4 grant funded the field research for the development of granulosis virus for controlling the codling moth discussed on later.

There are other opportunities to address safety and testing by borrowing from other fields, including the pharmaceutical industry and the environmental health sciences. The pharmaceutical industry uses a variety of "rapid screening" methods to asses both active pharmaceutical ingredients and processing methods. It is possible that some of these methods could be useful in evaluating biopesticides and the manufacturing process. But as we have discussed, biopesticides also need to broaden their testing range to include additional ecological and health impacts. Dovetailing with research underway in the environmental health sciences is absolutely essential. Encouraging cross-science communication and collaboration is very important for all of green chemistry; there are initial efforts underway to link these fields but these need to be systematized and institutionalized.

TRANSPARENCY

Efficacy and safety testing are only useful if people are aware of the results; there is a need for greater transparency about biopesticide products. The Biopesticide Industry Alliance (BIA) is currently engaged in developing industry standards to enable greater transparency, but it is our understanding that these standards will focus primarily on efficacy. Biopesticides could learn much from experiences in other product areas to develop Ecolabels – information tools based on efficacy but also on more nuanced environment and health information; this presents the greatest *opportunity* to generate better transparency around biopesticides.

Unaddressed short-comings in products (as in the example of concerns about inert ingredients) that must be addressed before a product is commercialized and used. Sustainable agriculture aims at reducing the incidence of pests and diseases to such a degree that they do not seriously damage crops without upsetting nature's balance. One of the aims of sustainable agriculture is to rediscover and develop strategies whose cost and ecological side-effects are minimal. The use of synthetic pesticides has undoubtedly resulted in achievement of green revolution in different countries through increased crop production. However, in recent years there has been considerable pressure on consumers and farmers to reduce or eliminate synthetic pesticides in agriculture. This concern has encouraged researchers to look for better alternatives to synthetic pesticides.

Medicinal plants represent a rich source of antimicrobial agents. Plants are used medicinally in different countries and are a source of many potent and powerful drugs (Srivastava *et al.*, 1996).

A wide range of medicinal plant parts is used for extract as raw drugs and they possess varied medicinal properties. The different parts used include root, stem, flower, fruit, twigs exudates and modified plant organs. While some of these raw drugs are collected in smaller quantities by the local communities and folk healers for local used, many other raw drugs are collected in larger quantities and traded in the market as the raw material for many herbal industries (Uniyal *et al.*, 2006). Although hundreds of plant species have been tested for antimicrobial properties, the vast majority of have not been adequately evaluated (Balandrin *et al.*, 1985). Considering the vast potentiality of plants as sources for antimicrobial drugs with reference to antibacterial and antifungal agents, a systematic investigation was undertaken to screen the local flora for antibacterial and antifungal activity.

Pesticidal compounds of plant origin are effective against pests, mostly through diverse modes of action and can express several properties such as growth retardation, feeding deterrent, oviposition deterrent and reduction in fertility. Such allelochemicals need proper attention of plant biologists to exploit plant-pest chemical ecology in integrated management of plant pests. Most of the essential oils of higher plant origin act in biorational mode of action interrupting the function of octapamine receptors found in insects but absent in mammalian system (Hollingsworth *et al.*, 1984). Hence, their exploitation in pest management would be an ideal eco-chemical approach.

Despite many years of effective control by conventional agrochemical insecticides, a number of factors are threatening the effectiveness and continued use of these agents. These include the development of insecticide resistance and use-cancellation or de-registration of some insecticides due to human health and environmental concerns. Therefore, an eco-friendly alternative is the need of the hour. Improvement in pest control strategies represents one method to generate higher quality and greater quantity of agricultural products. Therefore, there is a need to develop biopesticides which are effective, biodegradable and do not leave any harmful effect on environment. Their protection against pests is a priority and due to the adverse impact of chemical insecticides, use of biopesticides is increasing.

BIOPESTICIDES IN INDIA

Biopesticides represent only 2.89% (as on 2005) of the overall pesticide market in India and is expected to exhibit an annual growth rate of about 2.3% in the coming years (Thakore, 2006). In India, so far only 12 types of biopesticides have been registered under the Insecticide Act, 1968. Neem based pesticides, *Bacillus thuringensis*, NPV and *Trichoderma* are the major biopesticides produced and used in India. Whereas more than 190 synthetics are registered for use as chemical pesticides. Most of the biopesticides find use in public health, except a few that are used in agriculture. Besides, (i) transgenic plants; and (ii) beneficial organisms called bio-agents: are used for pest management in India.

Some success stories about successful utilization of biopesticides and bio-control agents in Indian agriculture include (Kalra and Khanuja, 2007).

- Control of diamondback moths by *Bacillus thuringiensis*
- Control of mango hoppers and mealy bugs and coffee pod borer by *Beauveria*

- Control of *Helicoverpa* on cotton, pigeon-pea, and tomato by *Bacillus thuringiensis*
- Control of white fly on cotton by neem products
- Control of *Helicoverpa* on gram by N.P.V.,
- Control of sugarcane borers by *Trichogramma* and
- Control of rots and wilts in various crops by *Trichoderma*-based products.

Reasons of using pestisides of *Piper nigrum* L.

Piper nigrum (family Piperaceae) is a valuable medicinal plant. It is one of the most commonly used spices and considered as "The King of spices" among various spices. Black pepper is grown in many tropical regions like Brazil, Indonesia and India. *Piper nigrum* L. is commonly known as Kali Mirch in Urdu and Hindi, Pippali in Sanskrit, Milagu in Tamil and Peppercorn, White pepper, Green pepper, Black pepper, Madagascar pepper in English. Hot and pungent peppercorns are obtained from Black pepper which is the most famous and one of the commonly used spices throughout the world. Black pepper is used as medicinal agent, a preservative, and in perfumery. Whole Peppercorn of *Piper nigrum* L. or its active components are being used in different types of foods and as medicine. Pepper is used worldwide in different types of sauces and dishes like meat dishes. It contains major pungent alkaloid Piperine (1-peperoyl piperidine) which is known to possess many interesting pharmacological actions. It is widely used in different traditional systems of medicine like Ayurvedic and Unani System of medicines (Ahmad *et al.*, 2012; Acharya *et al.*, 2012). Piperine exhibits diverse pharmacological activities like antihypertensive and antiplatelets (Taqvi *et al.*, 2008), antioxidant, antitumor (Manoharan *et al.*, 2009), antiasthmatics (Parganiha *et al.*, 2011), antipyretic, analgesic, anti-inflammatory, anti-diarrheal, antispasmodic, anxiolytic, antidepressants (Li *et al.*, 2007), hepato-protective (Matsuda *et al.*, 2008), immuno-modulatory, antibacterial, antifungal, anti-thyro ids, antiapoptotic, anti-metastatic, antimutagenic, anti-spermatogenic, antiColon toxin, insecticidal and larvicidal activities etc. Piperine has been found to enhance the therapeutic efficacy of many drugs, vaccines and nutrients by increasing oral bioavailability by inhibiting various metabolising enzymes (Johnson *et al.*, 2011). It is also known to enhance cognitive action and Fertility (Wattanathorn *et al.*, 2008). Piperine also found to stimulate the pancreatic and intestinal enzymes which aid to digestion. Many therapeutic activities of this spice are attributed to the presence of piperine apart from other chemical constituents. The fruits of *Piper nigrum* are used to produce white and green peppers. *Piper nigrum* L. is also used as a flavoring agent (Ahmad *et al.*, 2012).

Black pepper is one of the important spices rich in aromatic and medicinal components along with appreciable levels of several other functional components having health promoting properties (Meghwal and Goswami, 2012). The uses of black pepper in various fields such as food processing, pharmaceutical industry etc, is increasing steadily due to its recognition as an important source of natural antioxidant having anticarcinogenic activity (Srinivasan, 2007). Large number of studies has been undertaken in the laboratory against the causal organism affecting the tomato plant. However the effectiveness of the peppercorn extracts on individual crops in different agro-climatic zones and cultivars in field condition have not been investigated much. Hence the objective of the study was to determine to efficacy of efficacy of black pepper seed extracts as biopesticide agent on growth parameters and disease control in egg plant.

Taxonomical Classification of *Piper nigrum* L.

Kingdom: Plantae
Class: Equisetopsida
Sub class: Magnoliidae
Super order: Magnolianae
Order: Piperales
Family: Piperaceae
Genus: Piper
Species: nigrum

Pharmacognosy of the *Piper nigrum* L.

Pharmacognostical Characteristics *Piper nigrum* (Black pepper) plant is a flowering woody perennial climbing vine that belongs to Piperaceae family. Pepper plants easily grow in the shade on supporting trees, trellises or poles up to maximum height of 13 feets or 4 meters and roots may come out from leaf nodes if vine touch to the ground. The plants have heart shape as long as the leaves. The length of spikes goes up to 7-15 cm. The black pepper's fruits are small (3 to 4 mm in diameter) called a drupe and the dried unripe fruits of *Piper nigrum* are known as a peppercorn. The fully mature fruits are dark red in color and approximately 5 mm in diameter. A fruit contains a single seed. The plants bear fruits from 4th or 5th year, and continue to bear fruits up to seven years. A single stem contains 20-30 spikes of fruits. The collected spikes are sun dried to separate the peppercorns from the spikes. The fresh harvested unripe green fruits may freeze-dry to make green pepper. The fresh harvested unripe green fruits may sun-dried to make black pepper. The red skin of the ripen fruits is removed and the stony seeds are sun-dried to make white pepper.

Chemical Composition of *Piper nigrum* L.

The phytochemical investigations of *P. nigrum* revealed that it contains variety of phytochemicals. Piperine was the first pharmacologically active compound isolated from different members of Piperaceae family. Many investigators isolated different types of compounds viz Phenolics, flavonoids, alkaloids, amides and steroids, lignans, neolignans, terpenes, chalcones etc and many other compounds. Some of the compounds are Brachyamide B, Dihydro-pipericide, (2E, 4E)-N-Eicosadienoyl-pereridine, N-trans-Feruloyltryamine, N-Formylpiperidine, Guineensine, pentadienoyl as piperidine, (2E,4E)- Nisobuty- ldecadienamid, isobutyl-eicosadienamide, Tricholein, Trichostachine, isobutyl-eicosatrienamide, Isobutyl-octadienamide, Piperamide, Piperamine, Piperettine, Pipericide, Piperine, Piperolein B, Sarmentine, Sarmentosine, Retrofractamide A. The different pharmacological activities were reported due to the presence of these phytochemicals. Piperine reported to have four isomers viz; Piperine, Isopiperine, Chavicine and Isochavicine. Among all isolated compounds isolated from *P. nigrum*. Piperine, pipene, piperamide and piperamine were found to possess diverse pharmacological activities (Ahmad *et al.*, 2012).

BIOLOGICAL EFFECTS OF BLACK PEPPER ON INSECTS

Piperaceae family has provided many past and present civilizations with a source of medicines and food spices; the secondary metabolites of different species in the genus piper have been used for various biological activities including insect repellent activities. The active compounds having insecticidal activity are the piperamides extracted from different species of piper including Piper nigrum (Scott *et al.*, 2008). Black pepper is the main spice food stuff and Piperine is a pungent alkaloid of black pepper. Two important sesquiterpens, β-caryophyllene and nerolidol, the first having anaesthetic activity (Santra *et al.*, 2005) and second used for flavouring agent, it is also been reported that the piperine enhances the trans-dermal delivery of active drugs through skin membrane. A natural compound isolated from piper species known as nerolidol having pesticidal activity against various mites. Another active agent isolated from volatile oil of peppercorn known. The action of *Piper nigrum* products as pest control agents can be manifested at different levels and in different ways. This is a very important point to be noted since the farmer would be used to the "knock-out" effect of chemical pesticides. *Piper nigrum* extracts do not exhibit this type of effect on pests but affect them in several other ways.

INSECT GROWTH REGULATION

Regulation of the insects' growth is a very interesting property of black pepper products which is unique in nature, since the products work on juvenile hormones. The insect larva feeds and as it grows, it sheds its old skin. This particular shedding of old skin is the phenomenon of ecdysis or moulting and is governed by an enzyme, ecdysone. When the black pepper components, especially piperine, enter the body of the larva, the activity of ecdysone is suppressed and the larva fails to moult, remains in the larval stage and ultimately dies. If the concentration of azadirachtin is not high enough, the larva will die only after it has entered the pupal stage. If the concentration is lower still, the adult emerging from the pupa will be 100% malformed, and absolutely sterile.

FEEDING DETERRENT

The most important property of black pepper extract is feeding deterrence. When an insect larva sits on a leaf, it will want to feed on it. This particular trigger of feeding is given through the maxillary glands. Peristalsis in the alimentary canal is thus speeded up, and the larva feels hungry and starts feeding on the surface of the leaf. If the leaf is treated with a back pepper extracts, there will be an anti-peristaltic wave in the alimentary canal which produces something similar to a vomiting sensation in the insect. Because of this sensation, the insect does not feed on the black pepper-treated surface. Its ability to swallow is also blocked.

OVIPOSITION DETERRENT

It is one of the common way in which black pepper extract controls pests is by preventing the females from depositing eggs. After this treatment, the insects will not feed on them. Further damage to the grains will be halted and the female will be unable to lay its eggs during the egg-laying period of its life cycle. There are also other known modes of action:

(a) The formation of chitin or the hard part covering the insect

(b) Mating as well as sexual communication is disrupted

(c) Larvae and adults of insects are repelled

(d) Adults are sterilized and

(e) Larvae and adults are poisoned.

The use of *Piper nigrum* L. products does not give immediate results, unlike chemical insecticides. Some patience is required after the application of *Piper nigrum* L. products. Besides its insecticidal and nematicidal properties, neem is also a promising agent for control of plant diseases. It has also been demonstrated to possess anti-fungal properties. One of the problems with the use of chemical pesticides has been their impact on "non-target" species. Often they have proven harmful to various other species in the ecosystem that could be beneficial. However, *Piper nigrum* L. extracts are devoid of these effects. *Piper nigrum* L. seed extracts, when incorporated into potting soil containing earthworms, increased the earthworm population by 25%. *Piper nigrum* L. products have proven to be remarkably benign to spiders and also other insects such as bees that pollinate crops and trees, ladybug beetles that consume aphids and wasps which act as parasites on various crop pests. *Piper nigrum* L. products have to be ingested to be effective. Those insects which feed on plant tissues, therefore, easily succumb. However, natural predators like spiders feed only on other insects while bees feed on nectar. Hence they rarely come in contact with significant concentrations of *Piper nigrum* L. products.

MODE OF ACTION

Piper nigrum L. acts as a biopesticide at different levels and in various ways. Primarily it acts as antifeedant ie., when an insect larva is hungry and it wants to feed on the leaf but if the leaf is treated with neem product, because of the presence of Piperine containing (E, E)-1- piperoylpiperidine and (E, E)-1- [5-(1, 3- benzodioxol-5-yl)-1-oxo-2, 4-pentdienyl there is an antiperistalitic wave in the alimentary canal and this produces something similar to vomiting sensation in the insect. Because of this sensation the insect does not feed on the neem treated surface and ability to swallow is also blocked. Secondly it acts as oviposition deterrent ie., by not allowing the female to deposits eggs comes in very handy when the seeds in storage are coated with black pepper powder. It also acts as insect growth regulator. It is a very interesting property of black pepper product and unique in nature, i.e., it works on juvenile harmone.

SELECTION OF PLANT FOR STUDY

Brinjal or eggplant (*Solanum melongena* L.) is an important solanaceous crop of sub-tropics and tropics. The name brinjal is popular in Indian subcontinents and is derived from Arabic and Sanskrit whereas the name eggplant has been derived from the shape of the fruit of some varieties, which are white and resemble in shape to chicken eggs. It is a perennial but grown commercially as an annual crop. A number of cultivars are grown in India, consumer preference being dependent upon fruit color, size and shape. The varieties of *Solanum melongena* L. display a wide range of fruit shapes and colours, ranging from oval or egg-shaped to long club-shaped; and from white, yellow, green through degrees of purple pigmentation to almost black.

BOTANICAL DESCRIPTION

Brinjal or eggplant is an herbaceous annual with erect or semi spreading habits. It is a perennial plant but cultivated as annual. It develops into bushy plants with large, fuzzy leaves that grow to a height of about 60 to 120 centimeters. The plant is erect, compact, and well branched. It has a rather fibrous or lignified root system. The leaves are large, simple, lobed and alternate on the stems. The stems, leaves, and calyx of some cultivars are spined. The leaf pattern is mostly opposite, large, single lobed and the underside of the most cultivars is covered with dense wool like hairs. The leaves may be with or without spines at the midrib portions. The leaf blade and tip angle is very acute to very obtuse. Inflorescence is often solitary but sometimes it constitutes a cluster of 2 - 5 flowers. This character is dependent on the variety or hybrid. The flowers are large, violet-colored and either solitary or in clusters of two or more (Lawande and Chavan 1998). Flower is complete, actinomorphic and hermaphrodite. Calyx is five lobed, gamosepalous and persistent with or without spines depending on the cultivar types. It forms a cup like structure at the base. Corolla is five lobed gamopetalous with margins of lobes incurved. There are five stamens which are free and inserted at the throat of corolla. Anthers are cone shaped, free and with apical dehiscence. Ovary is hypogynous, bicarpellary, sycarpous and with basal placentation. The fruit is pendent and is fleshy berry borne signally or in clusters. The shape of fruit varies from ovoid, oblong, obovoid, or long cylindrical. The colour of the mature fruit varies from monocoloured purple, purple black, yellowish, white, green and variegated types of purple with white stripes, green with light green/white stripes or even combination of three colours. The seeds are borne on the fleshy placenta and the placentae with the seeds completely fill the locular cavity. The seed color is white, light yellow, brownish yellow, brown to black brown for different varieties.

CULTIVATION

Climatic and Soil Requirements

Brinjal is a warm season vegetable and susceptible to severe frost. Climatic conditions especially low temperature during the cool season cause abnormal development of the ovary (splitting) in flower buds which then differentiate and develop into deformed fruits during that season (Nothmann and Koller, 1973). The optimum temperature for growth and fruit set is 20-30°C. However the high night and day temperature condition of 22-24°C to 33-35°C markedly reduce fruit set and yield (Kalloo *et al*, 1990; Kumar *et al.*, 2000; Thapa, 2002). Many of the round varieties set fruits at slightly lower temperature but are highly susceptible to frost. The long fruited varieties set fruit at higher temperature and show tolerance to frost. The brinjal can be grown practically on all soils from light sandy to heavy clay. Light soils are good for an early crop, while clay loam and silt-loam are well suited for high yield. Generally, silt-loam and clay loam soils are preferred for brinjal cultivation. The soil should be deep, fertile and well-drained (pH 5.5-6.0).

Seedbed Preparation

Brinjal seeds were sown on nursery beds to raise seedlings for transplanting in the field. Raised beds are necessary to avoid problem of water logging in heavy soils. In sandy soils, however, sowing can be taken up in flat beds. Raised beds of size 7.2 × 1.2m and 10-15cm in height were prepared. Thus, ten such beds are sufficient to raise seedlings for planting one hectare area. An about 70cm distance was maintained between two beds to carry out operations of watering, weeding, etc.

Seedling Establishment

About 250-300g of seeds is sufficient for raising seedlings for one hectare of land. Prior to sowing seeds are treated with fungal culture of *Trichoderma viride* (4g/kg of seed) or Thiram (2g/kg of seed) to avoid damage from damping-off disease. Sowing should be done thinly in lines spaced at 5-7cm distance. Seeds are sown at a depth of 2-3cm and the beds should be maintained required temperature and moisture. The watering should be done by water can as per the need till germination is completed. During the last week in nursery, the seedlings may be hardened by slightly withholding water.

Land Preparation

The field was ploughed to fine filth by giving four to five ploughing with a sufficient interval between two ploughing. Planking should be done for proper leveling. The field was then divided into beds and channels.

Transplantation

Seedlings were transplanted in furrows in light soils and on side of the ridges in case of heavy soils. A pre-soaking irrigation was given 3-4 days prior to transplanting. At the time of transplanting, the roots of the seedlings should be dipped in a solution of Bavistin (2g/liter of water). Transplanting should preferably be done in the evening.

Preparation of Plant Extract

The seeds of *Piper nigrum* L. plant were collected from different localities. Then the seeds were out dried at room temperature for three weeks. The dried seeds were milled to a fine powder and stored at room temp in closed glass jar. Hundred grams from each of the dried, powdered plant sample were weighed and placed in to 1000 ml flask. The flask was closed with cotton balls and covered with aluminum foil, then filtered with the help of cheese cloth. The liquid extract which were placed in a 1000 ml each 10 ml solution of each was sprayed on the leaves of tomato plant from week to week. The liquid extract of black pepper seed extracts were sprayed on the leaves of egg plants. The following growth parameters were recorded from week to week as per observation. The growth parameters, effects of black pepper extracts on the growth and development and various controlled diseases of *Solanum melongena* L. plants were studied.

Water Extract

A water extract was prepared by mixing 100 gm of the powder with one liter of sterile distilled water in 1000ml flask, stirring vigorously, allowing one hour for settling and then filtering the extract through four folds of cheese cloth.

Application of Black pepper extracts on *Solanum melongena* L. through spraying

(a) Spraying should be undertaken in the morning or late in the evening. Under hot conditions, the frequency of spraying should be increased. In winter, spraying once in 10 days and every day in the rainy season is recommended.

(b) Insects lay eggs on the underside of the leaves. Hence it is important to spray under the leaves also.

(c) While using a power sprayer, the quantity of water used should be halved.

(d) It is better to use low concentrations of extracts frequently.

(e) As a general guideline, it can be said that each acre of land to be protected can be sprayed with 60 litres of ready-to-use solution (not the concentrate). Of course, the volume may have to be varied depending on the exact conditions prevailing, such as the intensity of the pest attack.

PARAMETERS FOR STUDIES

Morphological Analysis

Morphological measurements of *Solanum melongena* L. were taken at 10, 20, 30, 40, 50, 60 and 70 days after transplantation. Morphological measurements of *Solanum melongena* L. were taken at 10 days interval after transplantation. From day of transplantation to harvest time the experimental fields were maintained .The following parameters were measured as follows: shoot height, number of leaves, number of buds, number of flowers and number of fruits for this study.

Effect of *Piper nigrum* L. seed extracts on growth parameters of *Solanum melongena* L.

Shoot height (Table 7.1)

The effect of extraction of *Piper nigrum* L. seed on the height of brinjal plants were observed at 7, 14, 21, 28, 35, 42and 49 days after transplantation. The height of plants increased progressively from 7 days to 49 days in both control (untreated) and *Piper nigrum* L. treatment.

Table 7.1: Effect of *Piper nigrum* L. Seed Aqueous Extract on Plant Height of *Solanum melongena* L.

Height (cm)	10 Days	20 Days	30 Days	40 Days	50 Days	60 Days	70 Days
Control	3.80±0.34	4.75±0.42	5.50±0.47	10.7±0.49	12.6±2.24	14.5±2.57	15.5±2.57
P. nigrum	4.20±0.30	5.46±0.33	6.90±0.64	7.10±0.56	11.6±1.61	15.9±1.99	20.3±2.15

Number of leaves (Table 7.2)

The number of leaves of brinjal plant was observed at 10, 20, 30, 40, 50, 60 and 70 days. The final reading on the 70th day exhibited significant increase over control (untreated) in *Piper nigrum* L. treatment. The *Piper nigrum* L. treatment showed high increase in leaf number over control (untreated) on 10 to 70 days observation.

Table 7.2: Effect of *Piper nigrum* L. Seed Aqueous Extract on Number of Leaves of *Solanum melongena* L.

Leaf No.	10 Days	20 Days	30 Days	40 Days	50 Days	60 Days	70 Days
Control	3.50±0.21	3.70±0.21	3.90±0.23	4.30±0.21	5.80±0.54	7.30±0.86	8.30±0.98
P. nigrum	4.30±0.65	5.20±0.80	5.40±0.45	6.10±1.02	7.00±0.97	8.70±0.55	10.70±1.43

Number of Buds (Table 7.3)

The numbers of buds were observed at 10, 20, 30, 40, 50, 60 and 70 days. The *Piper nigrum* L. treatment showed high increase in number of buds over control (untreated) on 10, 20, 30, 40, 50, 60 and 70 days observation. Observation on 70th days showed high increase in number of buds in *Piper nigrum* L. treatments.

Table 7.3: Effect of *Piper nigrum* L. Seed Aqueous Extract on Number of Buds of *Solanum melongena* L.

Leaf No.	10 Days	20 Days	30 Days	40 Days	50 Days	60 Days	70 Days
Control	3.10±0.25	4.80±0.48	6.80±0.37	7.00±1.00	10.66±1.20	15.50±0.50	17.00±0.65
P. nigrum	5.5±1.62	6.2±1.78	7.2±1.78	8.9±0.84	12.9±1.03	18.0±0.74	20.8±0.67

Number of Flowers (Table 7.4)

Significant increases in numbers of flowers over untreated control were observed in *Piper nigrum* L. treatment. The *Piper nigrum* L. treatment showed significant increase in number of flowers on 10 to 70 days observation over untreated control.

Table 7.4: Effect of *Piper nigrum* L. Seed *aqueous* Extract on Number of Flowers of *Solanum melongena* L.

Flowers	10 Days	20 Days	30 Days	40 Days	50 Days	60 Days	70 Days
Control	4.16±0.79	5.00±1.00	6.57±1.15	6.83±1.07	10.00±0.77	12.80±0.96	15.60±0.88
P. nigrum	4.90±0.23	6.50±0.22	6.80±0.35	8.10±0.27	13.1±1.12	14.8±1.56	17.4±2.12

Number of Fruits (Table 7.5)

The numbers of fruits were observed at 10, 20, 30, 40, 50, 60 and 70 days. Observation on 7 to 70 days it showed significant increase in number of fruits in *Piper nigrum* L. treatments.

Table 7.5: Effect of *Piper nigrum* L. Seed Aqueous Extract on Number of Fruits of *Solanum melongena* L.

Fruits	10 Days	20 Days	30 Days	40 Days	50 Days	60 Days	70 Days
Control	5.00±0.81	5.00±0.81	6.25±0.88	4.40±0.74	5.00±1.29	4.40±0.74	5.00±1.29
P. nigrum	9.11±0.77	8.25±1.68	8.37±1.26	7.10±3.27	6.62±0.86	5.40±0.60	6.66±0.94

Effect of *Piper nigrum* L. seed extracts on diseases of *Solanum melongena* L.

Wilt (Table 7.6)

It was noticed that the application of *Piper nigrum* seed extract treatment on brinjal plant during the whole seven weeks suppressed the wilt disease in comparison to control(untreated). The *Piper nigrum* seed extract treatment showed minimum growth of diseases on 10, 20, 30, 40, 50, 60 and 70 days observation.

Table 7.6: Effect of *Piper nigrum* L. Seed Aqueous Extract on Wilt of *Solanum melongena* L.

Wilt	10 Days	20 Days	30 Days	40 Days	50 Days	60 Days	70 Days
Control	32.6±1.53	39.7±3.50	31.2±2.49	34.7±1.97	35.3±3.60	29.4±2.30	20.8±2.56
P. nigrum	15.8±1.26	13.6±1.68	12.3±1.79	11.8±1.90	20.9±1.39	23.0±2.63	18.2±0.93

Leaf Spot (Table 7.7)

The *Piper nigrum* seed extract treatment was effective in reducing growth of leaf spot diseases on all days of observations. The maximum growth of diseases was observed in untreated control. The black pepper extract treatment showed minimum growth of diseases on 10, 20 and 30 days observation. On the observation of 10 to 70 days, the number of diseases were reduced the growth of diseases.

Table 7.7: Effect of *Piper nigrum* L. Seed Aqueous Extract on Leaf Spot of *Solanum melongena* L.

Leaf Spot	10 Days	20 Days	30 Days	40 Days	50 Days	60 Days	70 Days
Control	93.6±3.16	89.7±3.32	80.7±5.70	65.2±4.52	61.7±3.17	70.4±3.26	66.8±4.17
P. nigrum	87.3±2.06	85.4±1.47	61.8±1.56	35.7±1.58	24.7±1.43	15.8±1.00	9.8±1.58

GROWTH AND YIELD

The experiment was conducted on growth and yield of tomato cultivation of neem extract and the results on effectiveness of various treatments were described. There was significant increase in the plant height, number of leaves, buds and fruits number at all growth stages from 10-70 days in neem extract treatment in comparison to control. All measured parameters gave significant differences from their respective controls (Table 7.1 to 7.5). Neem aqueous extract showed a promotive effect on shoot lengths (30.96%), leaf numbers (28.91%), number of buds (22.35%), number of flowers (11.53%) and number of fruits (33.2%) with increasing time compared to untreated or control ones. The promotive effect could be due to triterpene which acts by delaying the transformation of ammonium nitrogen into nitrate nitrogen as reported by Akhtar, (1999). The result suggests the applications are also growth promotive and cost effective and non-hazardous in agro-ecosystem. Results on growth parameters indicated significant differences in the shoot length, number of leaves, number of branches, number of flowers, number of fruits, number of nodes, number of tillers and number of panicles etc. in all treatments. Growth stimulating effect of ten medicinal plant extracts (*P. pinatta, A. marmelos, A. indica, B. campestris, P. nigrum, E. tirucalli, V. negundu, A. conyzoides, T. patula and Z. jujube*) on *Lycopersicum esculentum* L. have been observed (Pattnaik *et al*., 2012). Similar experiment carried out by Okunlola and Thomas (2013) showed the effect of *A. indica* and *Piper guineense* on the growth and yield of jute under sole and mixed cropping. All growth parameters increased in comparison to control. In another experiment ethanolic extracts of *Melia azedarch, Eucalyptus robosta, Sapium sebiferum* had no significant influence on growth and development of Soybean seedlings (Wan *et al*., 2012). Effect of tea seed extracts on growth of beet, mustard, oat and barley were studied. Different concentrations of these extracts increased the growth, yield and biomass of the crops. The growth stimulating effect is not exclusively by its adverse effect on pathogen or by an increase in nutrient uptake. However substances with hormone like properties can stimulate of effect biomass allocation in plants. In addition to hormones, medicinal plant extracts contain saponins and polyphenols which could be the active compounds causing the effect on growth (Anderson, 2010).

DISEASES

Because of its fleshy nature, tomato fruit is attacked by a number of insect pests and diseases. Pathogenic diseases develop through soil borne and above ground infections, and, in some instances, are transmitted through insect feeding. Major tomato diseases include those that attack the root system (fusarium wilt, verticiliun wilt, bacterial wilt, rhizoctonia), above-ground stems and foliage (early blight, leaf spot, bacterial canker, late blight), and fruit (bacterial spot, bacterial speck, anthracnose) (Pandey *et al*., 2006). Thus, the disease control programme is important at each stage of growth. Wilt is caused by the soil borne fungus *Fusarium oxysporum* f. sp. *Lycopersici*. The black pepper extracts substantially reduced the number of infected leaves and number of lesions on foliage, and curtailed disease development, which in turn, protected flowers and capsules from infection (Enikuomehin, 2005). Similarly our result also showed a positive effect on reducing Fusarium wilt by 14.28% (Table 7.6). The results obtained from El-Khalal, 2007; Croxton *et al.*, 2011 who reported that the growth rate of shoot and root was markedly inhibited in tomato seedlings in response to fusarium wilt diseases. This further strengthens our field experiment on wilt control of brinjal by aqueous black pepper extract. Leaf spot caused by the fungus *Septoria lycopersici* which are noticeable by small, circular spots on the upper surface of the lower leaves. Heavily infected leaves turn yellow, wither, and eventually fall off. Reduction of leaf spot disease was observed from 40th day onwards and maximum reduction was observed on 70^{h} day in comparison to control (85.32%) (Table 7.7). A study was undertaken to evaluate the effectiveness of 33 plant extracts against leaf spot of ground nut.

In eggplant (*Solanum melongena*) was moderatly efficient in controlling wilt & but highly efficient in controlling leaf spots. The difference in the inhibitory effect of various plant extract may be due to qualitative and quantitative difference in the secondary metabolites acting as antifungal/ antibacterial compounds. It is presumed that the phytochemical compounds present in higher concentration are more fungitoxic to control the pathogenecity of economically important crop plants. All treatments including black pepper treated varieties gave considerable reduction in disease incidence (Hussain *et al.*, 2013). Suppression of septorial leaf disease of tomato by aerated compost tea reduced 26.3% of diseases by foliar spray (Gangaiah *et al.*, 2004). It can be concluded that black pepper extract was found more effective in comparison to other plants. The natural lipophilic Piperine and piperiline were isolated from *Piper nigrum*, Piperine was hydrolyzed into piperic acid which was converted into 16 amides having insecticidal activity (Scott *et al.*, 2008; Santra *et al.*, 2005). The larvicidal activity of *Piper nigrum*, was also reported, larvicidal effects of crude extracts of dried ripened fruits of pepper against *Culex quinquifasciatus* larval instars.

In the recent past, efforts have been intensified to control the associated insect pests of garden egg using synthetic insecticides such as cyperforce, karate, cymbush, attack, decis to mention but a few where promising results were obtained. The hazardous effect of these pesticides has increasingly become a major concern to environmentalist. Thus other options for management of pests became imperative. However, the search for more sustainable nonconventional method using plant derived insecticides that are environmentally safe with simple application techniques for control of insect pests of garden egg gave rise to my desire to carry out this research work with the objective of contributing to increase in the production and yield of garden egg by reducing its infestation through application of locally available plant materials that are environmentally friendly, of very low cost/ cheap, using simple application technique that is always available.

Fig. 7.1: *Piper nigrum* L. Plant

Fig. 7.2: *Piper nigrum* L. Seeds

Fig. 7.3: Wilt Disease in Egg Plant

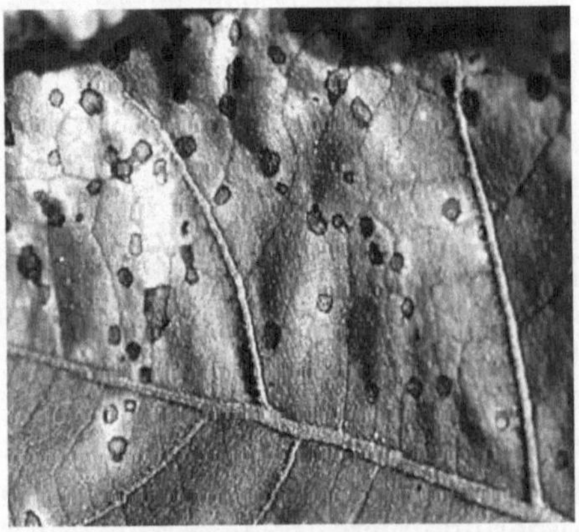

Fig. 7.4: Leaf Spot Disease in Egg Plant

CONCLUSION

Further studies on these effective botanicals should include bioassay-directed fractionation of the extracts which will lead to the isolation of the compounds that is showing considerable antifungal activity. The continuation of study on the plant is essential to isolate, identify, characterize and elucidate the structure of the bioactive compounds responsible for the observed antifungal activities. From this result, it is essential to investigate the specific constituents which are responsible for this observed activity and such characterization studies are underway. Hence, further work is necessary to evaluate its potentiality *in vivo* studies on other pathogens. Simultaneous investigations are also needed to characterize, formulate and market the active principles of these extracts which may provide leads for the discovery of novel antimycotic compounds. These biofungicidal botanicals are environmentally safe, therefore, they could successfully replace the toxic and hazardous synthetic compounds and exploited as an ideal treatment for future plant disease management programmes.

REFERENCES

1. Acharya, S.G., Momin, A.H. and Gajjar, A.V. (2012): Review of Piperine as A BioEnhancer, *Am J Pharm Tech Res.*, 2: 32-44.
2. Ahmad, N., Fazal, H., Abbasi, B.H., Farooq, S. and Ali, M. (2012): Biological Role of *Piper nigrum* L. (Black Pepper): A Review, *Asian Pacific J Trop Biomed*, S1945-S1953.
3. Akhtar, M. and Mahmood, I. (1995): Evaluation of a Neem Based Product Against Root-knot Nematode *Meloidogyne incognita*. Tests of Agrochemicals and Cultivars, *Annal. Appl. Biol.*, 16: 6-7.
4. Anderson, M. (2010): Plant Growth is Stimulated by Tea-seed Extract: A New Natural Growth Regulator? *Hort. Science*, 45(12): 1848-1853.
5. Balandrin, M.F., Klocke, J.A., Wurtele, E.S. and Bollinger, W.H. (1985): Natural Plant Chemicals: Sources of Industrial and Medicinal Materials, *Science*, 228 (4704): 1154-1160.
6. Benbrook, C. (2008): Personal Communication. Troy (OR): The Organic Center. Chief Scientist.
7. Broderick, N.A., Raffa, K.F. and Handelsman, J. (2006): Midgut Bacteria Required for *Bacillus thuringiensis* Insecticidal Activity, *Proc Natl Acad Sci.*, 103, 15196-15199.
8. Broderick, N.A., Robinson, C.J., McMahon, M.D., Holt, J., Handelsman, J. and Raffa, K.F. (2009): Contributions of Gut Bacteria to *Bacillus thuringiensis*-induced Mortality Vary Across a Range of Lepidoptera, *BMC Biol*, Vol. 7, pp. 11.
9. Croxton, S.D., Foshee, III, W.G., Blythe, E.K., Murphy, J.F. and Sibley, J.L. (2011): Evaluation of Selected Tempera Paints Applied to Tomatoes to Reduce the Occurrence of Tomato Spotted Wilt Virus. *International Journal of Vegetable Science*, 17: 177-189.
10. D'Amico V. (2007): Baculoviruses in Biological Control: A Guide to Natural Enemies in North America. Ithaca (NY): Cornell University. URL: http://www.nysaes.cornell.edu/ent/biocontrol/pathogens/baculoviruses.html (accessed 19 Aug 2008).
11. Desai, S. T. (1997): Chemical Industry in the Post Independence Era: A Finance Analysis Point of View, *Chemical Business*, 11(1): 25-28.
12. El-Khallal, S.M. (2007): Induction and Modulation of Resistance in Tomato Plants Against Fusarium Wilt Disease by Bioagent Fungi (*Arbuscular Mycorrhiza*) and/or Hormonal Elicitors (Jasmonic Acid & Salicylic Acid): 2-changes in the Antioxidant Enzymes, Phenolic Compounds and Pathogen Related-proteins. *Australian Journal of Basic and Applied Science*, 1 (4): 717-732.
13. Enikuomehin, O.A. (2005): Cercospora Leaf Spot Disease Management in Sesame (*Sesamum indicum* L.) with Plant Extracts. *Journal of Tropical Agriculture*, 43(1-2): 19-23.
14. Gangaiah, C., Carey, E. and Tisserat, N.A. (2004): Suppression of Septoria Leaf Spot Disease of Tomato Using Aerated Compost Tea. Kansas State University. ASHS Annual Meeting. Available on http://www.ashs.org/annualmeeting/conference/index.lasso.
15. Hollingworth, R.M., Johnstone, E.M. and Wright, N. (1984): In: Magee, PS, Kohn GK, Menn JJ (Eds), Pesticide Synthesis Through Rational Approaches, ACS Symposium Series No. 225: 103-125. American Chemical Society, Washington, DC.
16. Hussain, B., War, A.R. and Sharma, H.C. (2013): Jasmonic and Salicylic Acid-induced Resistance in Sorghum Against the Stem Borer *Chilo partellus*. *Phytoparasitica*. pp. 1-22.
17. Icoz, I. and Stotzky, G., (2007): Cry3Bb1 Protein from Bacillus Thuringiensis in Root Exudates and Biomass of Transgenic Corn does not Persist in Soil. Transgenic Research,/http://www.springerlink.com/content/pm447n1340n136t3/S.
18. Johnson, J.J., Nihal, M., Siddiqui, I.A., Scarlett, C.O., Bailey, H.H., *et al.* (2011): Enhancing the Bioavailability of Resveratrol by Combining it with Piperine, *Mol Nutr Food Res.*, 55: 1169-1176.
19. Kalloo, G., Baswana, K. and Sharma, N.K. (1990): Heat Tolerance in Eggplant (*Solanum melongena*). XXIII Intern. Hortic. Congr. Florence, Itlay, Abst. 1204.

20. Kalra, A. and Khanuja, S.P.S. (2007): Research and Development Priorities for Biopesticide and Biofertiliser Products for Sustainable Agriculture in India. In. Business Potential for Agricultural Biotechnology (Teng, P.S. ed.), Asian Productivity Organisation, pp. 96-102.
21. Krischik, V. and Davidson, J. (2007): Integrated Pest Management of Northwest Landscapes. Minneapolis (MN): Regents of the University of Minnesota. Chapter 1, 23-24. pp. 315.
22. Kumar, A., Dahiya, M.S. and Bhutani, R.D. (2000): Performance of Brinjal Genotypes in Different Environments of Spring Summer Season, *Haryana J. Hort.*, 11: 63-67.
23. Kumar, S., Chandra, A. and Pandey, K.C. (2008): *Bacillus thuringiensis* (Bt) Transgenic Crop: An Environmentally Friendly Insect-pest Management Strategy, *J Environ Biol*, 29, 641-653.
24. Li, S., Wang, C., Wang, M., Li, W., Matsumoto, K., *et al.* (2007): Antidepressant Like Effects of Piperine in Chronic Mild Stress Treated Mice and its Possible Mechanisms, *Life Sci.*, 80: 1373-1381.
25. Mandula, B. (2008): Personal Communication. Washington DC: US EPA Office of Pesticide Programmes, Biopesticide and Pollution Prevention Division, Retired Scientist.
26. Manoharan, S., Balakrishnan, S., Menon, V., Alias, L. and Reena, A. (2009): Chemopreventive Efficacy of Curcumin and Piperine during 7,12-dimethylbenz[a] anthracene-induced hamster buccal pouch carcinogenesis, *Singapore Med J.*, 50: 139-46.
27. Matsuda, H., Ninomiya, K., Morikawa, T., Yasuda, D., Yamaguchi I and Yoshikawa M. (2008): Protective Effects of Amide Constituents from the Fruit of Piper chaba on D-galactosamine/ TNF-alpha-induced Cell Death in Mouse Hepatocytes, *Bioorg Med Chem Lett.*, 18: 2038-2042.
28. Meghwal, M. and Goswami, T.K. (2012): Chemical Composition, Nutritional, Medicinal and Functional Properties of Black Pepper: A Review, *Open Access Scientific Reports*, 2012; 1: 172.
29. Milner, R.J., Baker, G.L., Hooper, G.H.S. and Prior, C. (1997): Development of a Mycoinsecticide for the Australian Plague Locust. In: Krall, S., Peveling, R., Diallo, D.B. (eds) New Strategies in Locust Control. Birkhäuser, Basel, pp. 177-183.
30. Montesinos, E. (2003): Development, Registration and Commercialization of Microbial Pesticides for Plant Protection, *Int Microbiol.*, 6: 245-252.
31. Nothmann, J. and Koller, D. (1973): Morphogenetic Effects of Low Temperature Stress on Flowers of Egg Plant, *Israel J. Botany*, 22: 231-235.
32. Okunlola, I.A. and Thomas, I. O. (2013): Effect of Mixed Cropping and Plant Extracts on the Growth, Yield and Pest Control of Jute (*Corchorus olitorius* L.). *Folia Hort.*, 25 (1): 49-60.
33. Pandey, A.K., Namgyal, D., Mehdi, M., Mir, M.S. and Shikh, B.A. (2006). A Case Study: Major Insect Pest Associated with Different Vegetable Crops in Cold Arid Region, Ladakh of Jammu and Kashmir. *J. Entomol. Res.*, 30: 169-174.
34. Parganiha, R., Verma, S., Chandrakar, S., Pal, S., Sawarkar, H.A. and Kashyap, P. (2011): *In vitro* Anti-asthmatic Activity of Fruit Extract of *Piper nigrum* (Piperaceae). *Inter J Herbal Drug Res.*, 1: 15-18.
35. Parmar, V.S., Jain, S.C., Bisht, K.S., Jain, R., Taneja, P., Jha, A., Tyagi, O.D. (1997): Phytochemistry of the Genus Piper. Phytochemistry, 46, 597-673.
36. Pattnaik, M., Kar, M. and Sahu, R.K. (2012): Bioefficacy of Some Plant Extracts on Growth Parameters and Control of Diseases in *Lycopersicum esculentum*, *Asian Journal of Plant Science and Research*, 2(2): 129-142.
37. Roh, J.Y., Choi, J.Y., Li, M.S., Jin, B.R. and Je, Y.H. (2007): *Bacillus thuringiensis* as a Specific, Safe, and Effective Tool for Insect Pest Control, *J Microbiol Biotechnol*, 17, 547-559.
38. Santra, M., Santra, D.K., Rao, V.S., Taware, S.P. and Tamhankar, S.A. (2005): Inheritance of β-carotene concentration in durum wheat (*Triticum turgidum* L. ssp. durum), *Eucalypta*, 144: 215-221.
39. Schnepf, E., Crickmore, N., van Rie, J., Lereclus, D., Baum, J. and Feitelson, J. (1998): *Bacillus thuringiensis* and its Pesticidal Crystal Proteins, *Microbiology and Molecular Biology Reviews*, 62: 775 - 806.

40. Scott, I.M., Jensen, H.R., Philogene, B.J.R. and Arnason, J.T. (2008): A Review of Piper spp. (Piperaceae). Phytochemistry, Insecticidal Activity and Mode of Action. *Phytochem. Rev.*, 2008; 7: 65-75.
41. Shelton, A.M., Tang, J.D., Roush, R.T., Metz, T.D. and Earle, E.D. (2000): Field Tests on Managing Resistance to Bt-engineered Plants, *Nat Biotechnol.*, 18, 339-342.
42. Singh, N.K., Kumar, P., Gupta, D.K., Singh, S. and Singh, V.K. (2011): UVspectrophotometric Method Development for Estimation of Piperine in Chitrakadi Vati, *Der Pharmacia Lettre*, 3, 178-182.
43. Sosa-Gomez, D.R. and Moscardi, F (1998): Laboratory and Field Studies on the Infection of Stink Bugs, *Nezara viridula*, *Piezodorus guildinii*, and *Euschistus heros* (Hemiptera: Pentatomidae) with *Metarhizium anisopliae* and *Beauveria bassianain, Brazil J Invertebr Pathol.*, 2: 115-120.
44. Srinivasan, K. (2007): Black Pepper and its Pungent Principle-piperine: A Review of Diverse Physiological Effects, *Crit. Rev. Food Sci. Nutr.*, 47(8): 735-48.
45. Srivastava, J., Lambert and Vietmeyer, V. (2006): Medicinal Plants: An Expanding Role in Development, World Bank Technical Paper. No. 320.
46. Steinwand, B. (2008): Personal Communication. Washington DC: US Environmental Protection Agency, Biopesticide Ombudsman.
47. Taqvi, S.I., Shah, A.J. and Gilani, A.H. (2008): Blood Pressure Lowering and Vasomodulator Effects of Piperine, *J Cardiovasc Pharmacol.*, 52: 452-458.
48. Thakore, Y. (2006): The Biopesticide Market for Global Agricultural Use, *Ind Biotechnol*, 2, 194-208.
49. Thapa and Himali. (2002). Comparative Performance of Some Brinjal Genotypes in the Summer Rainy and Autumn Winter Conditions. M.Sc (Hort.) Thesis, Bidhan Chandra Krishi Viswavidyalaya, Mohanpur,West Bengal, pp. 45.
50. Uniyal, S.K., Singh, K.N., Jamwal, P. and Lal, B. (2006): Traditional Use of Medicinal Plants Among the Tribal Communities of Chhota Bhangal, *Western Himalayan Journal of Ethnobiology and Ethnomedicine*, 2, 1-14.
51. US e-CFR: US Electronic Code of Federal Regulations. 2008. 40 CFR 158 Subparts U and V. URL: http://ecfr.gpoaccess.gov/cgi/t/text/textidx?c=ecfr&sid=013b05537f6069487ae3f2252ae1d5a &rgn=div5 &view=text&node=40:23.0.1.1.9&idno=40#40:23.0.1.1.9.1 (accessed 3 Jun 2008). Washington DC: US Office of the Federal Register.
52. US Environmental Protection Agency, Regulating Pesticides. (2008): What are Biopesticides? URL: http://www.epa.gov/pesticides/biopesticides/whatarebiopesticides.htm (accessed 28 Sept 2008). Washington, DC: US Environmental Protection Agency.
53. Wan, J., Xu, J., Yang, M., Yang, Z., Huang, Q. and Zhao, S. (2012): Effects of Three Plant Extracts on Growth and Development of Dodder and Soybean and on Protective Enzymes of Host, *Legume Genomics and Genetics*, 3(2): 8-13.
54. Wattanathorn, J., Chonpathompikunlert, P., Muchimapura, S., Priprem, A. and Tankamnerdthai, O. (2008): Piperine, the Potential Functional Food for Mood and Cognitive Disorders, *Food Chem Toxicol.*, 46: 3106-3110.
55. Zhang, G.Y., Sun, X.L., Zhang, Z.X., Zhang, Z.F. and Wan, F.F. (1995): Production and Effectiveness of the New Formulation of *Helicoverpa* Virus Pesticide-emulsifiable Suspension, *Virologica Sinica*, 10, 242-247.

Pages: 146-163

CROP PRODUCTIVITY AND PLANT DISEASE MANAGEMENT

Edited by: Dr. Alka Chauhan; Dr. Pawan Kumar 'Bharti'; Ms. Deepti Sadana

ISBN: 978-93-5056-791-3

Edition: 2016

Published by: Discovery Publishing House Pvt. Ltd., New Delhi (India)

CHAPTER – 8

Epidemiology, Symptomatology and Management of Mungbean Anthracnose Caused by *Colletotrichum truncatum* (Schw.) Andrus and Moore

[1]Vandana Shukla*; [2]Vijay Sharma
[3]Kadu Tanvi Pradeeprao and [4]Payal Devi

ABSTRACT

Mungean anthracnose caused by *Colletotrichum truncatum* (Schw.) Andrus and Moore is one of the most important seed borne disease of Mungbean [*Vigna radiata* (L.) Wilczek] in the world. The disease is prevalent in areas that experience cool and wet weather conditions, causing up to 24 to 67% yield loss. The disease causes symptoms to appear on leaves, stems, pods and seeds. The pathogen can survive in seeds for up to five years, and is also known to overwinter in crop debris. Seed infection is the primary means by which the pathogen spreads. Therefore, the production and the use of certified seeds are one of the important control measures that is effective in dealing

1 Department of Plant Pathology, Indira Gandhi Krishi Vishwa Vidyalaya, Raipur - 492 012, Chhattisgarh, (India)

2 Department of Genetics & Plant Breeding, Maharana Pratap University of Agriculture & Technology, Udaipur - 313 001, Rajasthan, (India)

3 Department of Plant Molecular Biology and Biotechnology, Indira Gandhi Krishi Vishwa Vidyalaya, Raipur - 492 012, Chhattisgarh, (India)

4 Department of Entomology, Indira Gandhi Krishi Vishwa Vidyalaya, Raipur - 492 012, Chhattisgarh, (India)

with the disease. Fungicidal seed treatment and foliar application as well as cultural and biological methods are very important for bean anthracnose management. Studies on the disease epidemiology and symptomatology of mungbean anthracnose caused by *C. truncatum* (Schw.) Andrus and Moore was revealed that, fungus can grow at wide range of temperatures between 15-30°C; with most favoured range of temperature and pH for the growth and sporulation of fungus were 25°C to 30°C and 5.5 to 7.0, respectively. Further information on epidemiology and management of *C. truncatum* is needed to devise more effective management strategies. In this review attention were given to the epidemiology and management options, with an emphasis on the future research priorities.

Keywords: Anthracnose, *Colletotrichum truncatum*, Epidemiology, Temperature, pH, Growth, Sporulation, IDM

INTRODUCTION

Mungbean [*Vigna radiata* (L.) Wilczek], is an important pulse crop of India. It is also commonly known as mung, mungbean, green gram in India and mungo in Philippines, is most prized among the six cultivated *Vigna* spp. Mungbean [*Vigna radiata* (L.) Wilczek] is annual autogamous diploid (2x=2n=22) grain legume crop belonging to Fabaceae family. India grows a variety of pulse crops under a wide range of agro-climatic conditions and is recognized globally as a major player in pulses contributing 25% of the global production. In India, mungbean is grown on 3.43 m ha and total production of 1.71 m tonnes of grains with productivity of 4.98 q/ha (Anonymous, 2012). In spite of being the largest producer in the world, India has to import pulses to the tune of two million tones every year to meet its domestic requirement (Ali and Kumar 2005). In India mung bean is mostly grown in states like Andhra Pradesh, Maharastra, Orissa, Rajasthan, Gujrat, Madhya Pradesh, West Bengal, Punjab, and Uttar Pradesh etc. Mungbean is grown in summer and Kharif season in northern India and in southern India; it is also grown in winter season. In West Bengal, mungbean is the principal pulse crop and mainly grown in pre-*kharif* and *kharif* season. It is a major source of dietary protein that complements carbohydrate-rich sources such as rice, maize, and cassava. It is also a rich source of dietary fibers, minerals and certain vitamins. The mungbean suffers from several diseases, especially anthracnose (*Colletotricum truncatum*), cercospora leaf spot (*C. canescens, C. cruenta*), powdery mildew (*Erysiphe polygoni*), root disease complex (*Pythium* spp., *Rhizoctonia solani, Fusarium* spp.) and the reniform (*Rotylenchulus reniformis*) and root knot (*Meloidogyne* spp.) nematodes.. In recent years, mungbean anthracnose caused by *Colletotrichum truncatum*(Schw.) Andrus and Moore has become one of the major diseases which is known to occur in many countries *viz*. India, Nigeria, Thailand, Philippines, Upper volta, Zambia, Palmira, Columbia, *etc*. (Agarwal, 1991). It occurs in all parts of the world, wherever mungbean is cultivated. In India, the mungbean anthracnose was first reported from Jorhat of Assam state in 1951(Majid, 1953). The disease has been reported from all major mungbean growing regions of India in mild to severe form. The disease causes qualitative as well as quantitative losses (Sharma *et al.,* 1971). Losses in yield due to anthracnose have been estimated to be in the range of 24 to 67 per cent (Deeksha and Tripathi, 2002) and 18.2 to 86.57 per cent disease index of anthracnose have been reported in northern Karnataka (Laxman, 2006). The yield losses caused by mungbean anthracnose are proportional to the disease severity and vary remarkably depending on the stage of infection, genotypes and environmental conditions. The disease is characterized by serious leaf spotting ultimately resulting in 'shot hole' symptoms and finally defoliation which affects the yield greatly. Infection of pods directly damages the seeds and reduces its germinability. Pod infection may result in complete loss in yield. When *C. trucatum* attack mungbean leaves, it causes dark brown necrotic lesions and decrease leaf photosynthesis activity (Bassanezi *et al.* 2001). Yield loss is due to early leaf senescence and plant death, shrunken seed and an increase in the amount of diseased seed that has lesions on its coat (Pastor-Corrale and Tu, 1989). Such beans have a repulsive appearance and are not popular with consumers. This lowers the marketability and thus the income arising from their sale. Management strategies used to minimize seed borne infection in the seed production field include host resistance, cultural and chemical control methods. Harvesting drying and post harvest processing and storage operations can also be used to reduce the spread and to eradicate seed borne pathogens.

The fungus is known to have races that vary from, country, region, location, and variety, to another (CIAT, 1997). *C. truncatum* pathogen is of particular concern because, unlike others a fungus, a strategy for the management of mungbean anthracnose disease is inadequate, especially given the limited and antiquated chemical options available. The earlier studies on anthracnose caused by *C. truncatum* involved only reports of field observations on disease occurrence and its symptoms. Few workers have cultured a pathogen in laboratory and observed the colony morphology. However, there has been no systematic study involving disease epidemiology, effects of abiotic factors like temperature, pH and relative humidity on growth and development of pathogen and efficacy of different commonly used fungicides and biological control agents in suppressing this pathogen, especially in case of mungbean. Considering the wide host range and damage potential of *C. truncatum*, the problem deserves immediate and effective measures of control so as to minimise the yield losses. Therefore, this review was initiated with the following objective: To review the epidemiology, symptomatology and to intervene the disease spread by suggesting eco-friendly management strategy for mungbean anthracnose.

DISTRIBUTION OF MUNGBEAN ANTHRACNOSE

At least, four species of *Colletotrichum* have been found associated with mungbean and blackgram, infecting leaves, stem and pods severely in different parts of the world (Saxena and Sinha, 1977; Hiremath, 1981). Three different species of *Colletotrichum viz., C. truncatum, C. lindemuthianum* and *C. dematium* were reported to cause leaf spots or anthracnose disease of mungbean in India (Saxena and Gupta, 1981; Bharadwaj and Singh, 1986; Thakur and Khare, 1989). In India, the mungbean anthracnose was first reported from Jorhat of Assam state in 1951 (Majid, 1953). Later, Rathaiah and Sharma (2004) reported anthracnose disease on mungbean, which is caused by *C. truncatum* in Assam and subsequently by Laxman (2006) from Karnataka.

Several diseases caused by *Colletotrichum* pathogens are of economic and social importance. Lentil anthracnose, caused by *C. truncatum*, has been reported in the United States (Ventte *et al*. 1994), Bulgaria (Kaiser 1998), Brazil and Pakistan (Bellar and Kebabeh 1983; Morrall 1997). In Canada, the disease was first reported in Manitoba (Morrall 1988), and then in Saskatchewan (Morrall and Pederson 1991). In 1999, an epidemic of lentil anthracnose developed under unusually wet and warm weather conditions, causing severe losses in yield and seed quality (Anderson *et al*. 1999).

Although still regarded as one of the most important bean diseases, economic importance of anthracnose in recent years has declined in developed countries through the effective use of clean seed and resistant variety (Pastor-Corrale and Tu, 1989; Awgichew, 1982; Allen, 1983). However, in developing countries, it remains serious and it is regarded as one of the principal diseases of beans throughout tropical regions including Latin America and Eastern Africa (Allen, 1983).

TAXONOMY AND VEGETATIVE CYCLE OF BEAN ANTHRACNOSE

Taxonomy

Colletotrichum truncatum (Schw.) Andrus and Moore (1935), the fungus belongs to the division Eumycota, sub division Deuteromycotina, class Coelomycetes, order Melanconiales, family Melanconiaceae. *Colletotrichum* Corda is the anamorph of the ascomycete *Glomerella* Spauld. & H. Schrenk, a well defined taxon within the Sordariomycetes (Erikisson and Winka, 1998). The telomorph *Glomerella cingulata* belongs to the phylum Ascomycota of kingdom fungi, class Sordariomycetes Eriksson & Winka (Erikisson and Winka 1998), order Glomerellales, family Glomerellaceae. *Colletotrichum* (sexual stage: *Glomerella*) is a genus of fungi that are obligate symbionts to plants in the form of endophytes. Many of the species in this genus are plant pathogens, although some species may express a mutualistic life-style in non-disease hosts.

VEGETATIVE CYCLE

Colletotrichum truncatum deploys a complex life cycle which has various development phases and two ways to take food. In every phase may be seen as unique, differentiated stages that let the fungus survive. Independently of the fungus development phase, the spore germination occurs in a similar manner. In the imperfect form of *C. lindemuthianum* the reproduction is asexual, the spores are produced inside acervulus and immerse in water soluble-formed mucilage (O'Connell *et al.*, 1996). The development of fungal spore shows a biphasic behaviour which means two life styles, as a saprophyte and biotroph; therefore, the fungus has been classified as hemibiotroph. In saprophytic life style the fungus grows in any carbon source including crystalline cellulose which may be easily converted into molecules fuel by extracellular lytic enzymes. On the other hand, as a biotroph fungus has the ability to feeding of nutriments outright of living plants.

As a saprophyte fungus, the spore germination process begins with the spore adhesion to the plant surface under adequate humidity conditions; specifically, correct aqueous content in the spore envelope (mucilage). At this level, the spores of the fungus round off by water absorption and active growth. Later, the germinating tube is formed (germinule phase), and the hyphae elongates to colonize the substrate. The aerial mycelia appear; then the fungal reproductive structures are formed where the spores are storage.

Finally, their life cycle is completed and it starts all over again. During the spore adhesion, the hydrophobicity of vegetal surface, the physical-chemistry bidirectional signalization and the mucilage play a major role (Sela-Buurlage *et al.*, 1991; Mercure, 1994). The mucilage is formed by heavy molecular weight glycoproteins, a variety of enzymes and germination inhibitors; but it does not contain chitin (O'Connell *et al.*, 1996; Hughes *et al.*, 1999). Besides, it acts as a structure that protects the spore of dehydration and even as a protective barrier against environmental toxic and defense plant metabolites. The 6ìm length fimbriae structures which are part of the germinule and the appresorium also participate in the adhesion process (O'Connell *et al.*, 1996). The *C. lindemuthianum* hyphae grow constantly reaching a size of 2 or 3 times bigger than their original size spore. It is believed that critical nutrient conditions and chemical bidirectional communication induce the formation of the dome in the hyphae tip or appresorium. At same time, it initiates the melanin synthesis and the formation of the septum that separates cytoplasm from appresorium and germinule. Also, the plasmatic membrane presents a biochemical differentiation process which separates into two domains, one in the domo or appresorium and the other in the infection peg (Pain *et al.*, 1996). The appresorium produces and accumulates melanin an important factor involved in the turgency pressure which is required for the *C. lindemuthianum* to penetrate into the plant cell (Kubo and Furusawa, 1991).

A new distribution and localization of plasmatic membrane proteins occur in the base of appresorial dome. It is necessary for the formation of a penetration pore, the synthesis of new cell walls layers, and the secretion of some other materials (O'Connell *et al.*, 1996). The melanin is storage in a cell wall layer which lies very close to the plasmatic membrane (Bailey *et al.*, 1992). The penetration pore is rounded by an internal wall layer with funnel shape called, appresorial cone. This structure is contiguous with the peg penetration wall and does not have chitin or melanin. The apical growth starts again with the infection peg emission and the injection of the plasmatic membrane and the citosol through the penetration pore then grows down to the intramural space between plasmatic membrane and cell wall. This will become the infection hyphae which is present in the biotrophic phase (Pain *et al.*, 1996). Knowledge about the biotrophical phase between *C. lindemuthinanum* and bean cells interaction recently has started. However, during this phase, the primary hyphae growing between the vegetal plasmatic membrane and the cell wall is known. This fungus does not form specialized structures such as haustorium, like the ones seen in some strict biotrophs (O'Connell, 1987; Green *et al.*, 1995). One characteristic of biotrophic intracellular interaction between plant cell and fungus, it is that, pathogen avoids or suppresses the initiation event of the plant defense responses, those that switch on the hypersensibility reaction or the synthesis and deposition of callose on cell wall (Heath and Skalamera, 1997).

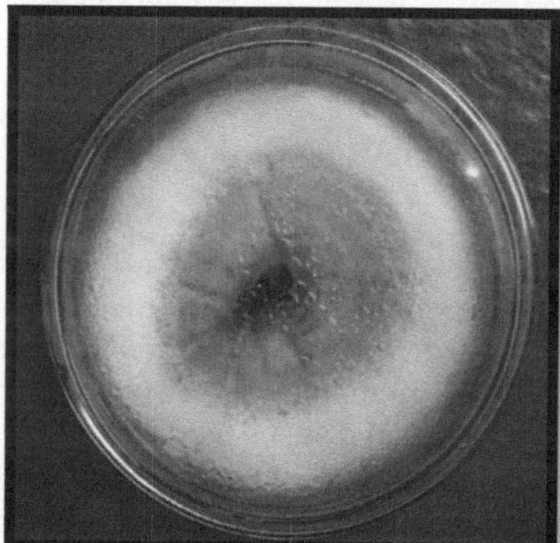

Pure Culture of C. Truncatum

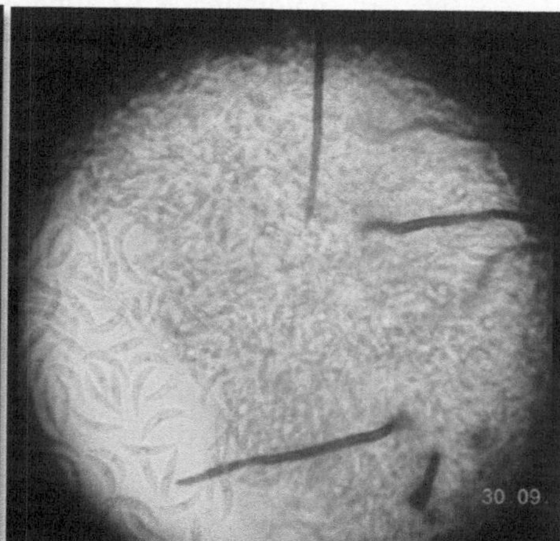

Setae and Conidia

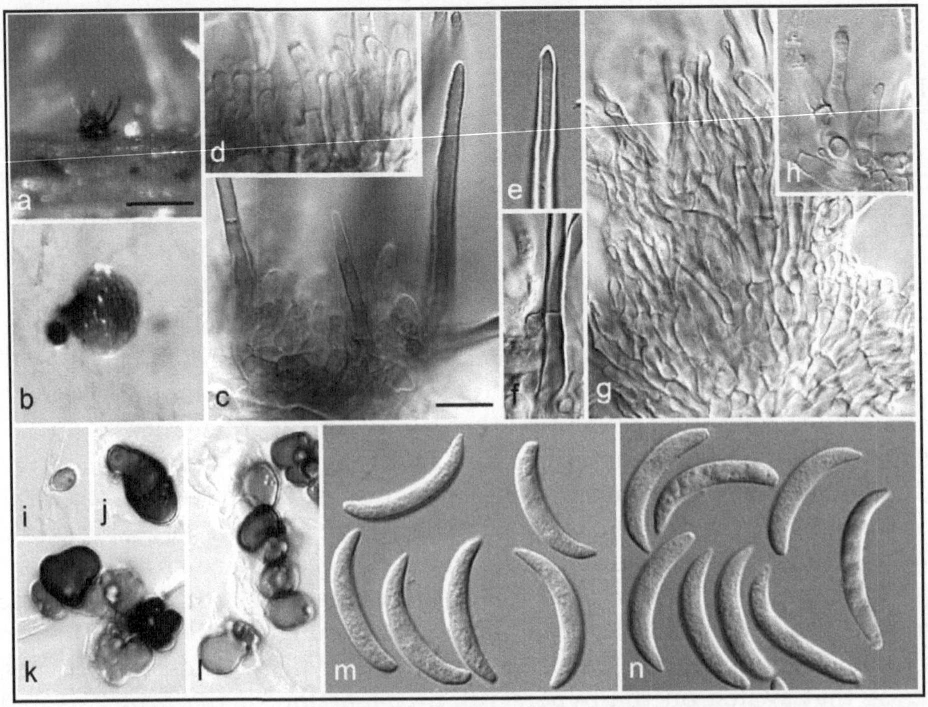

Fig. 8.1: *Colletotrichum truncatum* (a–h, m–n. from ex-epitype strain CBS 151.35, i–l. from CBS 120709). a–c. acervuli; d. conidiophores; e. tip of a seta; f. basis of a seta; g–h. conidiophores; i–l. appressoria; m–n. conidia; a, c–d, m: from *Anthriscus* stem; b, e–l: from SNA. a–b: DM; c–n: DIC. — Scale bars: a = 100 ¼m; c = 10 ¼m; a applies to a–b; c applies to c–n. (Damm *et al.* 2009)

PLANT INFECTION AND SYMPTOMS OF MUNGBEAN ANTHRACNOSE:

Leaf Infection and Symptoms

Singh and Shukla (1988) reported that *C. truncatum* causing serious leaf spotting in mungbean, the disease manifests mainly on the leaves but under severe conditions it may produce small, reddish brown, 1 to 4 mm diameter spots on petioles, light grey, water soaked, irregular, later on turning to rustic brown, 10 to 14 mm diameter spots on stems and small, reddish blotches on pods. The leaf spots later turn to form 'shot holes' and in severe cases pre-mature defoliation occurs. Lesions are most common on leaf petioles and on the lower surfaces of leaves and leaf veins (Hall, 1994). Although infection may occur on both sides of the leaf and on the petiole, early signs of infection usually appear on the lower leaf surface along the veins, which show brick red to purplish red discoloration. Later, such discoloration also appears on the upper leaf surface. At the same time, brown lesions of various sizes, with black, brown, or purplish red margins, develop around small veins (Alien *et al.,* 1996). During disease progression, vein necrosis appears first, then wilting and bleaching often occurs at the tip of the leaflet before spreading over the margin and finally over the centre of the blade (Godoy *et al.*, 1997). During this stage hyphae proliferate throughout host tissues, inside cells, in walls and through walls and in intercellular spaces.

POD INFECTION AND SYMPTOMS

Before attacking the pods, the anthracnose fungus will infect the stems first. Stem infection is manifested by dark brown eyespots which develop longitudinally along the stems (Tu and Aylesworth, 1980; Tu, 1983). In the young seedling, if the eyespots enlarge, the stem may break off, but for older stems, the eye-shaped lesion is limited to an approximate length of 5-7 mm, and the lesion often has a sunken cankerous center (Alien *et al.*, 1996). After infecting the stems, the infection will then be passed on to the pods on pods, the most striking disease symptoms are small brown specks on rusty brown spots. Rathaiah and Sharma (2004) indicated appearance of characteristic blood red ring like spots of 8 – 11 mm diameter on the upper surface of leaf. Blood red stains measuring upto 2.5 cm in length appeared on the pods.

As these spots enlarge, their centers turn brown and many tiny black specks appear randomly on the brown area, replacing the brown specks (Bailey *et al.*, 1992). Each of the tiny black specks contains a mass of pinkish spores, often visible as a viscous droplet in humid conditions. The lesions on the pod usually reach a diameter of 5-8 mm, are slightly sunken at the center and have a dark brown or purplish brown margin (Tu and Aylesworth, 1980).

SEED INFECTION AND SYMPTOMS

Seed infection is the major source of anthracnose transmission to the next crop generation and provides conditions which enable the fungus to survive unfavourable weather conditions. The fungus will remain alive as long as the seed remains viable, although not all infested and infected seed is capable of transmitting the disease (Bailey *et al.*, 1992). The variation in seed transmission relates to the degree of infestation as well as the severity and site of infection in the seed (Tu, 1983). Infection of the seed is as a result of infections passed on from the pods. The higher the number of pods infected, the higher is the number of seeds infected. On the seed, anthracnose is displayed as brown to light chocolate-colored spots on the seed coats and in highly infected seed, the lesions may extend into the cotyledons (Alien *et al.*, 1996).

EPIDEMIOLOGY OF MUNGBEAN ANTHRACNOSE

Optimum Conditions for Disease Development

Anthracnose is favoured by cool and wet weather. Temperatures of 13-26°C with an optimum of 17°C, relative humidity above 92% and free moisture favour the germination of spores and initial infection (Goodwin, 2003). During favourable environmental conditions typical anthracnose symptoms as lesions develop in all the above ground plant parts (Pastor-Corrale and Tu, 1989), from these lesions are washed down with water to other plant parts and serve as secondary sources of inoculum that initiate secondary infection in the field (Beshir, 2003). The spores can spread from infected to healthy plants by rain splash, wind-blown rain and through the movement of insects, animals and man, especially when the foliage is moist (Buruchara, 2010). Frequent showers, particularly those accompanied by driving winds and cool temperature, highly favour further disease development in the field and subsequent pod and seed infections that can bring on epidemics (Goodwin, 2003; Yusuf and Sangchote, 2005; Kumar *et al.*, 1999).

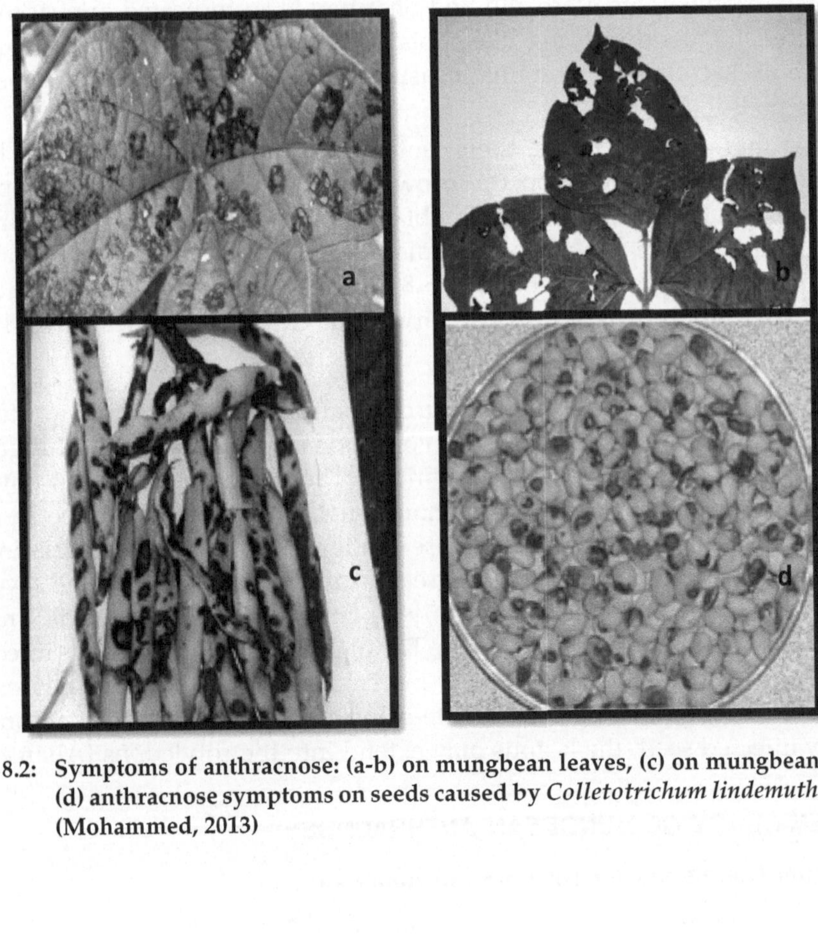

Fig. 8.2: Symptoms of anthracnose: (a-b) on mungbean leaves, (c) on mungbean pods, (d) anthracnose symptoms on seeds caused by *Colletotrichum lindemuthianum* (Mohammed, 2013)

Table 8.1: Reaction of Mungbean Genotypes Against Anthracnose Under Field Conditions

Disease Score	Disease Reaction	Name of the Genotypes
0	Immune	Nil
1	Resistant	LGG-460 and TMV-37
3	Moderately resistant	GM-9926
5	Moderately susceptible	PDM-262, PDM-11, PDM 84-143, IPM 02-3 RED, PDM-87, PDM-139, IPM 02- 14, BRS-2435, SAPTARI LOCAL, K-851, GM - 02-06, GM - 02-08, GM - 02-09, GM - 02-10, GM - 02- 14, GM - 02-16, GM - 0 2-17, GM - 02-19, GM - 02-21, GM - 03-04, GM - 03-08, GM - 03-11, GM - 03-12, GM - 03-15 and GM - 03-16
7	Susceptible	PDM-288, IPM 02-1, IPM 99-125, MEHA, IR-16, GM-3, GM- 4, GM-9703, GM – 9917, GM - 9918, GM – 9925, GM – 9926, GM - 02-01, GM - 02-02, GM - 02- 03, GM - 02-04, GM - 02-05, GM - 02-07, GM - 02-11, GM - 02-12, GM - 02-13, GM- 02-15, GM - 02-18, GM - 02-20, GM - 03-01, GM - 03-02, GM - 03-03, GM - 03-05, GM - 03-06, GM - 03-07, GM - 03-09, GM - 03-10, GM - 03-13 and GM - 03-14
9	Highly susceptible	GM- 9705, GM - 2k-5 and GM - 2k-14

(Yadav and Panday, 2014)

EFFECT OF TEMPERATURE

Among the external factors, temperature is an important factor governing distribution, growth, reproduction and survival of the fungus. Temperature affects almost every function of fungi including the growth and sporulation. Temperature has profound effect on the vegetative and reproductive activity of the fungi. Temperature plays an important role in infection and disease development. An effort was made to know the optimum temperature for the growth and sporulation. In the present study, it was observed that maximum fungal growth and sporulation of *C. truncatum* was recorded at 30°C followed by 25°C and it was least at 40°C. Ahmed (1982) reported that optimum temperature for growth and sporulation of *C. capsici* was found to be 30°C, whereas temperature of 5, 10 and 40°C did not favour growth of the fungus. Optimum range of temperature for the growth of *C. truncatum* as 25 to 30°C (Laxman, 2006; He Fan *et al.*, 2010; Hubballi *et al.*, 2010; Thangamani *et al.*, 2011). However, maximum growth of fungus was recorded at 30°C. In the present study, the excellent fungal growth and sporulation was observed at 30°C followed by 25°C. Hence, the temperature range of 25 to 30°C can be recommended to obtain excellent fungal growth and sporulation of *C. truncatum*.

EFFECT OF pH

Any living organism requires a particular medium for the growth and development. The pH of the media should be optimum for growth. A wide range of pH supported the growth of *C. truncatum*. Good growth was found at a range of 5.5 to 7.0 pH. The sporulation was also influenced by the pH and is known to play a crucial role. The excellent sporulation was found in 6.0 and 6.5 pH and good sporulation was noticed at 5.5 and 7.0 pH (Angadi, 1999; Laxman, 2006; Tao JinHua *et al.*, 2006; He Fan *et al.*, 2010; Kumara *et al.*, 2008; Satpathy *et al.*, 2012). Boyette *et al.* (2012) studied several factors influencing the conidial germination and pathogenicity of *Colletotrichum truncatum*. The conidia were germinated on 2% water agar over pH (3.5 to 9.0) and the optimal pH for the germination depended on the specific buffer used. Citrate and acetate buffers of low pH inhibited the germination.

The optimum pH range was obtained towards acidic pH side and sudden decline were observed towards basic pH side which indicated that fungus was acid tolerant. Cochrane (1958) and Bilgrami and Verma (1978) also opined that in contrast to bacteria and actinomycetes are relatively more tolerant to acid ions (H^+) than basic ions (OH^-). Hence, it can be recommended that to obtain good growth and sporulation of *C. truncatum*, the pH level from 5.5 to 7.0 can be maintained in the culture.

EFFECT OF LIGHT

Light is also playing an important role in disease development. Alternate cycles of light and darkness, as well as the continuous darkness supported maximum growth and excellent sporulation of the pathogen. However, maximum fungal growth was recorded in the treatment of alternate cycles of light and darkness, whereas least growth and sporulation was recorded in culture exposed to continuous light (Shirshikar, 1995; Kaushal *et al.*, 1998; Varaprasad, 2000; Thangamani *et al.*, 2012). He Fan *et al.* (2010) studied biological characterization of the pathogen isolated from papaya (*Carica papaya* L.) fruit induced by anthracnose. The results showed that for the pathogen *Colletotrichum gloeosporioides* Penz. the condition of constant darkness and light-dark alternation were effective for mycelial growth. Hubballi *et al.* (2010) collected ten isolates of *Colletotrichum gloeosporioides* from different noni growing areas of Tamil Nadu, Karnataka and Kerala in India and their pathogenicity was proved under glass house conditions and reported that exposure of the fungus to alternate cycles of 12 h light and 12 h darkness resulted in the maximum mycelial growth of *C. gloeosporioides* compared to the 24 h exposure to continuous light and 24 h exposure to continuous dark.

CONTROL OF MUNGBEAN ANTHRACNOSE DISEASE

Anthracnose is an important disease of mungbean. Many factors including seed transmissibility of the disease, survival ability of the causal fungus to up to 22 months in the crop residues coupled with occasional sclerotia development by the pathogen, and lack of cost effective chemical control method are some of the constraints that limit effective control of the disease. In an experiment to check the advancement of anthracnose of mungbean, several control strategies cutting across seed treatment, cultural measures, sanitation procedures, fungicide spraying and use of resistant cultivars have been employed . Such cultural method involves the use of clean seeds, field sanitation whereby previous mungbean residues are deeply buried or properly destroyed by burning, crop rotation with non-host crops of the disease, mixed or intercropping and destruction of alternate weed hosts of the pathogens among others (Awurum et al., 2001; Than et al., 2008). These and many other cultural practices are mainly prophylactic. They may not effectively check the disease during epidemics and thus, a significant drawback (Enyiukwu et al., 2014).

CULTURAL CONTROL

Infested mungbean debris should be removed or buried in the soil after harvest to reduce winter survival. The spores, present in diseased spots as a sticky mass, are more easily spread from diseased plants to healthy ones when plant parts are wet. Cleaning and bagging stations in areas where anthracnose may be play as sources of contaminated dust. Therefore, these stations should be cleaned from debris between shipments and the shipments isolated. Seed storage materials should also be disinfected and agricultural materials which are commonly used (leather, rubber, painted metal and denim) should also be disinfected. For this, a 10 percent bleach solution (0.525% sodium hypochlorite), followed by chlorine dioxide (Aquacare) and chloroxylenol (Dettol) was found to be the most effective (Buruchara *et al.*, 2010). Seeds produced under wet and humid conditions should not be use for sowing purpose because in most cases, they harbor the pathogen inside their seed coat (Sicard *et al.*, 1997). Seeds should not be stored for sowing purpose from previously infected fields with anthracnose (Bush, 2009). Thus, the production of disease free seeds in semi-arid areas, where conditions are not favourable for anthracnose infection could play vital role. A two-year crop rotation is highly recommended to minimize the chance of survival, and it can be done with non-host plants like cereals and *solanaceous* crops (Buruchara *et al.*, 2010). Rotation of non-host crop species may reduce the development of mungbean anthracnose mainly due to the reduction of initial infection that arises from the initial inoculum source.

Others cultural methods like screening the fields weekly for symptoms of anthracnose is recommended so that seeds from infected plants are not harvested (Batureine, 2009). Ensuring adequate plant spacing which promotes foliar drying (Bush, 2009), weed control will provide proper aeration and decrease moisture in the foliar canopy (Bush, 2009). Avoid sowing before the recommended planting dates, because cool conditions favour anthracnose development (Bush, 2009). Overhead irrigation should also be avoided, since it will liberate fungal spore masses on foliage (Buruchara *et al.*, 2010).

PHYSICAL METHODS

Soil solarization by covering the soil with transparent plastic sheet for one month before sowing resulted in the reduction of severity and incidence of anthracnose (Mohammad *et al.*, 2013). A hot-water seed treatment by soaking at 64 to 72°F for 15 hours followed by another soaking at 117°F for 25 minutes has been reported to kill the fungus in infested seeds without reducing germination (Bush, 2009).

BIOLOGICAL CONTROL

Seed dressing or application of spore suspension of *Trichoderma viride* as seed dip and soil drench was effective against seed borne infection of *C. lindemuthianum* reported by various workers (Bankole and Adebjano, 1996). A strong local protection against mungbean anthracnose was also obtained when susceptible mungbean leaves were treated with *Trichoderma harzianum* in a liquid mediu. Smearing infected seeds with cultures of *T. harzianum, T. viridae, T. hamatum* and *Gliocladium virens* for 15min and drying them overnight before sowing significantly inhibited infection of *C. lindemuthianum* and increased seed germination (Padder and Sharma, 2010). The main antagonistic activities of these bio-agents were through, mycellial growth inhibition, toxic volatile metabolite production and inhibition of spore germination (Anitha and Murugesan, 2001). Some plant extracts (botanicals) also showed promising results in the control of bean anthracnose of common beans. Neem (*Azadirachta indica*) seed extract effectively inhibited both germination of conidia and mycelial growth of *C. lindemuthianum* (Onifade, 2000). Seed treatment and field spray using the extracts of *Lawsonia inermis* significantly improved seedling emergence and reduced incidence of bean anthracnose (Ravi *et al.*, 2000).

HOST PLANT RESISTANCE

Resistance is the most effective and efficient method of anthracnose management (Esteban *et al.*, 2003). However, this has been complicated by the presence of several forms or races of the fungus, and the fact that plants resistant to one race may be susceptible to another. In the common bean *C. lindemuthianum* interaction, nine resistance genes have been reported so far in different parts of the world (Kelly and Young, 1996). Cultivars AB 136 and G 2333 could be used as sources of resistance in the bean breeding programme since they are found to be highly resistant or immune to different races of *C. lindemuthianum* found in Africa, North and Central America (Gonjalez *et al.*, 1998; Mahuku *et al.*, 2000). Cultivar mixtures containing at least 60% of a resistant cultivar have been reported to offer a good control of anthracnose (Beshir, 2003). Although planting resistant cultivars is the most effective, least expensive, and easiest for farmers to adopt (Pastor-Corrales *et al.*, 1995) the possible breakdown of resistance due to adaptation of the pathogen is the main drawback for its application. Varieties must be tested where they are to be grown to determine their tolerance to the locally prevalent races.

CHEMICAL CONTROL

Benlate (500 g a.i./kg WP) as a seed dressing at a rate of 2g/kg seed, difenoconazole (250 ml a.i./EC) at a rate of 87.5 g a.i./ha as a foliar spray and Benlate (500 g a.i./kg WP) seed dressing at a rate of 2 g/kg seed followed by foliar spray of difenoconazole (250 ml a.i./EC) at a rate of 87.5 g a.i./ha effectively reduced anthracnose severity and incidence and increased the yield per plot and 100 g seed weight (Beshir, 2003). Mancozeb seed treatment at a rate of 3g/kg seeds followed by carbendazim foliar spray at a rate of 0.5 kg/ha and Carbendazim seed treatment at a rate of 2g/kg seeds followed by carbendazim foliar spray at a rate of 0.5 kg/ha have been suggested to reduce anthracnose severity and incidence (Mohammad *et al.*, 2013).

INTEGRATED DISEASE MANAGEMENT

Bharadwaj and Thakur (1991) conducted field trials, where they used carbendazim (0.1%), captafol (0.25%) and mancozeb (0.25%) applied alone as single sprays at 60 days, two sprays at 45 and 60 days or three sprays at 45, 60 and 75 days or in sequence one after the other on a three sprays schedule at 45, 60 and 75 days after sowing for the control of leaf spot and pod blight of urdbean, caused by *C. dematium* f. sp. *truncatum*. All three fungicides reduced the disease severity on foliage, however, three sprays schedule was found more effective than the single or two spray carbendazim than mancozeb or captan. Laxman (2006) studied the efficacy of different fungicides and biorationals under field condition against greengram anthracnose and found that among different treatment, the least disease incidence was observed in propiconazole followed by hexaconazole and carbendazim. But, in case of biorationals, the least disease incidence was noticed in azadirachtin. *C. lindemuthianum* has high pathogenic variability and new races of the pathogen are reported frequently. Thus, integrated disease management is considered the most effective approach to minimize the yield losses to anthracnose (Menezes and Dianese, 1988). The integration of soil solarization, Mancozeb seed treatment at a rate of 3 g/kg seeds and Carbendazim foliar spray at a rate of 0.5 kg/ha were found to be effective in reducing bean anthracnose epidemics (Mohammad *et al.*, 2013). In case of chilli anthracnose caused by *C. capsici* the minimum disease intensity 19.67 % was recorded in carbendazim 0.05 % which was statistically at par with spraying of 0.2 % mancozeb (20.71 %), 0.2 % carbendazim + mancozeb (22.51 %) and 0.2 % copper oxychloride (23.16 %) (Chauhan *et al.*, 2014). Deeksha and

Tripathi (2002) studied on management of blackgram anthracnose and found that seed treatment followed by two prophylactic sprays of bavistin or tilt @ 0.1% each at 15 days interval showed minimum disease severity and maximum grain yield followed by contaf (0.1%) and Indofil M-45 (0.2%) sprayed plots. Botanicals and biopesticides (10% extracts of *Adenocalymma alliaceae, Azadirachta indica* and Lawsonia inermis, 0.4% talc formulation of *T. viride* and *Pseudomonas fluorescens* along with fungicides (Carbendazim (0.2%) and Mancozeb (0.4%) were evaluated in a greenhouse and field experiment in India and gave promising results (Ravi *et al.*, 2000).

CONCLUSION

Isolates of *C. truncatum* have shown differential response for the parameters *viz.* light, media pH and temperature regimes in respect of growth and sporulation. The optimum temperatures for maximum growth of *C. truncatum* were 28°C followed by 32°C with 6.0 media pH. Thus, the *C. truncatum* pathogen can grow maximum under the temperature ranging 25 to 30°C with media pH of 5.5 to 7.0. Thus it may be concluded that the temperature and media pH are the critical factors for the growth of pathogen, which might be the main reason for the expression of mungbean anthracnose symptoms under field conditions in various parts of India. Mungbean is important dietary components of India and other tropical countires. Anthracnose no doubt is one of the major constraints to its efficient production especially in India. Managing its yield and grain quality reducing disease involves a number of strategies. Managing the disease for sustainable mungbean grain production in the overall, should be holistic; taking into account integrated approach since no one control strategy is grossly effective at all times and conditions. Integrated management of mungbean anthracnose under tropical conditions requires knowledge of the biology of the pathosystem and the technologies available for control, their economical feasibility, and ecological acceptability.

REFERENCES

Agarwal, S.C. (1991): Diseases of Greengram and Blackgram, *International Book Distributors*, Dehradoon, pp: 321.

Ahmed, S.S. 1982. Studies on Seed borne Aspects of Anthracnose of Chillies Caused by *Colletotrichum capsici* (Sydow) Butler and Bisby. *M. Sc. (Agri.) Thesis*, Univ. Agric. Sci., Bangalore, Karnataka, India.

Ali, M. and Kumar, S. (2005): Pulses Yet to See a Break Through. *In Hindu Survey of Indian Agri.*, pp. 54-56.

Alien, D.J., Ampofo, J.K.O, Wortman, C.S. (1996): Pest, Disease, and Nutritional Disorders of the Common Bean in Africa: A Field Guide. *Centro International de Agricultura Tropical*, Cali Colombia.

Allen, D.J. (1983): The Pathology of Tropical Food Legumes: Disease Resistance in Crop Improvement. *John Wiley and Sons Inc*, New York.

Anderson, K.L., Buchwaldt, L., Chongo, G. and Gossen, B.D. (1999): Diseases of Lentil in Saskatchewan. *Can. Plant Dis. Surv.* 79: 127-128.

Angadi, H.D. (1999): Studies on Anthracnose of Chilli (*Capsicum annum*) and its Management. *M.Sc. (Agri.) Thesis*, Univ. Agric. Sci., Bangalore, Karnataka, India.

Anonymous, (2012): Project Co-ordinator's Report AICRP on MULLaRP Crops, IIPR, Kanpur.

Awgichew, K. (1982): Additional Index of Plant Disease in Ethiopia, Institute of Agricultural Research, Addis Ababa, Ethiopia.

Bailey, J.A., O'Connell, R.J., Nash, C. (1992): Infection Strategy of *Colletotrichum lindemuthiamun* Species. In: Bailey, J.A. and Jeger, M.J. (eds.). Colletotrichum: Biology, Pathology and Control CAB International, Wallingford, UK.

Bassanezi, R.B., Amorin, L., Filho, A.B., Hau, B. and Berger, R.D. (2001): Accounting for Photosynthetic Efficiency of Bean Leaves with Rust, Angular Leaf Spot and Anthracnose to Assess Crop Damage. *Plant Pathol*, 50: 443-452.

Bellar, M., and Kebabeh, S. (1983): A List of Diseases, Injuries, and Parasitic Weeds of Lentils in Syria (Survey 1979-1980). *LENS Newsl,* 10: 30-31.

Beshir, T. (2003): Biology and Control of Bean Anthracnose in Ethiopia. A Ph.D Thesis Submitted to the Faculty of Natural and Agricultural Ciences, University of Free State. Bloemfontein, South Africa.

Bharadwaj, C.L. and Singh, B.M., (1986): Strain Variation in *Colletotrichum dematium* f. sp. *truncatum* from Four Leguminous Hosts. *Indian J. Mycol. Plant Pathol,* 16: 139-141.

Bharadwaj, C.L. and Thakur, D.R. (1991): Efficacy and Economics of Fungicide Spray Schedules for Control of Leaf Spots and Pod Blights in Urdbean. *Indian Phytopath,* 44 (4): 470-475.

Bilgarami, K.S. and Verma, R.N. (1978): *Physiology of Fungi*, Vikas Publishing House Pvt. Ltd., New Delhi, pp: 498.

Boyette, C.D. and Hoagland, R.E. (2012): Interactions of Chemical Additives, pH and Temperature on Conidia Germination and Virulence of *Colletotrichum truncatum*, a Bioherbicide of *Sesbania exaltata. Allelopathy Journal,* 30 (1): 103-116.

Buruchara, R., Mukankusi, C. and Ampofo, K. (2010): Bean Diseases and Pest Identification and Management. Kampala, UG: International Center for Tropical Agriculture (CIAT); Pan-African Bean Research Alliance (PABRA)-Handbook for Small Scale Seed Producers.

Chauhan, Y.B., Patel, R.L., Chaudhary, R.F. and Rathod, N.K. (2014). Efficacy of Different Fungicides for the Management of Chilli Anthracnose Caused by *Colletotrichum capsici. The Bioscan,* 9(1): 399-402.

CIAT (1997): Bean Programme Annual Report 1995. Working Document.

Cochrane (1958): *Physiology of Fungi*, John Wiley and Sons Inc., New York, pp: 524.

Damm, U., Woudenberg, J.H.C., Cannon, P.F. and Crous, P.W. (2009): *Colletotrichum* Species with Curved Conidia from Herbaceous Hosts. *Fungal Diversity*, 39: 45-87.

Deeksha, J. and Tripathi, H.S. (2002): Cultural, Biological and Chemical Control of Anthracnose of Urdbean. *J. Mycol. Pl. Path..,* 32 (1): 52-55.

Eriksson, O.E, Winka, K. (1998): Families and Higher Taxa of Ascomycota. *Myconet,* 1: 17-*24.*

Godoy, C.V., Carneiro, S.M.T.P.G., Lamauti, M.T., Pria, M.D. and Amorim, L. (1997): Diagramatic Scales for Bean Disease: Development and Validation. *Zeitschrift fUr Pflanzenkrankheiten und Pflanzenschutz*, 104: 336-345.

Goodwin, M. (2003): Crop Profile-Dry Beans (Including White and Colored) *Phaseolus vulgaris.*

Green, J.R., Pain, N.A., Cannell, M.E., Leckie, C.P. and McCready, S. (1995): Analysis of Differentiation and Development of the Specialized Infection Structures Formed by Biotrophic Fungal Plant Pathogens Using Monoclonal Antibodies. *Canadian J Botany*, 73: 408-417.

Hall, R. (1994): Compendium of Bean Diseases. (2nd edn.), The American Phytopathological Society, APS Press, St. Paul, Minnesota.

He Fan, Fan HongYan, Luo Ni and Tao TingYan (2010): Study on Identification and Biological Characterization of Pathogen (*Colletotrichum gloeosporioides* Penz.) from Papaya. *Southwest China Journal of Agricultural Sciences,* 23 (3): 752-755.

Heath, M.C, Skalamera, D. (1997): Cellular Interaction Between Plants and Biotrophic Fungal Parasites. In: Tommerup IC, Andrews JH, ed. Academic Press. *Advances in Botany Research.* 24: 196.

Hiremath (1981): *Macrophomina* Stem Blight of Blackgram and its Effect in Some Varieties. *Curr. Res.,* 10 (1): 11-13.

http://www.ipmcenters.org/cropprofiles/docs/TNsnapbeans2012.pdf

Hubballi, M., Nakkeeran, S., Raguchander, T., Ananad, T. and Samiyappam, R. (2010): Effect of Environmental Conditions on Growth of Alternaria Alternata Causing Leaf Blight of Noni. *World J. Agricultural Sciences*, 6: 171-177.

Hughes, H.B., Carzaniga, R., Rawlings, S. L., Green, J. R. and O'Connell, R.J. (1999): Spore Surface Glycoproteins of Colletotrichum Lindemuthianum are Recognized by a Monoclonal Antibody which Inhibits Adhesion to Polystyrene. *Microbiology,* 145: 1927-1936.

Kaiser, W.J., Mihov, M., Muehlbauer, F.J. and Hanan, R.M. (1998): First Report of Anthracnose of Lentil Incited by *Colletotrichum truncatum* in Bulgaria. *Plant Dis,* 82: 128.

Kaushal, R.P., Kumar, A. and Tyagi, P.D. (1998): Role of Light, Temperature and Relative Humidity on Germination of *Colletotrichum truncatum* and Soybean Pod Infection Under Laboratory Conditions. *Journal of Mycology and Plant Pathology,* 28 (1): 1-4.

Kubo, Y., Furusawa, I. (1991): Melanin Biosyntheses: Pre-requisite for Successful Invasion of the Plant Host by Appressoria of *Colletotrichum* and *Pyricularia.* In: G.T. Cole & H.C. Hoch (Plenum, Eds). The Fungal Spore and Disease Initiation in Plants and Animals. New York.

Kumar A, Sharma PN, Sharma OP, Tyagi PD (1999): Epidemiology of Bean Anthracnose *Colletotrichum lindemuthianum* Under Sub-humid Mid-hills Zone of Himachal Pradesh. *Indian Phytopath.,* 52: 393-397.

Kumara, K.L.W. and Rawal, R.D. (2008): Influence of Carbon, Nitrogen, Temperature and pH on the Growth and Sporulation of Some Indian Isolates of *Colletotrichum gloeosporioides* Causing Anthracnose Disease of Papaya (*Carrica papaya* L). *Tropical Agricultural Research and Extension*, 11: 7-12.

Laxman, R. (2006): Studies on Leaf Spot of Greengram Caused by *Colletotrichum truncatum* (Schw.) Andrus and Moore. *M. Sc. (Agri.) Thesis*, Univ. Agric. Sci., Dharwad, Karnataka, India.

Majid, S. (1953): Annals Report of Department of Agriculture, Assam for Year Ending 31st March 1950. II. *The Grow More Food Campaign*, 11: 107.

Menezes, J.R. and Dianese, J.C. (1988): Race Characterization of Brazilian Isolates of *Colletotrichum lindemuthianum* and Detection of Resistance to Anthracnose in *Phaseolus vulgaris. Phytopathology,* 78: 650-655.

Mercure, E.W., Leite, B. and Nicholson, R.L. (1994): Adhesion of Ungerminated Conidia of *Colletotrichum graminicola* to Artificial Hydrophobic Surfaces. *Physiology and Molecular Plant Pathology*, 45: 421-440.

Mohammed, A., Ayalew, A. and Dechassa, N. (2013): Effect of Integrated Management of Bean Anthracnose (*Colletotrichum lindemuthianum* Sacc. and Magn.) Through Soil Solarization and Fungicide Applications on Epidemics of the Disease and Seed Health in Hararghe Highlands, Ethiopia. *J Plant Pathol Microb.*, 4: 182.

Morrall, R.A.A. 1988. A New Disease of Lentil Induced by *Colletotrichum truncatum* in Manitoba. *Plant Dis. Rep.* 72: 994.

Morrall, R.A.A. (1997): Evolution of Lentil Diseases Over 25 Years in Western Canada. *Can. J. Plant Pathol.,* 19: 197-207.

Morrall, R.A.A., and Pedersen, E.A. (1991): Discovery of Lentil Anthracnose in Saskatchewan in 1990. *Can. Plant Dis. Surv.,* 71: 105-106.

O'Connell, R.J. (1987): Absence of a Specialized Interface Between Intracellular Hyphae of *Colletotrichum lindemuthianum* and Cells of *Phaseolus vulgaris. New Phytopatologist*, 107: 725-734.

O'Connell, R.J., Pain, N.A., Hutchinson, K.A., Jones, G.L. and Green, J.R. (1996): Ultrastructure and Composition of the Cell Surfaces of Infection Structures Formed by the Fungal Plant Pathogen *Colletotrichum lindemuthianum. J Microscopy*, 181: 204-212.

O'Connell, R.J., Bailey, J.A. and Richmond, D.V. (1985): Cytology and Physiology of Infection of *Phaseolus vulgaris* by *Colletotrichum lindemuthianum. Physiol Plant Pathol.* 27: 75-98.

Pain, N.A., Green, J.R., Jones, G. L. and O'Connell, R. J. (1996): Composition and Organisation of Extracellular Matrices Around Germ Tubes and Appressoria of *Colletotrichum lindemuthianum. Protoplasma*, 190: 119-130.

Pastor-Corrales, M.A, Tu, J.C. (1989): Anthracnose. Schwartz HF, Pastor-Corrales MA eds. (2nd edn.), Bean Production Problems in the Tropics. CIAT, Cali, Colombia.

Rathaiah, Y. and Sharma, S.K. (2004): A New Leaf Spot Disease on Mungbean Caused by *Colletotrichum truncatum, J. Mycol. Pl. Path.,* 34 (2): 176-178.

Ravi, S., Sabitha, D., Valluvaparidasan, V. and Jayalakshmi, C. (2000): Production of *Colletotrichum lindemuthianum* Free French Bean Seeds. *Legume Research,* 23: 170-173.

Satpathy, M.R.., Beura, S.K. and Mohanty, R.C. (2012): Epidemiological Studies on Colletotrichum Lindemuthianum (Sacc. & Magn.) Scribber, the Incitant of Cowpea Anthracnose. *Journal of Mycopathological Research,* 50 (2): 329-331.

Saxena, R.M. and Gupta, J.S. (1981): Field Survey for Suspected Seed Transmitted Disease of Mungbean and Urdbean in Uttarpradesh. *Indian Phytopathol.,* 34 (3): 340-345.

Saxena, R.M. and Sinha, S. (1977): Seed Borne Infection of *Vigna mungo* in Uttar Pradesh. *Indian Phytopathol.,* 30 (4): 582-583.

Sela-Buurlage, M.B., Epstein, L. & Rodriguez, R.J. (1991): Adhesion of Ungerminates *Colletotrichum musae* Conidia. *Physiology and Molecular Plant Pathology.*, 39: 345-352.

Sharma, H.C., Khare, M.N., Joshi, L.K. and Kumar, S.M. (1971): Efficacy of Fungicides in the Control of Diseases of *Kharif* Pulses Mung and Urid. *All India Workshop on Kharif Pulses,* pp: 2.

Shirshikar, S.P. (1995): Studies on Seed Borne Nature and Cultural Aspects of *Colletotrichum truncatum* (Schw.) Andrus and Moore; Incitent of Anthracnose Disease of Soybean (*Glycine max* (L.) Merrill). *Ph.D. Thesis,* Univ. Agric. Sci., Bangalore, Karnataka, India.

Singh, R.R. and Shukla, P. (1988): *Colletotrichum* Leaf Blight of Blackgram. *Farm Sci. J.*, 3: 97-102.

Tao JinHua, Hu RuiLan, Chen FaHe and Feng ZuoShan (2006): Biological Characteristics of Loquat Anthrax Fungus (Colletotrichum Gloeosporioides Penz.). *Xinjiang Agricultural Sciences,* 43 (6): 472-476.

Thakur, M.P. and Khare, M.N. 1989. Evaluation of Mungbean Varieties for Resistance to Anthracnose. *Indian J. Plant Prot.,* 17 (1): 107-108.

Thangamani, P.R., Kuppusamy, P., Peeran, M.F., Gandhi, K. and Raguchander, T. (2011): Morphological and Physiological Characterization of Colletotrichum Musae the Causal Organism of Banana Anthracnose. *World Journal of Agricultural Sciences,* 7 (6): 743-754.

Tu, J.C. 1983. Epidemiology of Anthracnose Caused by *Colletotrichum lindemuthianum* on White Bean (Phaseolus vulgaris) in Southern Ontario: Survival of the Pathogen. *Plant Disease.* 67: 402-404.

Tu, J.C. and Aylesworth, J.W. (1980): An Effective Method of Screening White (pea) Bean Seedlings (*Phaseolus vulgaris* L.) for Resistance to *Colletotrichum lindemuthianum. Phytopathol.,* 99: 131-139.

Varaprasad, C.H. 2000. Studies on Blight Disease of Chickpea Caused by *Colletotrichum dematium* (Pers. Ex. Fr.) Grove. *M.Sc. (Agri.) Thesis*, Univ. Agric. Sci., Dharwad, Karnataka, India.

Ventte, J.R., Lamey, H.A. and Lamppa, R.L. (1994): First Report of Lentil Anthracnose (*Colletotrichum truncatum*) in the United States. *Plant Dis.,* 78: 1216.

Pages: 164-185

CROP PRODUCTIVITY AND PLANT DISEASE MANAGEMENT
Edited by: Dr. Alka Chauhan; Dr. Pawan Kumar 'Bharti'; Ms. Deepti Sadana
ISBN: 978-93-5056-791-3
Edition: 2016
Published by: Discovery Publishing House Pvt. Ltd., New Delhi (India)

CHAPTER – 9

Integrated Disease Management in India
An Overview

Sanjeev Kumar[1*] and **Archana Rani**[2]

INTRODUCTION

Plant diseases caused by a array of causal agents (fungi, bacteria, viruses, phytoplasmas and nematodes) is a group of biotic constraints that reduces crop yields worldwide. In India, from tropical to subtropical to temperate climates, crop losses are often elevated than in the developed countries, mainly because farming communities lack most proper solutions and resources dedicated to their study. As per the estimate by the Central Pollution Control Board of the Govt. of India, the highest food grain loss is due to weeds (28%), by diseases (25%), by insects (23%), during storage (10%), by rats (8%) and by others (6%). As reported by the Union Minister of Agriculture while responding to a starred question No. 62 in Rajya Sabha on 2 March 2007, the crop losses due to pests, diseases and weeds are approximately assessed to be ranging between 10-30% crop productions. If we consider, on a average, crop loss of 20%, and the present gross value of our agriculture

1 Office of Dean, Faculty of Agriculture, Jawaharlal Nehru Krishi Vishwa Vidyalaya, Krishi Nagar, Adhartal, Jabalpur - 482 004 (India)

2 Ph.D, Department of Agricultural Biotechnology and Molecular Biology, (FBS & H), Rajendra Agricultural University, Pusa - 848 125, Bihar (India)

produce as Rs. 7 lakh crore, the loss comes to Rs. 1,40,000 crore, which is very huge. Even if we could save 50 percent by using plant protection, it will add Rs. 70,000 core additional income to our farmers. At a same time, when all of us are concerned about National Food Security, can the country afford these losses? (Kumar and Gupta., 2012). The list of pathogens harmful to crops is large and extremely diverse. Crops can be attacked at different growth stages: at seedling establishment (root and seed rots), young seedlings (root and collar rots, seedling blights, wilts), pre-flowering (wilts, leaf blights, yellowing and mottling of the foliage, stunting), flowering (bud rots, flower blight), post flowering (rusts, blights) and post harvest (fruit rots). The same disease can induce diverse symptoms at different growth stages. Man made activities such as crop intensification and introduction of new crops or new cultivars of existing crops to new regions as well as changes in cropping practices, including plant breeding led to the development of serious epidemics around the globe, mainly because such activities could disturb the balance, which naturally existed for many generations (Buddenhagen, 1977).

Of late, application of pesticides was the dominant form of disease control in developed and, increasingly, in developing, countries like India. However, numerous tribulations have been associated with such an approach, such as the frequent emergence of fungicide resistance in pathogens and the detrimental effects of fungicides to human health and the environment. The concept of Integrated Disease Management (IDM), where diseases are managed by integrating a range of control methods and practices, is becoming more popular among farmers and researchers. IDM calls for minimal use of pesticides, and only if deemed obligatory, giving predilection to other control methods such as host-plant resistance, cultural practices and biological control. Even though the use of IDM strategy is well established and results obtained are encouraging, in practice and in the majority of cropping systems today, emphasis is still being placed on a single technology, may it be host-plant resistance, pesticide applications or cultural practices and rarely the combination of all (Thomas and Waage, 1996). The outcome of such practices is mostly not sustainable. Implementation of IDM in India is gaining momentum, but still requires more serious efforts to realize impact at the country or regional level. The implementation of IDM in India at present still follows a top-down approach, which is mainly linked to the traditional extension system. This does not provide farmers with the needed empowerment that is considered crucial for the development of sustainable IDM, nor does it provide the extension personnel, especially with the reduction in extension funding, with appropriate knowledge and skills needed to achieve that objective. This paper intend to summarize the developing IDM strategies and their components for major crops in India, the constraints for their wide use and training needs which are essential for their large scale implementation.

Justification for IDM

A unilateral approach using pesticides has limitations; thus a socially acceptable and economically practical approach to crop protection is needed. What are the problems with pesticides?

- Economic and energy costs
- Resistance to pesticides
- Disruption of natural control
- Target pest resurgence
- Induced secondary pest outbreaks
- Human health hazards acute and chronic effects user and consumer risks
- Environmental pollution and effects on wildlife
- Effects on pollinators

Definitions of IDM

"Selection, integration, and implementation of disease control based on predicted economic, ecological, and sociological consequences".

"A comprehensive approach to disease control that uses combined means to reduce the status of disease to tolerable levels while maintaining a quality environment".

"The optimization of disease control in an economically and ecologically sound manner, accomplished by the coordinated use of multiple tactics to assure stable crop production and to maintain disease loss below the economic injury level while minimizing risks to man and the environment".

"A sustainable approach to manage diseases by combining biological, cultural, physical and chemical tools in a way that minimizes economic, health and environmental risks".

Objective of IDM

The basic objectives of any IDM programme should be to achieve at least the following:

- Reduce the possibility of introducing diseases into the crop
- Avoid creating conditions suitable for disease establishment and spread
- Simultaneous management of multiple pathogens
- Regular monitoring of pathogen effects, and their natural enemies and antagonists aswell
- Use of economic or treatment thresholds when applying chemicals
- Integrated use of multiple, suppressive tactics.

Concept of IDM

IDM is not implemented in isolation from other management activities; rather, it is one component of the total crop production system of physical, biological, and management functions all interacting to determine the yield of a cultivated crop. Thus, IPM, like nutrient management, is a component of integrated crop management (lCM).

Integrated means that a broad interdisciplinary approach is taken using scientific principles of crop protection to combine into a single cropping system a variety of management strategies and tactics to reduce pest populations.

Strategies are the general approaches used to implement coordinated systems of multiple tactics. Examples are containment, preventive, corrective or remedial, and eradication.

Tactics are the specific methods used to achieve pest control. These include cultural, biological, physical, genetic, chemical, and regulatory procedures.

Management implies a process by which information is collected and used to make good management decisions to reduce losses from disease in a planned, coordinated way. IDM requires a more tolerant management approach than traditional pesticide based programmes. Eradicating all diseases from a crop is the not the objective IDM emphasizes disease suppression rather than eradication. This approach allow for the conservation of natural control factors and the establishment of a pest refuge for resistance management.

Disease: Disease is one of those terms that are very difficult to define. It is realized that disease (literally dis-ease) implies lack of 'comfort' and therefore, involves deviation form normal functioning. From time to time several definitions which have been proposed, Das Gupta (1977) defined disease as a malfunctioning process involving more or less continuous interaction between host and pathogen occurring through a large number of quantitative changes between qualitative states of healthy and diseasesd conditions.

Major Underlying Principles of IDM:

- The **management unit is the agroecosystem** and any management action may produce unexpected and undesirable effects – this notion forms the basis of the systems or holistic approach to IDM.
- **Any disease exists at some tolerable level** – this notion forms the basis of the economic injury level concept.
- **Natural control factors regulate disease index and are maximized** in IDM as the primary means of management; if this strategy fail to maintain disease index below economic levels, then pesticides in combination with other tactics are used as a last resort.
- **Less than 100% control is desirable to leave a permanent pest/disease residue** for natural enemies and as a refuge for susceptible pests/dseases to reduce the chances of resistance development.

Why should we adopt IDM

- To avoid the collapse of control system based on single technology.
- To avoid disease control to enter exploitation, crisis and disaster phage.
- **Explotation phage**: The disease control programme is dependent solely on chemical pesticides which are exploited to the maximum resulting in high yield.
- **Crisis phage**: After many years of in exploitation phage and heavy use of pesticides resistance, pathogen resurgence and out break of secondary diseases occur which increases the production cost.
- **Disaster phage**: The use of pesticide increases the cost of production to the point where crop could no longer be grown profitably. High residue of pesticide in the food makes the produce unacceptable to consumers.

Currently most control is in exploitation phage and IDM should be quickly adopted to avoid the crisis and disaster phage

Advantages

Integrated approach integrates preventive and corrective measures to keep pathogen from causing significant problems, with minimum risk or hazard to human and desirable components of their environment. Some of the benefits of an integrated approach are as follows:

- Promotes sound structures and healthy plants
- Promotes the sustainable bio based disease management alternatives.
- Reduces the environmental risk associated with management by encouraging the adoption of more ecologically benign control tactics
- Reduces the potential for air and ground water contamination
- Protects the non-target species through reduced impact of plant disease management activities.
- Reduces the need for pesticides and fungicides by using several management methods.
- Reduces or eliminates issues related to pesticide residue
- Reduces or eliminates re-entry interval restrictions
- Decreases workers, tenants and public exposure to chemicals
- Alleviates concern of the public about pest & pesticide related practices.
- Maintains or increases the cost-effectiveness of disease management programmes

COMPONENTS OF IDM

The major components of disease management summarized here are: host-plant resistance, cultural practices, biological control and chemical control. Even though these components will be dealt with individually, it should be mentioned that often the different components are complementary to each other with strong interaction among and between them and the environment and that it is essential to break away from relying on a single-technology and to adopt a more ecological approach built around a fundamental understanding of population biology at the local farm level and to rely on the integration of control components which are readily available to the resource-poor farmers (Thomas, 1999).

Acceptable Pest Level

IDM holds that eradication or wiping out the entire population is impossible. Therefore, the emphasis should be on keeping the pathogen population at an acceptable level that is achievable, economically affordable and environmentally safe.

Monitoring Pathogens

As mentioned, monitoring is a critical component of an effective IPM programme. Monitoring can be direct (looking for the pathogen or disease) or indirect (recording environmental conditions that affect disease development). Financial considerations weigh heavily in the choice of monitoring practices. Direct disease monitoring can be based on symptoms or signs of the pathogen. Pathogen identification is generally difficult because they are usually microscopic and can be detected typically after the disease process has begun. Most monitoring is actually for disease symptoms, with the control strategy aimed at reducing further spread. Even when visible symptoms are evident, disease levels may be so low as to make detection very difficult.

To optimize the chances of detection, one should concentrate on those areas where disease is most likely to occur; for example, low areas or areas of lush growth. If this is not possible, an array of sampling designs may be used, such as a diagonal across the field, a random walk, a stratified design where each subsection of the field is sampled, or a stratified random design where a random sample is taken in each subsection of the field. The appropriate sampling design depends on the level of disease expected, the distribution of the disease, and sampling schemes already in place for other pests. Disease distribution within a field is dependent, in large part, on the source of inoculum for the pathogen. If the disease is seed-borne, in many cases the first diseased plants are more uniformly distributed in the field. If the disease is soilborne, it may often be found in clusters in the field.

If insects transmit the disease, the distribution may be more random, or a field edge effect may be apparent. Thus, it is important to understand the pathogen's biology when developing an appropriate sampling strategy for it.Indirect disease monitoring most often involves stand-alone computer systems with probes or whole units in the field. Data commonly gathered include temperature, relative humidity, and leaf wetness and can be used to update real-time indices of disease likelihood at a given time. The algorithms for the models are often developed from controlled environmental chamber experiments where the minimum, maximum, and optimal temperatures and relative humidity for fungal growth, germination, and/or disease development are identified. Leaf wetness, either monitored directly or by predicting dew point based on the relative humidity and temperature conditions, is used if the pathogen requires free water for germination. Predicting disease events through environmental monitoring has been very successful in a few cases and is used widely for those crops and diseases where sufficient research exists.

Host-plant Resistance

First major component under IDM is the use resistant or tolerant varieties. Swaminathan, M.S., noted Indian agriculture scientist, stated undoubtedly the most attractive form of defense is provided by disease resistance, for as long as it remains effective it provides protection at no cost to the farmer or the community. Host plant resistance is an imperative tool to manage diseases of major food crops in India, especially rice, wheat, chickpea, pigeonpea and cowpea etc.. The use of resistant varieties is very much welcomed by under privileged farmers as it does not need added cost and it is eco-friendly. The resistance is often durable, thanks to proper management of genetic diversity by employing gene rotation, multilines and cultivar mixtures, a strategy that proved effective in reducing disease damage in natural ecosystems (Wolf, 1985).

Such success stimulated interest in extending the principles of genetic diversity for disease control to other crops in India. Late blight is considered as one of the most vital biotic impediment for potato production in India. Usually this disease is managed by numerous fungicide spays, but the emergence of fungicide resistance in many locations and the escalating cost of their application, encouraged the look for other management strategies. The development of high yielding varieties resistant to late blight with acceptable quality such as 'Kufri Badshah, Kufri Jyoti, Kufri Jawahar, Kufri Chipsona-1, Kufri Chipsona-2, Kufri Pukhraj, Kufri Megha, Kufri Giriraj, Kufri Sherpa, and Kufri Himalini was very much welcomed by the farming community in India.

Late leaf spot caused by *Phaeoisariopsis personata* and rust caused by *Puccinia arachidis* are two most destructive foliar diseases of peanut worldwide. Host plant resistance has been used recently as one control component and a number of peanut cultivars such as ICGV 89104 and ICGV 91114 are now available. Field trials conducted in India showed that these cultivars yield 55-60% more than local cultivar, and the severity of both diseases is significantly lower in these than in the local cultivar (Pande *et al.*, 2001). Similarly, peanut varieties resistant to peanut rosette virus disease which causes serious losses in Africa have been developed (Reddy, 1998). So Intensive research in needed in India in this line because HPR is the basic component to which other components can be integrated.

Cultural Practices

Cultural practices serve an important role in integrated disease management. Cultural practices such as cultivation techniques, mulching, intercropping, plant density, planting date, crop rotation, strip farming, timing of harvest, barrier crops, crop mixtures, rouging, healthy planting material, soil solarization, soil amendments and fertilizer management, andwater management have been used singly and in combination as tools for disease management. The benefits of cultural control begin with the establishment of a growing environment that favors the crop over the pathogen. Reducing plant stress through environmental modification promotes good plant health and aids in reducing damage from some plant diseases.

Sanitation practices aimed at excluding, reducing, or eliminating pathogen populations are critical for management of infectious plant diseases. It is important to use only pathogen-free transplants. In order to reduce dispersal of soilborne pathogens between fields, stakes and farm equipment should be decontaminated before moving from one field to the next. Reduction of pathogen survival from one season to another may be achieved by crop rotation and destroying volunteer plants. Removal of cull piles and prompt crop destruction should be done as general practice. Avoid soil movement from one site to another to reduce the risk of moving pathogens. For example, sclerotia of *Sclerotinia sclerotiorum* and *Sclerotium rolfsii* are transported primarily in contaminated soil.

Minimizing wounds during harvest and packing reduces postharvest disease problems. Depending on crops and other factors, soil sanitation can be achieved to some degree by solarization. Crop rotation is a very important practice, especially for soilborne disease control. For many soilborne diseases, at least a 3-year rotation using a non-host crop greatly reduces pathogen populations. This practice is beneficial for Phytophthora blight of pepper and Fusarium wilt of watermelon, but longer rotation periods (up to 5-7 years) may be needed. Land previously cropped to alternate and reservoir hosts should be avoided whenever possible. Vegetable fields should be located as far away as possible from inoculum and insect vector sources. Weed control is important for the management of viral diseases.

Weeds may be alternate hosts for many important vegetable viruses. Eliminating weeds might reduce primary inoculum. Non-host cover crops help to reduce weed populations and primary inoculum of soilborne pathogens. Excessive handling of plants, such as in thinning, pruning, and tying, may be involved in spreading pathogens, particularly bacteria. It is advisable to handle plants in the field when plants are driest. Because some pathogens can only enter the host through wounds, situations that promote plant injury should be avoided.

During the pruning process and harvest, workers should periodically clean their hands and tools with a disinfectant, such as isopropyl alcohol. If applicable, plants can be staked and tied for improved air movement in the foliar canopy. A more open canopy results in less wetness, discouraging growth of most pathogens. Soil aeration and drying can be enhanced by incorporating composted organic amendments in the soil. The pathogen inoculum can be reduced by removing plant material (infected and healthy) after harvest. Between-row cover crops reduce plant injury from blowing sand.

Biological Control

Biological control has an important role to play in IDM for the effective management of diseases in an eco-friendly manner. Several hundred species of natural enemies have been recorded suppressing the diseases and pests in natural field conditions. Some of the important bioagents are *Trichoderma, Pseudomonas, Bacillus, Aspergillus* etc. Biocontrol can be achieved either by introducing biocontrol agents directly into natural ecosystem or by adopting practices, which favour population build up of biocontrol agents under natural conditions.

Combination of both the approaches is probably the best solution. Of late, there has been a tremendous progress in this area. Success in using microorganisms against plant pathogens started with the control of crown gall with *Agrobacterium radiobacter* K84 (Kerr, 1980), and that of seedling blights caused by *Pythium* and *Rhizoctonia* with *Trichoderma harizanum, Gliocaladium virens* and *Streptomyces griseus* (Cook *et al*., 1996). Biocontrol agents like *Trichdoerma* and *Pseudomonas* have multiple activities like antifungal, antinematode, symbiotic, plant growth promontory, plant defense inducing, composting phosphorus solubilization and probably anti weed. Plant growth promoting rhizobacteria like *Pseudomonas* with biocontrol ability play important role in controlling soil and seed borne and sometimes foliar disease. They are extremely useful in high humidity and water logged condition and in alkaline soils, where fungal biocontrol agents like *Trichoderma* spp. are less effective. They are useful for forestry, pulses and vegetable crops, particularly for nurseries and therefore now well accepted in organic farming and integrated disease management programme.

While it is unlikely that biological control will completely replace chemical pesticides in the foreseeable future, we can expect that there will be some decline in the use of chemicals, particularly in developed countries. Thus far, most approaches have involved the single antagonist concept, although a biological systems approach, where disease is suppressed from several angles, might provide a better alternative. Similarly, the use of biological control agents could be used as one component of an integrated management programme to achieve the best possible results.

Regulatory Measures

The use of quarantines and pest eradication programmes is essential to limit the introduction or spread of deleterious plant pests and/or patho-gens. Strict government inspections and quarantines of imported plants, plant products, and soil can be an effective way to keep a pest or pathogen out of a region or area. However, given the global nature of modern society, the possibility of moving and introducing pests dangerous to people, plants, and animals is real. Government eradication programmes are conducted when a serious insect or disease pest breaks out. Often the trouble is eliminated before it has a chance to spread. Such programmes require highly trained personnel who know the potential insect and disease problems and are able to recognize the pathogens and the symptoms of their activities. On the grower level, many greenhouses and nurseries also use quarantine measures. They often keep the new material separated from the old. If a disease were to come in on the new material it would not impact the rest of the greenhouse or nursery.

Chemical Control

The chemical pesticides will remain a major component of IDM. For many decades' fungicides played an important role in disease control. In the 1960s, systemic fungicides started gradually to replace the older non-systemic chemicals with more effectiveness and specificity in disease control. Very quickly, triazole fungicides gained 24% of the total fungicides market (Hewitt, 1998). However, the non-systemic fungicides such as mancozeb and chlorothalonil plus copper and sulpher-based products continued to have a good share of the market,especially in India because of their lower cost. More recently, new classes of fungicides were developed with significant impact on disease control.

These include anilinopyrimidines, phenoxyquinolines, oxazolidinediones, spiroketalamines, phenylpyrroles, strobilurins and activators of systemic acquired resistance. However, the development of pathogen populations showing reduced sensitivity to many of the newly developed products posed a serious challenge that the traditional fungicides (e.g. sulpher, folpet, etc.) did not face. The availability of a variety of new products, with narrow and broad specificity, offer important disease control options, however, their practical application continues to face the risk of selection of resistant pathogen populations (Gullino *et al.*, 2000). Experience accumulated over the last few decades clearly showed that fungicidal application had a better impact when used within an IDM strategy (De Waard *et al.*, 1993). In addition, public concern has increasingly influenced the fungicide industry in developing effective products with low mammalian toxicity and environmental impact and low residues in food, to meet international health standards and compatibility in integrated pest management programmes (Knight *et al.*, 1997).

Why the Implementation of IDM at Farmers' Level is Limited in India

- Precise and standard surveillance and monitoring methods are yet to be worked out.
- Preventive measures like summer ploughing, proper showing dates, use of trap crops, crop barriers, collection of damaged parts of plant and their destruction etc. are normally not practiced by farmers.
- Dearth of disease resistant as well as multiple disease resistant varieties is a felt need. Though there is Bt. Cotton, but genetically engineered seeds of other crops are not commercially available.
- ETLs have not been worked out for all diseases/pests for different crops region- wise.
- Non availability of timely inputs like biopesticides. Quality control is another problem associated with biocontrol agents, particularly with fungal antagonist and viral preparations.
- Non availability of timely inputs like biopesticides.
- Quality control is another problem associated with biocontrol agents, mainly with fungal antagonist and viral preparations.
- There is a false notion that IDM means no pesticides, where as just the reverse is true, IDM cannot go without pesticides. Many countries which have already adopted IDM are still using maximum quantity of pesticides.
- Selective pesticides, which are effective against crop disease and pests and safe against natural enemies, are still not very much available.
- Forecasting and forewarning models are also lacking.
- The techniques of mass production of several potential bio-control agents are still not well developed.
- Concentrations of pesticide spray material are never proper, being either above the required dose, which becomes phototoxic or leaves great residue, or most of the time it si sub lethal causing development of resistance in pathogens.
- Indian farmers are by and large, are less educated and have a different kind of social and cultural environment, which is also a constraint in introducing modern technology. The pace of human resource development to train extension officers and farmers should be given top most priority.

- A few demonstrations here and there in the country may not make much of the dent in acceptance of IDM by farmers, unless efforts for extension and large scale technology transfer at field level are ensured. A strong infrastructure, including dedicated barefoot extension workers, is required. The relatively low status of plant protection workers in the administrative hierarchy is also a constraint to general improvement in IDM.
- Institutional constraints are also a feature. Fragmentation between disciplines, between research, extension and implementation and between institutes, all lead to a lack of institutional integration.
- Even if the IDM is adopted in principle, the funding for research, extension and accelerated training of farmers is a major constraint. In fact IDM should be taken as an investment like any other form of investment.

SUGGESTIVE MEASURES FOR SUCCESSFUL IMPLEMENTATION OF IDM STRATEGIES

The eventual aim of promoting IDM is to empower its users to engage sustainable agricultural production with long-term affirmative impacts on human, poverty and environmental health. The impact of successful implementation of IDM approaches beyond pilot scale cannot be achieved if IDM is not strategically positioned within national policies for agricultural production and protection, and within the broader context of agricultural and rural development, and human and environmental health (SP-IPM, 2008). There are a number of the national policies and related regulations that have direct impact on IDM adoption and scaling up in India. This can be summarized as follows:

Technical Efficacy

For IDM to be a success, it ought to be sound on technical and economic parameters. Technical feasibility of IDM is judged on two criteria: change in the pesticide use, and yield change over the conventional chemical control. As far as change in pesticide use is concerned, it is the basic goal of IDM to reduce pesticide use, and this evidence is well established under experimental as well as field conditions. Its effect on yield could be either way. Nevertheless, evidences presented in this study suggest substantial yield saving advantage of IDM over chemical control in food as well as non-food crops.

Economic Feasibility

Technical feasibility is a essential but not a adequate condition for commercialization and adoption of a technology. The necessary condition is the net benefits it entails to the producers over the conventional technology. Net benefits can be measured in terms of the difference in per hectare net revenue due to application of new technology and/or changes in unit cost of production. Studies suggest IDM as a cost-effective technology. The magnitude of net benefits however would depend on the type of input used in IDM package, its application rate and price. Evidences show that even under experimental conditions some technically feasible IDM packages turn out to be economically infeasible because of higher prices of some of its constituents.

COMMUNITY PARTICIPATION

Successful disease control demands collective efforts. Yet, most of the times disease control efforts are individualistic, giving rise to a number of disease control related problems, such as pest resistance, resurgence and secondary outbreak, destruction of natural enemies of pests. Collective disease management assumes greater significance in the context of IDM. There are a number of management practices such as observance of synchronicity in sowing dates, use of resistant varieties, crop rotations, etc. that require close cooperation among farmers to achieve maximum disease control efficiency. Further, IDM relies on inputs derived from living organisms, and the application of different control methods in a locality, in particular chemical pesticides, would adversely affect the activities of the biological inputs.

Though, a majority of the farmers could be aware of the benefits of collective action, a number of socio-economic factors act as a disincentive to participate in it. Birthal (2003) empirically examined the factors constraining community participation and found that social heterogeneity was the main hindrance. Further, the farmers applying IPM technologies were more willing to participate. The need therefore is to evolve institutional mechanisms that promote group action. The current concept of Farmers' Field School though is based on the principles of collective action; it is often observed that either the groups are not formed, or even if the groups are formed, they disappear once the programme is withdrawn.

Community participation is key to successful adoption of IDM, and needs to be sustained by devising an appropriate exit policy. Local bodies, such as Panchayats, Non-Governmental Organisations, Self Help Groups, etc. should be encouraged to shoulder this responsibility. Incentives and awards should be given to those farmers/groups who are following IDM/IPM approach.

SUPPLY OF BIOPESTICIDES

Biopesticides capture only 2 percent of the agrochemical market. Most of the production takes place in public sector units. So is their distribution. Of over 400 biocontrol laboratories in India, 70 percent are in the domain of public sector. Most of the laboratories are small and cater to the location-specific needs only of a small area. The average gross cropped area per biocontrol laboratory is large. This shows that production of biopesticides is thinly spread. However, the continental dimensions of the agricultural sector offer vast scope for expansion of biopesticide industry. Some inherent technical characteristics of bio-pesticides however act as disincentive to the entry of private sector. Unlike chemical pesticides, most of the bio-pesticides are not broad spectrum and are slow in action. Many of these like *Trichogramma* and *Trichoderma* have a short shelf-life, ranging from a few weeks to few months. Thus, production of biopesticides is fraught with risk. Other constraints in expansion of biopesticide industry are uncertain demand, and lack of appropriate infrastructure for transportation, storage and marketing. Rural unemployed and educated youths should be encouraged to establish small-scale biopesticide production units at village or block level. Measures, such as training to the potential entrepreneurs, provision of institutional credit, subsidies, insurance against low off take of inputs due to low pest infestation, and exemption from taxes and duties would stimulate production of biopesticides. Further, bio-pesticide manufacturing units are under strict registration and quality control requirements. The process of registration is cumbersome and costly, which discourages potential entrepreneurs. In view of the role of biopesticides in ecological conservation and human health safety, registration requirements should be relaxed, though without reconciliation with quality standards.

ECONOMIC INCENTIVES

Price of a technology is vital determinant in farmers' decision for its adoption. At present, bulk of the supply of biopesticides comes from public sector, often provided at subsidized prices under IPM programmes. The evidences show that benefits of adoption of IDM are marginally higher than the conventional chemical pest control . An increase in the price of biopesticides due to cost considerations or withdrawal of subsidies would upset the economics of IDM. Since biopesticides generate considerable social and environmental benefits, the government should think of classifying them into 'green box' for provision of subsidies. Simultaneously, the incentives/ subsidies, if any, on synthetic pesticides be withdrawn and the resultant savings be diverted towards promotion of IDM. Linking of agricultural credit and insurance to IDM can also facilitate its faster diffusion. Withdrawal of subsidies on chemical pesticides and diversion of the same towards production and use of biopesticides, and linking institutional credit and insurance with IDM adoption would induce farmers switching over to IDM.

DEVELOPMENT OF MARKET FOR PESTICIDE-FREE PRODUCTS

Economic incentives may not be sustained for a long. An alternative is to develop markets for pesticide-free or low-pesticide residue produce by creating consumer awareness about health benefits of such produce. At present, there are no premium markets and standards for organic food in India. Since in the short-run there is a possibility of shortfall in yield on switching over to IDM, farmers even if they are willing to adopt IDM may not do so. In developed countries market for pesticide free products is developing and these products fetch premium prices. This however is lacking in India. This would require not only development of certification procedures and labeling system to gain confidence of the consumers. The cost of certification is high for an individual farmer. The cost can be brought down considerably if a group approach is followed. Evolving simple and cost-effective certification and labeling systems to enable farmers to produce pesticide-free products and to gain confidence of the consumers will boost adoption of IDM.

Seed Certification, Including Vegetative Propagation Material

Several of the plant pests and diseases are transmitted through seeds or vegetative material and the use of clean planting material would then be a foremost component of any IDM programme. National policies associated to the quality control, availability and cost of such material for farmers is vital for IDM adoption. This encompasses systems for inspection and certification of seeds and vegetative material and nursery control. Such policies, if not properly assessed and designed in terms of their economic feasibility, practicality and accessibility to farmers could be a impediment to IDM programmes. This is particularly true in India where subsistence farmers may not be able to afford the cost of certified seeds and seedlings or have inadequate transportation access to sources of seeds.

AGRICULTURAL EXTENSION POLICY

Unlike many other technologies that require only limited information and delivery for adoption, IDM is akin to a new technology and knowledge intensive. Its effective implementation requires extension workers to have a sound understanding of the characteristics of the technology, its target host and relationship with natural enemies, and its method of application before the technology is delivered to the farmers. Lack of understanding of any of these would adversely affect its adoption. The extension workers should act more as a collaborator, consultant, and facilitator in dissemination of the knowledge, with the farmer playing a more active role.

IDM can be popularized with farmers only if critical inputs are available to them at the appropriate time. Kiosks should be opened in village to function as the discussion forum for farmers. Video materials on IDM should be shown in villages. Farmers adopting IDM and getting higher yields need to be suitably rewarded. More coverage on IDM need to be given in print as well as electronic media. More access by farmers for sorting out their problems related to plant protection. Extension system needs to overhauled in knowledge about IPM inputs,methodology of IPM and timely delivery of services to the farmers to accelerate the adoption of IPM.

Plant Quarantine

Quarantine systems are the basis for trans-boundary pest and disease prevention through control of the sources of pest introductions and incursions. est and disease surveys as well as pest risk analysis (PRA) studies are critical for preparing and updating quarantine pest lists. Although most of the developing countries have quarantine regulations in place, their effectiveness is very limited often due to scarce financial, human and infrastructural resources. Field surveys and PRA are sporadic when done and pest lists are commonly based on literature reviews and information from researchers. Early detection and reporting of the introduction or emergence of a new disease through regular surveys is indispensable for checking disease spread before it reaches epidemic levels. *Citrus tristeza virus* (CTV) which affect citrus production in many countries, including the Mediterranean region is a good example of the spread of a disease where not only the pathogen, but also its vector is covered by quarantine regulation and control (Moreno *et al.*, 2008).

JUDICIOUS USE OF PESTICIDES

The indiscriminate use of pesticides poses a great threat to IDM hence pesticide use should be selective and need based. Pesticides formulations, especially dusts, are still applied by hand by most of the farmers. Similarly concentrations of pesticide spray are never proper. They are either above or below the required dose. There is a great need to make farmers aware about pesticide application technology. There is a wide gap between pesticide application technology and its dissemination to farmers. If India is to grow more food and increase productivity, then pesticides are going to play a major role till we perfect other disease control options. Use of ICT will result in safe and judicious use of pesticides and will also reduce the pesticide load in the environment and subsequent residue problems

ENFORCEMENT OF PESTICIDE REGULATIONS

Of late, the central government has banned a number of pesticides for use in agriculture in consideration of their adverse effects on environment and human health. In spite of this, many of these are available in the market. For instance, DDT and BHC, which are permitted for use for malaria control, are extensively used in agriculture. Further, many pesticides that have been banned elsewhere in the world are available to Indian farmers. Lower prices of such pesticides induce farmers to use them. A number of spurious pesticides are available in the market because of lack of strict enforcement of regulations and/or regulatory loopholes. Strict enforcement of the regulations governing production, use, distribution and quality of pesticides would help weed out spurious elements from the industry and would benefit the farmers.

PRIVATE SECTOR INVESTMENT POLICY

This could have a negative or a positive effect on the adoption of IDM practices. This is usually related to the private sector involved in inputs for IDM or IPM technologies including bio-pesticides, disease-free seeds/ vegetative material (certified and tissue cultured material), biological control agents, etc. Regulations are critical to promote or hinder the involvement and support that the private sector could provide to IDM promotion. Since IDM or IPM is very location-specific, the scope of activities and market of this private sector are usually limited, and well-designed government incentives or tax breaks may be needed to allow this sector to survive (SP-IPM, 2008).

TRADE AND EXPORT POLICY

Policies at the global and national levels are increasingly interdependent as they influence pest management through regulation of international trade, food and environmental safety and intellectual property rights (Sorby *et al.*, 2003). IDM policies should accordingly be addressed at the global policy level. The management of trans-boundary diseases traveling across continents by wind or accidentally through travelers (such as the soybean or wheat rusts) should be of global concern and international cooperation would be needed to timely share information on the disease spread or the emergence of new virulent strains of pathogens. Concerted international efforts should be undertaken to support countries in need to monitor and manage the disease at its origin before it gets out of control. Examples of such systems include the global wheat rust monitoring system.

FOOD SAFETY, PUBLIC HEALTH AND ENVIRONMENTAL POLICIES

Food safety regulations and standards regarding pesticide residues and other food contaminants such as mycotoxins are usually a positive driving force for farmer to implement IDM strategies. Other related public health and environmental health issues include soil and water contamination with pesticides, agro-chemicals and other contaminants. Through regulatory systems for the use of pesticides or GMOs governments minimize environmental and public health hazards and determine a proper balance between the costs and benefits of these technologies (Schillhorn van Veen, 1999). However, the implementation of such a regulatory system is faced with several problems especially in the developing countries and these include: (i) involvement of several ministries and agencies with different/ limited mandates, power or authority and responsibilities; (ii) limited human, financial and infrastructure capacities for testing and action taking, and (iii) lack or limited systems fornational coordination and information sharing

LAND USE POLICY

Land tenure planning is often limiting factors in the adoption of IDM technologies by farmers. Land ownership and land size have direct effects on the risk level that farmers would be ready to assume as well as on the motivation of farmers to invest in new technologies and adopt strategies with longer-term returns on investment. Crop and genetic diversity within the larger landscape, including gene deployment strategies, reduction of the number of varieties cultivated in agro-ecological areas, monoculture in time and space, management of field hedges harboring natural enemies or the management of alternate and secondary hosts of pathogens are all factors that would directly affect the effectiveness and successes of IDM strategies and their scaling up at a regional or national level.

EDUCATION AND TRAINING POLICY

In view of the WTO requirements concerning pesticide residue in edible commodities and in the context of changed scenario of environmental security, people need to be educated about IDM at all level right from school stage. A multidisciplinary course on IPM at undergraduate need to in introduced. A Centre of Excellence in IDM will give fillip to plant protection programmes in the country.

CONVERGENCE AND SYNERGIES

A consortium of partners involving research scientists, state agriculture universities, extension departments, farmer's associations, nongovernmental organisations, seed and bio input industries, and product buyers should be set up to demonstrate, implement, train and promote IDM at farmer's fields. Such synergies would benefit all the players. Farmers can have latest upgraded technology and also an assured availability of input products' at their fields. Seed and bio input companies will be benefited by having an increased market penetration and assured sale. In return buyers of agricultural produce will have timely availability of high quality produces for their outlets at competitive prices. Scientists will be exposed to actual problems faced by various parties and will have effective outlet for their research outputs with respect to products and technologies.

SCALING UP

Scaling up IDM activities in India for a wider impact remains a challenge. This process, however, remains country and location-specific. IDM projects and programmes would require to identify and establish at an early stage of implementation linkages with organisations or individuals that can provide mechanisms for future scaling up (Vande Fliert *et al.*, 2000). Key persons and institutions should be involved in the design, planning and evaluation of the programme, as well as in critical events throughout the implementation of the programme. An analysis of potential organisations (public, private, NGOs, etc.) that are critical for the scaling-up should be done assessing their mandates, roles and responsibilities and capacities. Raising the awareness of decision makers at the national and district levels is also key to ensure the political support for sustainability of activities. Reporting is not enough and decision makers should be able to visit and see an FFS first hand and talk directly with farmers (Pontius *et al.*, 2002).

CONCLUSION

India has successfully reduced pesticide consumption without adversely affecting the agricultural productivity. This was facilitated by appropriate policies that discouraged pesticide use, and favoured IDM/IPM application. In spite of it, adoption of IDM is low owing to a number of socio-economic, institutional and policy constraints. On the supply side, lack of commercial availability of biopesticides and inappropriate institutional technology transfer mechanisms are the critical hindrance to increased application of IDM. The presence of private sector in biopesticide production and marketing is marginal, and needs to be improved through economic incentives. On the demand side, farmers though are aware of technological failure of pesticides to control diseases, and their negative externalities to environment and human health, disease risk is too high to experiment with newer approaches to disease management. IDM is a complex process and farmers lack understanding of disease cycle and their bioagents and methods of application of new technology components. The socio-economic environment of farming is also an important factor in adoption of IDM. There are a number of IDM practices that work best when applied by the entire community and in a synchronized mode. This is unlikely to happen without demonstrating benefits of group approach, and external motivation and support to the farmers. Though many technology programmes are based on community approach, they do not have any proper exit policy to sustain the group approach. The IDM policy should also provide incentives to farmers to adopt IDM as a cardinal principle of plant protection.Training and awareness raising of farmers, disease survey teams, agricultural development officers, extension agents and policy makers remains to be an important factor for the successful implementation of IDM strategies. All direct stakeholders including farmers, extension workers, and local crop protection technicians should have a practical understanding of the ecology, etiology and epidemiology of the major diseases of the crop. Intensive training using participatory approaches should be used to empower farmers with the appropriate knowledge to become better managers of their own fields translating this knowledge into appropriate decision- making tools and practical-control tactics.

REFERENCES

Adesina, A.A. and M.M. Zinnah. 1993. Technology Characteristics, Farmers' Perceptions and Adoption Decisions. Agricultural Economics 9: 297-311.

Agnihotri, N.P. 2000. Pesticide Consumption in Agriculture in India- An Update. Pesticide Res. Jour.112: 150-155.

Akoroda M., 2010. Global Perspectives on Cassava Production. *FAO African Regional Conference, Luanda, Angola,* 2010 (http://km.fao.org/biosecwiki/images/ 4/47/Cassava- Global ARC26-compressed1.pdf).

Antholt C.H., 1992. Relevancy, Responsiveness and Cost-effectiveness: Issues for Agricultural Extension in the 21st Century. *Journal of Extension Systems* 8: 37-44

Atwal, A.S. 1986. Future of Pesticides in Plant Protection. In: Plant Protection in the Year 2000 A.D. (Ed. G.S. Venkataraman). Indian National Science Academy, New Delhi.

Azzam O., Chancellor T.C.B., 2002. The Biology, Epidemiology, and Management of Rice Tungro Disease in Asia. *Plant Disease* 86: 88-100.

Baker K.F., Cook R.J., 1974. Biological Control of Plant Pathogens. Freeman W.H. & Co., San Francisco, USA.

Bonman J.M., Mackill D.J., 1988. Durable Resistance to Rice Blast Disease. Oryza 25: 103-110.

Birthal, P.S. 2003. Economic Potential of Biological Substitutes for Agrochemicals. NCAP Policy Paper 18. National Centre for Agricultural Economics and Policy Research, New Delhi.

Birthal, P.S., O.P. Sharma, and Sant Kumar. 2000. Economics of Integrated Pest Management: Evidence and Issues. Indian Journal of Agricultural Economics, 55(4): 644-659.

Buddenhagen I.W., 1977. Resistance and Vulnerability of Tropical Crops in Relation to Their Evolution and Breeding. *Annals of the New York Academy of Science* 287: 309-326.

Chester R., 2005. Achieving Scale in Agriculture: Past Efforts, Present Promise. Discussion Paper. Center for Environmental Strategies, Academy for Educational Development, USAID, Washington DC, USA.

Cook R.J., Bruckart W.L., Coulson J.R., Goettel M.S., Humber R.A., 1996. Safety of Microorganisms Intended for Pest and Plant Disease Control: A Framework for Scientific Evaluation. *Biological Control* 7: 333-351.

De Waard M.A., Georgopoulos S., Hollomon G.D.W., Ishii H., Leroux P., Ragsdale N.N., Schwinn F.J., 1993. Chemical Control of Plant Diseases: Problems and Prospects. *Annual Review of Phytopathology* 31: 403-421.

Dhaliwal, G.S. and R. Arora. 1996. Principles of Insect Management. Commonwealth Publishers, New Delhi.

FAO, 2004. FAOSTAT: FAO Statistical Data bases. Rome, Italy (http://faostat.fao.org).

Gullino M.L., Leroux P., Smith C.M., 2000. Uses and Challenges of Novel Compounds for Plant Disease Control. *Crop Protection* 19: 1-11.

Gullino ML, Leroux P and Smith CM. 2000. Uses and Challenges of Novel Compounds for Plant Disease Control. *Crop Protection* 19: 1-11.

Harman G.E., Bjorkman T., 1998. Potential and Existing Uses of *Trichoderma* and *Gliocladium* for Plant Disease Control and Growth Enhancement. In: Harmon G.E., Kubicek C.P. (eds). *Trichoderma and Gliocladium,* Vol. 2: Enzymes, Biological Control and Commercial Applications, pp. 229-265. Taylor and Francis, London, UK.

Hewitt H.G., 1998. Fungicides in Crop Protection. CAB International, Wallingford, UK.

Karamura E., Osiru M, Blomme G., 2005. Containing Banana *Xanthomonas* Wilt. *InfoMusa* 14: 45-46.

Hodson, D. and Nazari K. 2010. Serious Outbreaks of Wheat Stripe or Yellow Rust in Central and West Asia and North Africa – March/April 2010. Borlaug Global Rust Initiative, Newsroom, Rust in the news, April 2010 News Items. http://globalrust.org/traction/ permalink/Pathogen206

Kenmore, P.E. 1991. Indonesia's Integrated Pest Management: A Model for Asia. FAO Inter-Country Programme for Integrated Pest Control in Rice in South and Southeast Asia. Manila, Philippines.

Kerr A., 1980. Biological Control of Crown Gall Through Production of Agrocin 84. *Plant Disease* 64: 25-30.

Khoury W. El and Makkouk K. 2010. Integrated Plant Disease Management in Developing Countries. Journal of Plant Pathology (2010), 92 (4, Supplement), S4.35-S4.42 *Edizioni ETS Pisa, 2010*

Knight S.C., Anthony V.M., Brady A.M., Greenland A.J., Heaney S.P., Murray D.C., Powell K.A., Schultz M.A., Spinks C.A., Worthington P.A., Youle D., 1997. Rationale and Perspectives on the Development of Fungicides. *Annual Review of Phytopathology* 35: 349-372.

Kumar S., 2010a. Integrated Management of Maydis Leaf Blight of Maize. Annals of Plant Protect. Sci. 18(2): 536-537.

Kumar S 2013b., Trichoderma ; A Biological Weapon for Managing Plant Diseases and Promoting Sustainability. Int. J. Agric. Sci. Vet. Med. 1(3): 1-16.

Kumar S 2014c., Plant Disease Management: Advances and Challenges. Afr. J. Agric. Sci. 9(15):1207-1217. http://dx.doi.org/10.5897/AJAR2014.7311

Kumar S, Gupta OM., 2012. Expanding Dimension of Plant Pathology. JNKVV Res. J. 46(3):286-293.

Jha AMM (2009). Potential of Trichoderma spp. as Biocontrol Agents Against Pathogens Causing Maydis Leaf Blight of Maize. J. Biol. Control 23(1): 89-91.

Kumar S, Upadhyay JP, Rani A 2009., Evaluation of Trichoderma Species Against Fusarium Udum Butler Causing Wilt of Pigeon Pea. J. Biol. Control 23(3): 329-332.

Kumar Sanjeet, Upadhyay JP, Kumar S 2002., Biocontrol of Alternaria Leaf Spot of Vicia Faba Using Antogonistic Fungi J. Biol. Control 20(2): 247-251.

Kumar S, Upadhyay JP 2003., Compatibility of Rhizobium and Trichoderma *in vitro* and *in vivo*. RAU J. Res. 13(1-2): 61-64.

Lapar, M.L.A. and S. Pandey. 1999. Adoption of Soil Conservation: The Case of the Philippine Uplands. Agricultural Economics 21: 241-256.

Leung H., Zhu Y., Revilla-Molina I., Fan J. X., Chen H., Pangga I., Vera Cruz C.M., Mew T. W. 2003. Using Genetic Diversity to Achieve Sustainable Rice Disease Management. *Plant Disease* 87: 1156-1169.

Lumsden R.D., Walter J.F., 1995. Development of Biocontrol Fungus *Gliocladium virens*: Risk Assessment and Approval for Horticultural Use. In: Hokkanen M.T., Lynch J.M. (eds). Biological Control: Benefits and Risks, pp. 263-269. Cambridge University Press, Cambridge, UK.

Mancini F., van Bruggen A.H.C., Jiggins J.L.S., 2006. Evaluating Cotton Integrated Pest Management (IPM) Farmer Field School Outcomes Using the Sustainable Livelihoods Approach in India. *Experimental Agriculture* 43: 97-112.

Mew T.W., Vera Cruz C.M., Medalla E.S., 1992. Changes in Frequency of *Xanthomonas oryzae* pv *oryzae* in Response to Rice Cultivars Planted in the Philippines. *Plant Disease* 76: 1029-1032.

Moreno P., Ambros S., Albiachi-Marti M.R., Guerri J., Pena L., 2008. *Citrus tristeza virus:* A Pathogen that Changed the Course of the Citrus Industry. *Molecular Plant Pathology* 9: 251-268.

Hodson, D. and Nazari K., 2010. Serious Outbreaks of Wheat Stripe or Yellow Rust in Central and West Asia and North Africa – March/April 2010. Borlaug Global Rust Initiative, Newsroom, Rust in the News, April 2010 News Items. http://globalrust.org/traction/ permalink/Pathogen206

Nelson R., Orrego R., Ortiz O., Tenorio J., Mundt C., Fredrix M., Vien N.V., 2001. Working with Resource-poor Farmers to Manage Plant Diseases. *Plant Disease* 85: 684-695. Ou S.H., 1985. Rice Diseases. 2nd Ed. Commonwealth Mycological Institute, Kew, UK. Overton J., 1996. Ecologically Based Pest Management-New Solutions for a New Century. National Academy Press, Washington DC, USA.

Palti J., 1981. Cultural Practices and Infectious Crop Diseases. Springer-Verlag, Beriln, Germany.

Pande S., Narayan Rao J., Upadhyaya H.D., Lene J.M., 2001. Farmer's Participatory Integrated Management of Foliar Diseases of Groundnut. *International Journal of Pest Management* 47: 121-126.

Paroda, R.S. and P. Kumar. 2000. Food Production and Demand Situations in South Asia. Agricultural Economics Research Review 13(4): 1-25.

Pradhan, S. 1983. Agricultural Entomology and Pest Control. Indian Council of Agricultural Research, New Delhi.

Prashar M (2013) Tackling Threat of Ug99 or Wheat Rust Variants. J. Mycol. Pl. Pathol. 42(1): 28.

Reddy DVR. 1998. Control Measures for the Economically Important Peanut Viruses. In: Hadidi A., Khetarpal R.K., Koganezawa H. (eds). Plant Virus Disease Control, pp. 541-546. APS Press, St, Paul, MN, USA.

Saxena, S. 2001. Pesticide Industry in a Climate of Signal Shifts. Agriculture Today, April.

Schillhorn Van Veen T., Forno D.A., Joffe S., Umali-Deininger D., Cooke S., 1997. Integrated Pest Management: Strategies and Policies for Effective Implementation. Environmentally Sustainable Development Studies and Monographs Series No. 13. World Bank, Washington DC, USA.

Schillhorn Van Veen T., 1999. Agricultural Pest Management at a Crossroads: New Opportunities and New Risks. Food and Fertilizer Technology Centre for Asia and the Pacific Region, Extension Bulletin 01-04-1999.

Singh, S.P. 1997. Progress and Problems in the Use of Biocontrol Agents. In: The National Conference on Biopesticides. Ministry of Agriculture, Govt. of India, New Delhi, and All India Biotech Association, New Delhi. April 10, 1997.

Sorby K., Fleischer G., Pehu E., 2003. Integrated Pest Management in Development: Review of Trends and Implementation Strategies. Agriculture and Rural Development Working Paper 5. World Bank, Washington DC, USA.

SP-IPM, 2008. Incorporating Integrated Pest Management into National Policies. IPM Research Brief No. 6. SP-IPM Secretariat, International Institute of Tropical Agriculture (IITA), Ibadan, Nigeria.

Sulaiman R., Hall A., 2002. Beyond Technology Dissemination: Reinventing Agricultural Extension. *Outlook on Agriculture* 31: 225-233.

Thind T.S. (2012) Fungicides in Crop Health Security-the Road Ahead *Indan Phytopath* 65(2): 109-115.

Thomas M.B., Waage J.K., 1996. Integration of Biological Control and Host Plant Resistance Breeding: A Scientific and Literature Review. Technical Center for Agriculture and Rural Cooperation of the European Union, Wageningen, The Netherlands.

Thomas M.B., 1999. Ecological Approaches and the Development of "Truly Integrated" Pest Management. *Proceedings of the National Academy of Science USA* 96: 5944-5951.

Thurston H.D., 1990. Plant Disease Management Practices of Traditional Farmers. *Plant Disease* 74: 96-101.

Thurston H.D., 1992. Sustainable Practices for Plant Disease Management in Traditional Farming Systems. Western Press, Boulder, CO, USA.

Tripathi L., Mwangi M., Abele S., Aritua V., Tushemereirwe W., Bandyopadhyay R., 2009. Xanthomonas Wilt: A Threat to Banana Production in East and Central Africa. *Plant Disease* 93: 440-449.

Van de Fliert E., Asmunati R.,. Tantowijoyo W. 2000. Participatory Approaches and Scaling-up. In: Stür W.W., Horne P.M, Hacker J.B., Kerridge P.C. (eds). Working with Farmers: The Key to Adoption of Forage Technologies. *ACIAR Proceedings. No. 95, International Workshop, Cayagan de Oro City, Mindanao 1999*: 83-90.

Van de Fliert E., 2003. Recognising a Climate for Sustainability: Extension Beyond Transfer of Technology. *Australian Journal of Experimental Agriculture* 43: 29-36.

Waddington S.R., Li X., Dixon J., Hyman G., de Vicente C., 2010. Getting the Focus Right: Production Constraints for Six Major Food Crops in Asian and African Farming Systems. *Food Security* 2: 27-48.

Wolfe M.S., 1985. The Current Status and Prospects of Multiline Cultivars and Variety Mixtures for Disease Resistance. *Annual Review of Phytopathology* 23: 251-273.

[illegible] Nutrient Management in India.

[illegible] Rice-Wheat [illegible] and [illegible] South Asia. Agricultural [illegible] 1999.

[illegible] Indian Council of Agricultural Research, New Delhi.

[illegible] 1998. Wheat [illegible] Journal [illegible].

[illegible] Management [illegible] Agronomy [illegible].

[illegible] Climate [illegible] Chain, Agriculture [illegible].

[illegible] Development [illegible] Environment [illegible] World Bank, Washington, DC, USA.

[illegible] Food and Fertilizer [illegible].

[illegible] Delhi [illegible].

[illegible] Research and Extension Strategies, Agriculture and Rural Development [illegible] World Bank, Washington, DC, USA.

[illegible] 2008. [illegible] Research [illegible] Indian [illegible].

[illegible] Agricultural Extension [illegible].

[illegible] 2012. [illegible] in Crop Health [illegible].

[illegible] India [illegible].

[illegible] Journal [illegible].

[illegible] 1993 [illegible].

[illegible] Wiley [illegible].

[illegible] Water [illegible].

[illegible] USA [illegible].

[illegible]

Index

❑ ❑ ❑ ❑ ❑ ❑